D0983684

THE POEMS AND
SONGS OF
Robert Burns

ROBERT BURNS

From the portrait by Alexander Reid in the Scottish National Portrait Gallery

THE POEMS AND
SONGS OF
Robert Burns

Edited by

JAMES KINSLEY

Professor of English Studies in the
University of Nottingham

Volume II

TEXT

OXFORD
AT THE CLARENDON PRESS
1968

Oxford University Press, Ely House, London W.1

GLASGOW NEW YORK TORONTO MELBOURNE WELLINGTON
CAPE TOWN SALISBURY IBADAN NAIROBI LUSAKA ADDIS ABABA
BOMBAY CALCUTTA MADRAS KARACHI LAHORE DACCA
KUALA LUMPUR HONG KONG TOKYO

PRINTED IN GREAT BRITAIN

CONTENTS

VOLUME I

VOLUME II

CONTENTS

CONTENTS

VII

POEMS
1790

ELLISLAND

282. [To a Gentleman who had sent him a News-paper, and offered to continue it free of expense]

KIND Sir, I've read your paper through,
  And faith, to me, 'twas really new!
How guessed ye, Sir, what maist I wanted?
This mony a day I've grain'd and gaunted,
To ken what French mischief was brewin;   5
Or what the drumlie Dutch were doin;
That vile doup-skelper, Emperor Joseph,
If Venus yet had got his nose off;
Or how the collieshangie works
Atween the Russians and the Turks;   10
Or if the Swede, before he halt,
Would play anither Charles the twalt:
If Denmark, any body spak o't;
Or Poland, wha had now the tack o't;
How cut-throat Prussian blades were hingin;   15
How libbet Italy was singin;
If Spaniard, Portuguese, or Swiss,
Were sayin or takin aught amiss:
Or how our merry lads at hame,
In Britain's court kept up the game: 20
How royal George, the Lord leuk o'er him!
Was managing St. Stephen's quorum;
If sleekit Chatham Will was livin,
Or glaikit Charlie got his nieve in;
How daddie Burke the plea was cookin,   25
If Warren Hastings' neck was yeukin;
How cesses, stents, and fees were rax'd,
Or if bare a——s yet were tax'd;
The news o' princes, dukes, and earls,
Pimps, sharpers, bawds, and opera-girls;   30

To a Gentleman. *Text from Currie, 1801 (iv. 355–6). Henley and Henderson record a MS (not traced) without variation. Title in Currie* The following Poem was written to a Gentleman . . . expense. *Date in Currie* Ellisland . . . 1790

If that daft buckie, Geordie W***s,
Was threshin still at hizzies' tails,
Or if he was grown oughtlins douser,
And no a perfect kintra cooser,
A' this and mair I never heard of;   35
And but for you I might despair'd of.
So gratefu', back your news I send you,
And pray, a' gude things may attend you!

Ellisland, Monday morning

283. Elegy on Peg Nicholson—

Tune, Chevy Chase

Peg Nicholson was a good bay mare,
  As ever trode on airn;
But now she's floating down the Nith,
  And past the Mouth o' Cairn.

Peg Nicholson was a good bay mare,   5
  And rode thro' thick and thin;
But now she's floating down the Nith,
  And wanting even the skin.

Peg Nicholson was a good bay mare,
  And ance she bore a priest;   10
But now she's floating down the Nith,
  For Solway fish a feast.

Peg Nicholson was a good bay mare,
  And the priest he rode her sair:
And much oppressed and bruised she was—   15
  As priest-rid cattle are, &c. &c.

Elegy on Peg Nicholson. *Text from Cromek*, Reliques, *1808 (p. 108; letter to William Nicol, 9 February 1790; MS not traced)*

284. I love my Love in secret

M Y Sandy gied to me a ring,
Was a' beset wi' diamonds fine;
But I gied him a far better thing,
I gied my heart in pledge o' his ring.

    My Sandy O, my Sandy O,   5
    My bony, bony Sandy O;
Tho' the love that I owe to thee I dare na show,
Yet I love my love in secret my Sandy O.

My Sandy brak a piece o' gowd,
While down his cheeks the saut tears row'd;   10
He took a hauf and gied it to me,
And I'll keep it till the hour I die.
    My Sandy O &c.

I love my Love in secret. *Text from SMM, 1790 (204; unsigned)*

285. Tibbie Dunbar

Tune Johny McGill

O WILT thou go wi' me, sweet Tibbie Dunbar;
   O wilt thou go wi' me, sweet Tibbie Dunbar:
Wilt thou ride on a horse, or be drawn in a car,
Or walk by my side, O sweet Tibbie Dunbar.—

I care na thy daddie, his lands and his money;   5
I care na thy kin, sae high and sae lordly:
But say thou wilt hae me for better for waur,
And come in thy coatie, sweet Tibbie Dunbar.—

Tibbie Dunbar. *Text from the Hastie MS, f. 53ᵛ, collated with SMM, 1790 (207;*
Written for this work by Robert Burns)

286. The Taylor fell thro' the bed, &c.

Beware of the ripells

T̲h̲e̲ Taylor fell thro' the bed, thimble an' a',
The Taylor fell thro' the bed thimble an' a';
The blankets were thin and the sheets they were sma',
The Taylor fell thro' the bed, thimble an' a'.

The sleepy bit lassie she dreaded nae ill,   5
The sleepy bit lassie she dreaded nae ill;
The weather was cauld and the lassie lay still,
She thought that a Taylor could do her nae ill.

Gie me the groat again, cany young man,
Gie me the groat again, cany young man;   10
The day it is short and the night it is lang,
The dearest siller that ever I wan.

There's somebody weary wi' lying her lane,
There's somebody weary wi' lying her lane,
There's some that are dowie, I trow wad be fain   15
To see the bit Taylor come skippin again.

The Taylor fell thro' the bed. *Text from SMM, 1790 (212; unsigned). Cancelled fragment of ll. 9–12 in the Hastie MS, f. 26:*

> Gie me my groat again, canny young man;
> Gie me my groat again, canny young man;
> The night it is short and the day it is lang,
> It's a dear-won tipence to lie wi' a man.

287. Ay waukin O

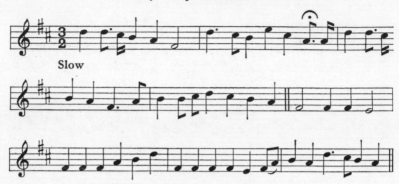

Slow

SIMMER'S a pleasant time,
   Flowers of every colour;
The water rins o'er the heugh,
   And I long for my true lover!
         Chorus
   Ay waukin, Oh,   5
     Waukin still and weary:
   Sleep I can get nane,
     For thinking on my Dearie.—

When I sleep I dream,
   When I wauk I'm irie;   10
Sleep I can get nane,
   For thinking on my Dearie.—
       Ay waukin &c.

Lanely night comes on,
   A' the lave are sleepin:
I think on my bonie lad,   15
   And I bleer my een wi' greetin.—
       Au waukin &c.

Ay waukin O. *Text from the Alloway MS, collated with the Adam MS and SMM,*
1790 (213; unsigned). Title in Adam Song for Miss Craig with the dutiful regards of
Rob! Burns. *The Cowie MS of* **157** *has a draft of ll. 13–16 on the verso with A' the*
house *at l. 14. A MS owned by G. R. Roy has two similar drafts, agreeing with Cowie*
at l. 14. One has That has my heart a keeping *in l. 16*

288. Beware o' bonie Ann

Slow

Y E gallants bright I red you right,
   Beware o' bonie Ann;
Her comely face sae fu' o' grace,
   Your heart she will trepan.
Her een sae bright, like stars by night,   5
   Her skin is like the swan;
Sae jimply lac'd her genty waist,
   That sweetly ye might span.

Youth, grace and love attendant move,
   And pleasure leads the van: 10
In a' their charms and conquering arms,
   They wait on bonie Ann.
The captive bands may chain the hands,
   But loove enslaves the man:
Ye gallants braw, I red you a',   15
   Beware o' bonie Ann.

Beware o' bonie Ann. *Text from SMM, 1790 (215; signed X)*

289. My Wife's a wanton, wee thing

My Wife's a wanton, wee thing,
  My wife's a wanton, wee thing,
My wife's a wanton, wee thing,
  She winna be guided by me.

She play'd the loon or she was married,   5
She play'd the loon or she was married,
She play'd the loon or she was married,
  She'll do it again or she die.

She sell'd her coat and she drank it,
She sell'd her coat and she drank it,   10
She row'd hersell in a blanket,
  She winna be guided for me.

She mind't na when I forbade her,
She mind't na when I forbade her,
I took a rung and I claw'd her,   15
  And a braw gude bairn was she.

290. [Lassie lie near me]

Lang hae we parted been,
  Lassie my dearie;
Now we are met again,
  Lassie lie near me.
    Cho: Near me, near me,   5
      Lassie lie near me;
      Lang hast thou lien thy lane,
      Lassie lie near me.

My Wife's a wanton, wee thing. *Text from SMM, 1790 (217; unsigned), collated with MMC, pp. 116–17*

Lassie lie near me. *Text from SMM, 1790 (218; unsigned), headed* Old Words *alternative to Blacklock's song* Laddie lie near me
    6 me;] me *SMM*

A' that I hae endur'd,
Lassie, my dearie,   10
Here in thy arms is cur'd,
Lassie lie near me.
    Cho: Near me, &c.

291. The Gardener wi' his paidle—or, The Gardener's March—

Slowish

WHEN rosy May comes in wi' flowers
    To deck her gay, green, spreading bowers;
Then busy, busy are his hours,
    The Gardener wi' his paidle.—

The chrystal waters gently fa';   5
The merry birds are lovers a';
The scented breezes round him blaw,
    The Gardener wi' his paidle.—

The Gardener wi' his paidle. *Text from the Hastie MS, f. 52, collated with SMM,
1790 (220; signed Z)*

When purple morning starts the hare
To steal upon her early fare;   10
Then thro' the dews he maun repair,
The Gardener wi' his paidle.—

When Day, expiring in the west,
The curtain draws of Nature's rest;
He flies to her arms he lo'es the best,   15
The Gardener wi' his paidle.—

292. On a bank of Flowers

O N a bank of flowers in a summer day,
   For summer lightly drest,
The youthful blooming Nelly lay,
With love and sleep opprest.

On a bank of Flowers. *Text from SMM, 1790 (223;* Written for this Work by Robert Burns), *collated with SC, 1799 (88)*

When Willie wand'ring thro' the wood,   5
   Who for her favour oft had su'd;
He gaz'd, he wish'd, he fear'd, he blush'd,
   And trembled where he stood.

Her closed eyes like weapons sheath'd
   Were seal'd in soft repose;   10
Her lips, still as she fragrant breath'd
   It richer dy'd the rose.
The springing lilies sweetly prest,
   Wild, wanton kiss'd her rival breast;
He gaz'd, he wish'd, he fear'd, he blush'd,   15
   His bosom ill at rest.

Her robes light waving in the breeze,
   Her tender limbs embrace;
Her lovely form, her native ease,
   All harmony and grace: 20
Tumultuous tides his pulses roll,
   A faltering, ardent kiss he stole;
He gaz'd, he wish'd, he fear'd, he blush'd,
   And sigh'd his very soul.

As flies the partridge from the brake   25
   On fear-inspired wings,
So Nelly starting, half-awake,
   Away affrighted springs:
But Willy follow'd,—as he should,
   He overtook her in the wood;   30
He vow'd, he pray'd, he found the maid
   Forgiving all and good.

293. My love she's but a lassie yet—

M Y love she's but a lassie yet,
    My love she's but a lassie yet;
We'll let her stand a year or twa,
    She'll no be half sae saucy yet.—

I rue the day I sought her O,   5
I rue the day I sought her O,
Wha gets her needs na say he's woo'd,
    But he may say he's bought her O.—

Come draw a drap o' the best o't yet,
Come draw a drap o' the best o't yet: 10
Gae seek for Pleasure whare ye will,
    But here I never misst it yet.—

We're a' dry wi' drinking o't,
We're a' dry wi' drinking o't:
The minister kisst the fidler's wife,   15
    He could na preach for thinkin o't.—

My love she's but a lassie yet. *Text from the Hastie MS, f. 53, collated with SMM,
1790 (225; unsigned), and SC, 1798 (35). SC has ll. 1–8, followed by sixteen lines*
Written for this Work By H. MacNeil, Esq.

294. Cauld frosty morning

Cauld frosty morning. *Text from the Hastie MS, f. 54, collated with SMM, 1790* (227; *signed Z*). *The Law MSS contain a draft* (*see* Burns Chronicle, *1926, p. 64*):

> Twas past one o'clock in a cold frosty morning,
>   As I lay a musing most pleasantlie,
> I heard the town clock give its usual warning,
>   Which I had intended should waken me.
> Then I arose, resolving that I would go
>   Visit a friend who oftimes had call'd me, O,
> To see whether she would prove kind to me or no;
>   This was the reason that wakened me.
>   Machline, Aug: 1788.

'T WAS past ane o'clock in a cauld frosty morning,
    When cankert November blaws over the plain,
I heard the kirk-bell repeat the loud warning,
    As, restless, I sought for sweet slumber in vain:
Then up I arose, the silver moon shining bright;   5
    Mountains and valleys appearing all hoary white;
Forth I would go, amid the pale, silent night,
    And visit the Fair One, the cause of my pain.—

Sae gently I staw to my lovely Maid's chamber,
    And rapp'd at her window, low down on my knee;   10
Begging that she would awauk from sweet slumber,
    Awauk from sweet slumber and pity me:
For, that a stranger to a' pleasure, peace and rest,
    Love into madness had fired my tortur'd breast;
And that I should be of a' men the maist unblest,   15
    Unless she would pity my sad miserie!

My True-love arose and whispered to me,
    (The moon looked in, and envy'd my Love's charms;)
'An innocent Maiden, ah, would you undo me!'
    I made no reply, but leapt into her arms: 20
Bright Phebus peep'd over the hills and found me there;
    As he has done, now, seven lang years and mair:
A faithfuller, constanter, kinder, more loving Pair,
    His sweet-chearing beam nor enlightens nor warms.

5 Then up *SMM*: Up *MS*   24 sweet-chearing] *correcting* all . . . *in MS*

295. Jamie come try me

Slow

JAMIE come try me,
  Jamie come try me,
If thou would win my love
Jamie come try me.

If thou should ask my love,   5
  Could I deny thee?
If thou would win my love,
  Jamie come try me.

If thou should kiss me, love,
  Wha could espy thee?   10
If thou wad be my love,
  Jamie come try me.
      Jamie come &c.

Jamie come try me. *Text from SMM, 1790 (229; unsigned), collated with the*
Rosenbach MS

296. The Captain's Lady

Mount your baggage

O MOUNT and go,
  Mount and make you ready,
O mount and go,
  And be the Captain's Lady.

When the drums do beat,   5
  And the cannons rattle,
Thou shalt sit in state,
  And see thy love in battle.
    Cho: O mount and go &c.

When the vanquish'd foe
  Sues for peace and quiet,   10
To the shades we'll go
  And in love enjoy it.
    Cho: O Mount &c.

The Captain's Lady. *Text from SMM, 1790 (233; unsigned). SMM repeats the verse, correcting* shall (*l. 7*) *to* shalt *in the repeat*

297. Johnie Cope

S I R John Cope trode the north right far,
Yet ne'er a rebel he cam naur,
Until he landed at Dunbar
Right early in a morning.
 Hey Johnie Cope are ye wauking yet, 5
 Or are ye sleeping I would wit;
 O haste ye get up for the drums do beat,
 O fye Cope rise in the morning.

He wrote a challenge from Dunbar,
Come fight me Charlie an ye daur; 10
If it be not by the chance of war
I'll give you a merry morning.
 Hey Johnie Cope &c.

When Charlie look'd the letter upon
He drew his sword the scabbard from—

Johnie Cope. *Text from SMM, 1790 (234; unsigned)*
 7 beat,] beat *SMM*

'So Heaven restore to me my own,   15
'I'll meet you, Cope, in the morning.'
   Hey Johnie Cope &c.

Cope swore with many a bloody word
That he would fight them gun and sword,
But he fled frae his nest like an ill scar'd bird,
And Johnie he took wing in the morning.   20
   Hey Johnie Cope &c.

It was upon an afternoon,
Sir Johnie march'd to Preston town;
He says, my lads come lean you down,
And we'll fight the boys in the morning.
   Hey Johnie Cope &c.

But when he saw the Highland lads   25
Wi' tartan trews and white cockauds,
Wi' swords and guns and rungs and gauds,
O Johnie he took wing in the morning.
   Hey Johnie Cope &c.

On the morrow when he did rise,
He look'd between him and the skies;   30
He saw them wi' their naked thighs,
Which fear'd him in the morning.
   Hey Johnie Cope &c.

O then he flew into Dunbar,
Crying for a man of war;
He thought to have pass'd for a rustic tar,   35
And gotten awa in the morning.
   Hey Johnie Cope &c.

Sir Johnie into Berwick rade,
Just as the devil had been his guide;
Gien him the warld he would na stay'd
To foughten the boys in the morning.   40
   Hey Johnie Cope &c.

22 town;] town *SMM*

Says the Berwickers unto Sir John,
O what's become of all your men,
In faith, says he, I dinna ken,
I left them a' this morning.
    Hey Johnie Cope &c.

Says Lord Mark Car, ye are na blate,   45
To bring us the news o' your ain defeat;
I think you deserve the back o' the gate,
Get out o' my sight this morning.
    Hey Johnie Cope &c.

298. [O dear Minny, what shall I do?]

O DEAR minny, what shall I do?
O dear minny, what shall I do?
O dear minny, what shall I do?
Daft thing, doylt thing, do as I do.—

43 faith,] faith *SMM*   45 Car,] Car *SMM*

O dear Minny. *Text from the Hastie MS, f. 102, collated with SMM, 1790 (236;*
Old Words *to the song* O dear Peggy, love's beguiling)
  4 doylt] *correcting* droll *in MS*

If I be black, I canna be lo'ed;   5
If I be fair, I canna be gude;
If I be lordly, the lads will look by me:
O dear minny, what shall I do.—
  O dear minny &c.

299. [Carl an the king come]

Chorus

CARL an the king come,
Carl an the king come;
Thou shalt dance and I will sing,
Carl an the king come.

An somebodie were come again,   5
Then somebodie maun cross the main,
And every man shall hae his ain,
Carl an the king come.
  Cho: Carl an &c.

Carl an the king come. *Text from SMM, 1790 (239; Old Words to the song* Peggy,
now the king's come)

I trow we swapped for the warse,
We gae the boot and better horse;   10
And that we'll tell them at the cross,
Carl an the king come.
 Cho: Carl an &c.

Coggie an the king come,
Coggie an the king come,
I'se be fou and thou'se be toom,   15
Coggie an the king come.
 Cho: Coggie an &c.

300. There's a youth in this City

A Gaelic Air

Slowish

There's a youth in this City. *Text from the Hastie MS, f. 51ᵛ, collated with SMM,
1790 (258; signed Z). Title from SMM; MS headed* Tune—Niel Gow's lamentation for the death of his brother. Note—it will be proper to omit the name of the
tune altogether, and only say—A Gaelic Air.—*The MS has two false starts to
stanza 2: (a) ll. 13–14, cancelled; (b)* ~~Tho' lan~~

1

THERE's a youth in this city, it were a great pity
    That he from our lasses should wander awa;
For he's bony and braw, weel-favour'd with a',
    And his hair has a natural buckle and a'.—
His coat is the hue of his bonnet sae blue;   5
    His facket is white as the new-driven snaw;
His hose they are blae, and his shoon like the slae;
    And his clear siller buckles they dazzle us a'.—

2

For beauty and fortune the laddie's been courtin;
    Weel-featur'd, weel-tocher'd, weel-mounted and braw;   10
But chiefly the siller, that gars him gang till her;
    The Pennie's the jewel that beautifies a'.—
There's Meg wi' the mailin that fain wad a haen him;
    And Susie whase daddy was laird o' the Ha':
There's lang-tocher'd Nancy maist fetters his fancy—   15
    But th' laddie's dear sel he lo'es dearest of a'.—

301. My heart's in the Highlands

Tune, Failte na miosg

Slow

M Y heart's in the Highlands, my heart is not here;
My heart's in the Highlands a chasing the deer;
Chasing the wild deer, and following the roe;
My heart's in the Highlands, wherever I go.—

My heart's in the Highlands. *Text from the Hastie MS, f. 55ᵛ, collated with SMM, 1790 (259; signed Z). Title from SMM, which sets the song in two eight-line stanzas*
3 Chasing] *correcting* A chasing *in MS*: A chasing *SMM*   wild] *interpolated in MS*

Farewell to the Highlands, farewell to the North;   5
The birth-place of Valour, the country of Worth:
Wherever I wander, wherever I rove,
The hills of the Highlands for ever I love.—

Farewell to the mountains high cover'd with snow;
Farewell to the Straths and green vallies below: 10
Farewell to the forests and wild-hanging woods;
Farewell to the torrents and loud-pouring floods.—

My heart's in the Highlands, my heart is not here,
My heart's in the Highlands a chasing the deer:
Chasing the wild deer, and following the roe;   15
My heart's in the Highlands, wherever I go.—

302. John Anderson my Jo

Jо н n Anderson my jo, John,
  When we were first acquent;
Your locks were like the raven,
Your bony brow was brent;

11 forests and wild-] *correcting* torrents and low *in MS*

John Anderson my Jo. *Text from SMM, 1790 (260; signed B), collated with SC,
1799 (51). See Commentary*

But now your brow is beld, John,   5
   Your locks are like the snaw;
But blessings on your frosty pow,
   John Anderson my Jo.

John Anderson my jo, John,
   We clamb the hill the gither;   10
And mony a canty day, John,
   We've had wi' ane anither:
Now we maun totter down, John,
   And hand in hand we'll go;
And sleep the gither at the foot,   15
   John Anderson my Jo.

303. Awa whigs awa

Awa whigs awa,
   Awa whigs awa,
Ye're but a pack o' traitor louns,
   Ye'll do nae gude at a'.

Our thrissles flourish'd fresh and fair,   5
   And bonie bloom'd our roses;
But whigs cam like a frost in June,
   And wither'd a' our posies.
      Cho: Awa whigs &c.

Awa whigs awa. *Text from SMM, 1790 (263; unsigned)*

Our ancient crown's fa'n in the dust;
    Deil blin' them wi' the stoure o't,   10
And write their names in his black beuk
    Wha gae the whigs the power o't!
      Cho: Awa whigs &c.

Our sad decay in church and state
    Surpasses my descriving:
The whigs cam o'er us for a curse,   15
    And we hae done wi' thriving.
      Cho: Awa whigs &c.

Grim Vengeance lang has taen a nap,
    But we may see him wauken:
Gude help the day when royal heads
    Are hunted like a maukin.   20
      Cho: Awa whigs &c.

304. I'll mak you be fain to follow me

Lively

As late by a sodger I chanced to pass,
  I heard him a courtin a bony young lass;
My hinny, my life, my dearest, quo he,
I'll mak you be fain to follow me.

I'll mak you be fain. *Text from SMM, 1790 (268; unsigned)*

Gin I should follow you, a poor sodger lad,   5
Ilk ane o' my cummers wad think I was mad;
For battles I never shall lang to see,
I'll never be fain to follow thee.

To follow me, I think ye may be glad,
A part o' my supper, a part o' my bed,   10
A part o' my bed, wherever it be,
I'll mak you be fain to follow me.
Come try my knapsack on your back,
Alang the king's high-gate we'll pack;
Between Saint Johnston and bony Dundee,   15
I'll mak you be fain to follow me.

305. Merry hae I been teethin a heckle

Tune, Boddich na' mbrigs, or Lord Breadalbine's March

O MERRY hae I been teethin a heckle,
   An' merry hae I been shapin a spoon:
O merry hae I been cloutin a kettle,
   An' kissin my Katie when a' was done.

Merry hae I been. *Text from SMM, 1790 (270; unsigned)*

O, a' the lang day I ca' at my hammer, 5
    An' a' the lang day I whistle and sing;
O, a' the lang night I cuddle my kimmer,
    An' a' the lang night as happy's a king.

Bitter in dool I lickit my winnins
    O' marrying Bess, to gie her a slave: 10
Blest be the hour she cool'd in her linnens,
    And blythe be the bird that sings on her grave!
Come to my arms, my Katie, my Katie,
    An' come to my arms and kiss me again!
Druken or sober, here's to thee, Katie! 15
    And blest be the day I did it again.

306. The White Cockade

Lively

M<small>Y</small> love was born in Aberdeen,
   The boniest lad that e'er was seen,
But now he makes our hearts fu' sad,
He takes the field wi' his White Cockade.

6 sing;] sing *SMM*   15 sober,] sober *SMM*

The White Cockade. *Text from SMM, 1790 (272; unsigned)*

O he's a ranting, roving lad,   5
He is a brisk an' a bonny lad,
Betide what may, I will be wed,
And follow the boy wi' the White Cockade.

I'll sell my rock, my reel, my tow,
My gude gray mare and hawkit cow;   10
To buy mysel a tartan plaid,
To follow the boy wi' the White Cockade.
    Cho: O he's a ranting, roving lad.

307. My Eppie

Chorus

AN O, my Eppie,
   My Jewel, my Eppie!
Wha wad na be happy
   Wi' Eppie Adair!

My Eppie. *Text from the Hastie MS, ff. 54ᵛ–55ʳ, collated with SMM, 1790 (281; unsigned). Title in SMM Eppie Adair*

I

By Love, and by Beauty;   5
By Law, and by Duty;
I swear to be true to
    My Eppie Adair!

2

A' Pleasure exile me;
Dishonour defile me,   10
If e'er I beguile thee,
    My Eppie Adair!

308. The Battle of Sherra-moor

Tune, Cameronian Rant

O CAM ye here the fight to shun,
    Or herd the sheep wi' me, man,
Or were ye at the Sherra-moor,
    Or did the battle see, man.

The Battle of Sherra-moor. *Text from SMM, 1790 (282;* Written for this Work by
Rob! Burns), *collated with Currie (iv. 360–2). Title in Currie* On the Battle of Sheriff-
Muir, Between the Duke of Argyle and the Earl of Mar. *No chorus in Currie*

I saw the battle sair and teugh,   5
And reekin-red ran mony a sheugh,
My heart for fear gae sough for sough,
To hear the thuds, and see the cluds
O' Clans frae woods, in tartan duds,
Wha glaum'd at kingdoms three, man.   10
        Cho: la la la, &c.

The red-coat lads wi' black cockauds
    To meet them were na slaw, man,
They rush'd, and push'd, and blude outgush'd,
    And mony a bouk did fa', man:
The great Argyle led on his files,   15
I wat they glanc'd for twenty miles,
They hough'd the Clans like nine-pin kyles,
They hack'd and hash'd while braid swords clash'd,
And thro' they dash'd, and hew'd and smash'd,
Till fey men di'd awa, man.   20
        Cho: la la la, &c.

But had ye seen the philibegs
    And skyrin tartan trews, man,
When in the teeth they dar'd our Whigs,
    And covenant Trueblues, man;
In lines extended lang and large,   25
When baiginets o'erpower'd the targe,
And thousands hasten'd to the charge;
Wi' Highland wrath they frae the sheath
Drew blades o' death, till out o' breath
They fled like frighted dows, man.   30
        Cho: la la la, &c.

O how deil Tam can that be true,
    The chace gaed frae the north, man;
I saw mysel, they did pursue
    The horse-men back to Forth, man;

13 push'd,] push'd *SMM*   17 kyles,] kyles *SMM*   17 om. *in Currie*
26 baiginets o'erpower'd] bayonets opposed *Currie*   targe *Currie*: charge *SMM*
34 man;] man *SMM*

And at Dunblane in my ain sight   35
They took the brig wi' a' their might,
And straught to Stirling wing'd their flight,
But, cursed lot! the gates were shut
And mony a huntit, poor Red-coat
For fear amaist did swarf, man.   40
      Cho: la la la, &c.

My sister Kate cam up the gate
    Wi' crowdie unto me, man;
She swoor she saw some rebels run
    To Perth and to Dundee, man:
Their left-hand General had nae skill;   45
The Angus lads had nae gude will,
That day their neebour's blude to spill;
For fear by foes that they should lose
Their cogs o' brose, they scar'd at blows
And hameward fast did flee, man.   50
      Cho: la la la, &c.

They've lost some gallant gentlemen
    Amang the Highland clans, man;
I fear my Lord Panmuir is slain,
    Or in his en'mies hands, man:
Now wad ye sing this double flight,   55
Some fell for wrang and some for right,
And mony bade the warld gudenight;
Say pell and mell, wi' muskets knell
How Tories fell, and Whigs to h—ll
Flew off in frighted bands, man.   60
      Cho: la la la, &c.

44 To . . . and to] Frae . . . unto *Currie*   49 they scar'd at blows] all crying woes, *Currie*   50 hameward fast did flee] so it goes you see *Currie*   54 in his en'mies] fallen in whiggish *Currie*   55 flight] fight *Currie*   57 And] But *Currie*   59 fell,] fell *SMM*   58–60 Say . . . man.] *Currie has*
    Then ye may tell, how pell and mell,
    By red claymores, and muskets knell,
    Wi' dying yell, the tories fell,
    And whigs to hell did flee, man.

309. Sandy and Jockie

Jenny's Lamentation

T WA bony lads were Sandy and Jockie;
Jockie was lo'ed but Sandy unlucky;
Jockie was laird baith of hills and of vallies,
But Sandy was nought but the king o' gude fellows.
Jockie lo'ed Madgie, for Madgie had money, 5
And Sandie lo'ed Mary, for Mary was bony:
Ane wedded for Love, ane wedded for treasure,
So Jockie had siller, and Sandy had pleasure.

Sandy and Jockie. *Text from SMM, 1790 (283; unsigned)*
 2 unlucky;] unlucky, *SMM*

310. Young Jockey was the blythest lad

YOUNG Jockey was the blythest lad
   In a' our town or here awa;
Fu' blythe he whistled at the gaud,
   Fu' lightly danc'd he in the ha'.
He roos'd my een sae bonie blue,   5
   He roos'd my waist sae genty sma;
An ay my heart came to my mou,
   When ne'er a body heard or saw.

My Jockey toils upon the plain
   Thro' wind and weet, thro' frost and snaw;   10
And o'er the lee I leuk fu' fain
   When Jockey's owsen hameward ca'.
An ay the night comes round again
   When in his arms he taks me a';
An ay he vows he'll be my ain   15
   As lang 's he has a breath to draw.

Young Jockey was the blythest lad. *Text from SMM, 1790 (287; signed Z)*

311. A waukrife Minnie

Lively

WHARE are you gaun, my bony lass,
  Whare are you gaun, my hiney.
She answer'd me right saucilie,
  An errand for my minnie.

O whare live ye, my bony lass,   5
  O whare live ye, my hiney.
By yon burn-side, gin ye maun ken,
  In a wee house wi' my minnie.

But I foor up the glen at e'en,
  To see my bony lassie;   10
And lang before the grey morn cam,
  She was na hauf sae saucey.

O weary fa' the waukrife cock,
  And the foumart lay his crawin!
He wauken'd the auld wife frae her sleep,   15
  A wee blink or the dawin.

An angry wife I wat she raise,
  And o'er the bed she brought her;
And wi' a meikle hazel rung
  She made her a weel pay'd dochter.   20

O fare thee weel, my bony lass!
  O fare thee weel, my hinnie!
Thou art a gay and a bony lass,
  But thou has a waukrife minnie.

A waukrife Minnie. *Text from SMM, 1790 (288; unsigned)*

312. Song

Tune, For a' that an' a' that

T Ho' women's minds, like winter winds,
  May shift, and turn an' a' that,
The noblest breast adores them maist,
  A consequence I draw that.

Chorus
For a' that, an' a' that,
  An' twice as meikle's a' that,
My dearest bluid to do them guid,
  They're welcome till 't for a' that.   5

Great love I bear to all the Fair,
  Their humble slave an' a' that;   10
But lordly WILL, I hold it still
  A mortal sin to thraw that.
    For a' that, &c.

In rapture sweet this hour we meet,
  Wi' mutual love an' a' that,
But for how lang the flie may stang,   15
  Let Inclination law that.
    For a' that, &c.

Song. *Text from the Alloway MS, collated with the Adam MS and SMM, 1790 (290; signed X). Title in SMM* For a' that an' a' that.
  6 meikle's] mickle as *SMM*   7–8, 23–24 My . . . that.] *SMM has*
> The bony lass that I lo'e best
>   She'll be my ain for a' that.   *See Commentary*

11 lordly WILL,] lordly, Will, *SMM*   12 *additional stanza in nineteenth-century editions:*
> But there is ane aboon the lave,
>   Has wit, and sense, an' a that;
> A bonie lass, I like her best,
>   And wha a crime dare ca' that?
>   For a' that, &c.   *See Commentary*

15 for] for, *SMM*

Their tricks and craft hae put me daft,
 They've taen me in, an' a' that,
But clear your decks, and here's, the Sex!
 I like the jads for a' that!   20
 For a' that, an' a' that,
 An' twice as meikle's a' that,
 My dearest bluid to do them guid,
 They're welcome till 't for a' that.

313. Killiecrankie

WHARE hae ye been sae braw, lad!
 Whare hae ye been sae brankie O?
Whare hae ye been sae braw, lad?
 Cam ye by Killiecrankie O?

An ye had been whare I hae been,   5
 Ye wad na been sae cantie O;
An ye had seen what I hae seen,
 I' th' braes o' Killiecrankie O.

Killiecrankie. *Text from SMM, 1790 (292; signed Z). A holograph draft of ll. 1–8,
formerly owned by the Earl of Lincoln, has* lass *for* lad *in ll. 1–3*

I faught at land, I faught at sea,
  At hame I faught my Auntie, O;   10
But I met the Devil and Dundee
On th' braes o' Killiecrankie, O.
  An ye had been, &c.

The bauld Pitcur fell in a furr,
  An' Clavers gat a clankie, O;
Or I had fed an Athole Gled   15
On th' braes o' Killiecrankie, O.
  An ye had been, &c.

314. The Campbells are comin

Chorus

T H E Campbells are comin, Oho, Oho!
  The Campbells are comin, Oho, Oho!
The Campbells are comin to bonie Lochleven,
The Campbells are comin Oho, Oho!

The Campbells are comin. *Text from the Hastie MS, f. 57, collated with SMM, 1790*
(299; unsigned). Lines 1–4 follow the last stanza in the MS. Note in SMM, Index
Said to be composed on the imprisonment of Mary Queen of Scots in Lochleven
Castle

Upon the Lomonds I lay, I lay,   5
Upon the Lomonds I lay, I lay,
I looked down to bonie Lochleven,
And saw three bonie perches play—
            The Campbells &c.

Great Argyle he goes before,
He maks his cannons and guns to roar,   10
Wi' sound o' trumpet, pipe and drum
The Campbells are comin Oho, Oho!
            The Campbells are &c.

The Campbells they are a' in arms
Their loyal faith and truth to show,
Wi' banners rattling in the wind   15
The Campbells are comin Oho, Oho!

315. Scots Prologue, *For Mrs. Sutherland's Benefit Night*, Spoken at the Theatre Dumfries

WHAT needs this din about the town o' Lon'on?
How this new Play, and that new Sang is comin?
Why is outlandish stuff sae meikle courted?
Does Nonsense mend, like Brandy, when imported—
Is there nae Poet, burning keen for Fame,   5
Will bauldly try to gie us Plays at hame?
For Comedy abroad he need na toil,
A Knave an' Fool are plants of ev'ry soil:
Nor need he hunt as far as Rome or Greece,
To gather matter for a serious piece;   10
There's themes enow in Caledonian story,
Wad shew the Tragic Muse in a' her glory.

Scots Prologue. *Text from Stewart, 1802 (pp. 253–4), collated with the Lochryan MS (Loch; letter to Mrs. Dunlop, March 1790) and Cromek*, Reliques (*pp. 409–11*) Title *Mrs. Loch*: *Mr. Stewart Cromek* Spoken at the Theatre] *om. Loch Cromek. Loch adds* March 3ᵈ 1790
    4 Brandy] whisky *Cromek*   6 bauldly . . . Plays] try to gie us sangs and plays *Cromek*   8 Knave an' Fool] fool and knave *Cromek*   9 hunt] stray *Loch*   or] and *Cromek*   12 Wad] Should *Loch*: Would *Cromek*

Is there no daring Bard will rise and tell
How glorious Wallace stood, how hapless fell?
Where are the Muses fled, that should produce   15
A *drama* worthy of the name of Bruce?
How on *this* spot he first unsheath'd the sword
'Gainst mighty England and her guilty Lord,
And after many a bloody, deathless doing,
Wrench'd his dear country from the jaws of Ruin!   20
O! for a Shakespeare or an Otway scene,
To paint the lovely hapless Scottish Queen!
Vain ev'n the omnipotence of Female charms,
'Gainst headlong, ruthless, mad Rebellion's arms.
She fell—but fell with spirit truly Roman,   25
To glut that direst foe,—*a vengeful woman;*
A *woman*—tho' the phrase may seem uncivil,
As able—and as wicked as the devil!
[One Douglas lives in Home's immortal page,
But Douglases were heroes every age: 30
And tho' your fathers, prodigal of life,
A Douglas followed to the martial strife,
Perhaps, if bowls row right, and Right succeeds,
Ye yet may follow where a Douglas leads!]

    As ye have generous done, if a' the land   35
Would take the Muses' servants by the hand,
Not only hear—but patronise—defend them,
And where ye justly can commend—commend them;
And aiblins when they winna stand the test,
Wink hard, and say, 'The folks hae done their best.'   40
Would a' the land do this, then I'll be caition,
Ye'll soon hae Poets o' the Scottish nation,
Will gar Fame blaw until her trumpet crack,
And warsle Time, and lay him on his back.

    For us and for our Stage, should ony spier,   45
'Whase aught thae Chiels maks a' this bustle here?'

15 should] could *Cromek*   17 on *this* spot] here, even here *Cromek*
22 paint] draw *Cromek*   23 ev'n] all *Cromek*   26 that . . . *vengeful*] the
vengeance of a rival *Cromek*   28 wicked] cruel *Cromek*   29–34 One . . .
leads! *Cromek*: om. *Loch Stewart*   36 the Muses' servants] their native Muses
Loch   42 Ye 'll] Ye 'd *Loch*   43 Will] Would *Loch*

My best leg foremost, I'll set up my brow,
We have the honor to belong to you!
We're your ain bairns, e'en guide us as ye like,
But, like guid mothers, shore before ye strike;   50
And grateful still, I trust, ye'll ever find us:
For gen'rous patronage, and meikle kindness,
We've got frae a' professions, sorts, an' ranks:
God help us!—we're but poor—ye 'se get but thanks!

316. Lament of Mary Queen of Scots on the Approach of Spring

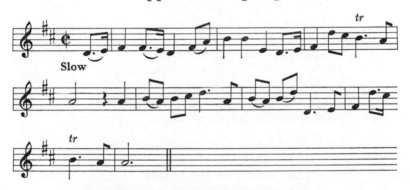

Now Nature hangs her mantle green
On every blooming tree,
And spreads her sheets o' daisies white
Out o'er the grassy lea:

48 *Loch adds* (bowing to the Audience)   49–50 We're . . . strike;] *om. Loch*
51 trust,] hope *Cromek*   52 gen'rous] a' the *Cromek*

Lament of Mary Queen of Scots. *Text from the Edinburgh edition, 1793, collated with the Bixby MSS (A, B), the Alloway MS (Al), the Lochryan MS (Loch; letter to Mrs. Dunlop, 6 June 1790), the Fintry MS (letter to Mrs. Graham, 10 June 1790), the Afton Lodge MS, the Watson MS (1132; letter to Clarinda, 11 December 1791), MSS Adam, Esty, Glenriddell (Glen; pp. 114–17; transcript), Kilmarnock (Kil), Huntington Library (HL), and Texas, SMM, 1796 (404; signed B), and the edition of 1794. See Commentary. Title* Queen Mary's Lament *in Bixby (A, B)* Loch Fintry HL;
The Lament . . . Scots *in Texas;* The Lament . . . Scots.—A Ballad *in Afton, Watson*
2 every] ilka *SMM*   blooming] *correcting* spreading *in Watson Kil*   3 o']
of *HL*   4 Out o'er] *correcting* On every *in Bixby A*

Now Phœbus chears the crystal streams,   5
And glads the azure skies;
But nought can glad the weary wight
That fast in durance lies.

Now laverocks wake the merry morn,
Aloft on dewy wing;   10
The merle, in his noontide bower,
Makes woodland echoes ring;
The mavis mild wi' many a note,
Sings drowsy day to rest:
In love and freedom they rejoice,   15
Wi' care nor thrall opprest.

Now blooms the lily by the bank,
The primrose down the brae;
The hawthorn 's budding in the glen,
And milk-white is the slae: 20
The meanest hind in fair Scotland
May rove their sweets amang;
But I, the Queen of a' Scotland,
Maun lie in prison strang.

I was the Queen o' bonie France,   25
Where happy I hae been;
Fu' lightly rase I on the morn,
As blythe lay down at e'en:
And I'm the sovereign of Scotland,
And mony a traitor there;   30
Yet here I lie in foreign bands,
And never ending care.

But as for thee, thou false woman,
My sister and my fae,
Grim vengeance, yet, shall whet a sword   35
That thro' thy soul shall gae:

6 azure] *correcting* vernal *in Fintry*   7 weary] careful *Watson*: carefu' *Bixby*
(*A, B*) *Loch Fintry Adam Esty Afton HL Texas*   12 woodland] a' the *Watson*
13 many] mony *HL*   21 fair] *correcting* a' *in Fintry Esty*   22 their] thir
Bixby (*A, B*) *Fintry Afton Adam Esty HL Texas*: thae *Watson*: these *Kil*   24 strang]
strong *Bixby* (*A, B*) *Loch Afton Watson Texas*   27 rase] rose *Bixby* (*A, B*) *Watson*
Afton Adam Esty HL Texas   the] *om.* 93   29 of] o' *HL*   31 Yet] But *Loch*
33 woman] womán *Al Watson Esty HL Texas*

The weeping blood in woman's breast
　Was never known to thee;
Nor th' balm that draps on wounds of woe
　Frae woman's pitying e'e.   40

My son! my son! may kinder stars
　Upon thy fortune shine!
And may those pleasures gild thy reign,
　That ne'er wad blink on mine!
God keep thee frae thy mother's faes,   45
　Or turn their hearts to thee:
And where thou meet'st thy mother's friend,
　Remember him for me!

O! soon, to me, may summer-suns
　Nae mair light up the morn!   50
Nae mair, to me, the autumn winds
　Wave o'er the yellow corn!
And in the narrow house o' death
　Let winter round me rave;
And the next flowers, that deck the spring,   55
　Bloom on my peaceful grave.

37 weeping] *correcting* pitying *in Bixby A*   38 Thy *cancelled start in Bixby A*
Is quite unknown to thee *correcting* Thy breast did never know *in Al*   39 Nor]
corrected to And *in Al*   draps on] *correcting* draps frae *in Fintry and* drops from
in Al and melts at *in Kil*   wounds of woe] *correcting* woman's een *in Al*
40 Frae . . . e'e] *correcting* To heal the wounds of woe *in Al*   45 God keep]
Heaven shield (*correcting* keep) *Watson*   49 summer-suns] *correcting* kinder
stars *in Bixby A*   51 to . . . winds] the winds of autumn wave *Afton Glen Kil*
52 Wave o'er] Out o'er *Afton*: Across *Glen Kil*   53 o'] of *HL*   54 round]
o'er *Watson*   55 flowers, that deck] *correcting* morn that decks *in Fintry*
56 Bloom on my] *correcting* Shine o'er the *in Bixby A*: Bloom o'er ~~the~~ my *HL*
Bixby B: Bloom o'er my *Adam Esty Glen*

317. Song—

Tune, Cornwallis lament for Coln! Moorhouse

Plaintive

SENSIBILITY how charming,
  Dearest Nancy, thou canst tell;
But distress with horrors arming,
  Thou hast also known too well.—

Fairest flower, behold the lily,   5
  Blooming in the sunny ray.
Let the blast sweep o'er the valley,
  See it prostrate on the clay.—

Hear the woodlark charm the forest,
  Telling o'er his little joys: 10
Hapless bird! a prey the surest
  To each pirate of the skies.—

Song. *Text from the Hastie MS, f. 68ʳ, collated with MSS Watson (1131; letter to
Clarinda, July 1791?), Lochryan (letter to Mrs. Dunlop, 9 July 1790; quoting ll. 5–8,
13–16), Afton Lodge (1791), f. 31ᵛ, Alloway, and SMM, 1792 (329; assigned to
Burns in the Index). First-line title in SMM, set in eight-line stanzas. Title in Afton MS
On Sensibility—To a Freind.*

1 Sensibility] Sweet Sensibility *Watson*   2 Dearest Nancy, thou canst] Thou,
my Friend, canst truly *Watson Afton Al*   6 sunny ray] summer day *Loch*
8 on] in *Loch*

Dearly bought the hidden treasure,
Finer Feelings can bestow:
Chords that vibrate sweetest pleasure,   15
Thrill the deepest notes of woe.—

318. Epistle to Rob![Graham Esq: of Fintry on the Election for the Dumfries string of Boroughs, Anno 1790—

FINTRY, my stay in worldly strife,
Friend o' my Muse, Friend o' my Life,
Are ye as idle 's I am?
Come then, wi' uncouth, kintra fleg,
O'er Pegasus I'll fling my leg,   5
And ye shall see me try him.—

13 Dearly bought] Envy not *Loch*   14 Feelings] Feeling *Loch*

Epistle to Rob! Graham Esq: of Fintry. *Text from the Glenriddell MS (Glen; pp. 81–86), collated with the Alloway MS (Al; Sketch, 50 lines), the Fintry MS (sent to Graham, dated Ellisland 10ᵗʰ June 1790), the Afton Lodge MS (ff. 23ᵛ–27ʳ), the Dumfries MS (Dum; ll. 1–60 only, apparently part of the MS belonging to Mrs Mc-Murdo and used by Allan Cunningham), Dewar's transcript of a holograph fragment sold at Sotheby's on 13 November 1934 (ll. 61–67 and 94–100; apparently part of MS Dum), and Cunningham, iii. 155–60 (Cun). Title in Afton and Cun* Epistle . . . on the close of the disputed Election between Sir J. Johnston and Capt!! Miller, for the Dumfries district of Boroughs.—*Footnotes to ll. 31–53, 108 from Fintry*
6 *Four rejected stanzas follow in Al:*

                    But where shall I gae rin or ride,
                    That I may splatter nane beside?
                            I wad na be uncivil:
                    For mankind's various paths and ways,   10
                    There's ay some doytan body strays,
                            And I ride like a devil.—

                    Say, I break off wi' a' my birr,
                    And down yon dark, deep alley spur,
                            Where Theologics dander: 15
                    Alas! curst wi' eternal fogs,
                    And damn'd in everlasting bogs,
                            As sure's the creed I'll blunder!

                    I'll stain a Band, or jaup a gown,
                    Or rin my reckless, guilty crown   20
                            Against the haly door:
                    Sair do I rue my luckless fate,
                    When, as the Muse and Deil would hae't,
                            I rade that road before.—

I'll sing the zeal Drumlanrig bears,
Wha left the all-important cares
        Of fiddles, wh–res and hunters;
And, bent on buying Borough-towns,   10
Cam shaking hands wi' wabster-louns,
        And kissin barefit bunters.—

Confusion thro' our Boroughs rode,
Whistling his roaring pack abroad
        Of mad, unmuzzled lions;   15
As Queensberry BUFF AND BLUE unfurled,
And Westerha and Hopeton hurled
        To every whig defiance.—

But cautious Queensberry left the war,
Th' unmanner'd dust might soil his star,   20
        Besides, he hated *Bleeding*:
But left behind him heroes bright,
Heroes in Cesarean fight,
        Or Ciceronian pleading.—

Suppose I take a spurt, and mix   25
Among the wilds o' Politicks,
        Electors and Elected:
Where dogs at Court (sad sons o' bitches!)
Septennially a madness touches
        Till all the Land's infected.—   30

9 fiddles, wh–res and hunters] Princes and their Darlings *Dum Cun*   10 buy-
ing] winning *Dum Cun*   12 bunters] Carlins *Dum Cun*   12 *Two stanzas
and a couplet follow in Al, and the MS breaks off:*

All-hail! Drumlanrig's haughty Grace,
Discarded remnant of a Race,
        Once godlike great in story:
Thy fathers' virtues all contrasted;
The very name of D— blasted;
        Thine that inverted glory.—

Hate, Envy, oft the Douglas bore,
But thou hast superadded more,
        And sunk them in Contempt:
Follies and Crimes have stained the name,
But Queensb'ry thine the virgin claim,
        From aught of Good exempt.—

Great was the drinking, dancing, singing,
Bonfireing, racketing and ringing,

13 Confusion] Combustion *Fintry Afton Dum Cun*

O, for a throat like huge Monsmeg,   25
To muster o'er each ardent Whig,
          Beneath Drumlanrig's banner!
Heroes and heroines commix,
All in the field of Politics
          To win immortal honor.—   30

Mᶜmurdo* and his lovely Spouse,
(Th' enamour'd laurels kiss her brows)
          Led on the Loves and Graces:
She won each gaping Burgess' heart,
While he, sub rosa, play'd his part   35
          Among their wives and lasses.—

Craigdarroch led a light-arm'd Core,
Tropes, metaphors and figures pour
          Like Hecla streaming thunder:
Glenriddel†, skill'd in rusty coins,   40
Blew up each Tory's dark designs,
          And bar'd the treason under.—

In either wing two champions fought;
Redoubted STAIG‡, who set at nought
          The wildest savage Tory: 45
While WELSH§, who never flinch'd his ground,
High-wav'd his magnum bonum round
          With Cyclopean fury.—

Miller‖ brought up th' artillery ranks,
The many-pounders of the banks,   50
          Resistless desolation!
While Maxwelton¶, that baron bold,
'Mid LAWSON's** port entrench'd his hold,
          And threaten'd worse damnation.—

* The Duke's Factor and Cousin   † Robᵗ Riddel Esqʳ of Glenriddel
‡ Provost of Dumfries and Director of the Bank of Scotland
§ Sherriff Substitute
‖ Patrick Miller Esqʳ of Dalswinton the Candidate's father
¶ Sir Robᵗ Lowrie   ** A famous wine Merchᵗ

35 sub rosa] in ambush *Fintry*: all-conquering *Dum Cun*   46 While] And
Fintry Dum Cun   never] ne'er yet *Fintry Afton Dum Cun*

To these what Tory hosts oppos'd,   55
With these what Tory warriors clos'd,
          Surpasses my descriving:
Squadrons, extended long and large,
With headlong speed rush to the charge,
          Like furious devils driving.—   60

What Verse can sing, or Prose narrate,
The butcher deeds of bloody Fate,
          Amid this mighty tulzie!
Grim Horror girn'd; pale Terror roar'd,
As Murder at his thrapple shor'd;   65
          And Hell mix'd in the brulzie.—

As Highland craigs by thunder cleft,
When lightenings fire the stormy lift,
          Hurl down wi' crashing rattle;
As flames among a hundred woods,   70
As headlong foam a hundred floods,
          Such is the rage of battle.—

The stubborn Tories dare to die,
As soon the rooted oaks would fly
          Before th' approaching fellers: 75
The Whigs come on like ocean's roar,
When all his wintry billows pour
          Against the Buchan bullers.—

Lo, from the shades of Death's deep night,
Departed Whigs enjoy the fight,   80
          And think on former daring:
The muffled Murtherer of CHARLES*
The Magna charta flag unfurls,
          All deadly gules it's bearing.—

* Charles 1st was executed by a man in a mask.—

---

59 headlong] furious *Fintry Dum Cun*   60 furious] raging *Fintry Dum Cun*

Nor wanting ghosts of Tory fame;   85
Bold SCRIMGEOUR* follows gallant GRAHAM†,
      Auld Covenanters shiver!
(Forgive, forgive! much wrong'd Montrose!
Now, Death and Hell engulph thy foes,
      Thou liv'st on high for ever.)   90

Still o'er the field the combat burns,
The Tories, Whigs, give way by turns,
      But Fate the word has spoken:
For Woman's wit, and strength of Man,
Alas! can do but what they can;   95
      The Tory ranks are broken.—

O, that my een were flowing burns!
My voice, a lioness that mourns
      Her darling cub's undoing!
That I might greet, that I might cry,   100
While Tories fall, while Tories fly
      From furious whigs pursuing.—

What Whig but melts for good SIR JAMES!
Dear to his Country by the names,
      Friend, Patron, Benefactor!   105
Not Pulteney's wealth can Pulteney save;
And Hopeton falls, the generous, brave;
      And STEWART‡ bold as Hector!

Thou, Pit, shalt rue this overthrow,
And Thurlow growl a curse of woe,   110
      And Melville melt in wailing:
How Fox and Sheridan rejoice!
And Burke shall shout, O Prince, arise!
      Thy power is all-prevailing!

---

* Viscount Dundee   † Montrose—   ‡ Wᵐ Stuart of Hill-side Esqʳ

---

85 fame] name *Fintry*   94 and] or *Afton*   102 From] And *Fintry*
Afton Cun   113 shout] sing *Afton Cun*

For your poor friend, the Bard, afar   115
He hears and sees the distant war,
            A cool Spectator purely:
So, when the storm the forest rends,
The Robin in the hedge descends,
            And patient chirps securely.—   120

Now, for my friends' and brethren's sakes,
And for my native LAND-O'-CAKES,
            I pray with holy fire;
Lord, send a rough-shod troop o' hell,
O'er a', wad Scotland buy, or sell,   125
            And grind them in the mire!!!
                    I am, &c.

319. On the Birth of a Posthumous Child, born in peculiar circumstances of Family-Distress

SWEET floweret, pledge o' meikle love,
    And ward o' mony a prayer,
What heart o' stane wad thou na move,
    Sae helpless, sweet, and fair.

November hirples o'er the lea,   5
    Chill, on thy lovely form;
And gane, alas! the sheltering tree,
    Should shield thee frae the storm.

May HE who gives the rain to pour,
    And wings the blast to blaw,   10
Protect thee frae the driving shower,
    The bitter frost and snaw.

116 He . . . distant war] He only hears and sees the war *Fintry Afton Cun*
120 patient] sober, *Fintry Cun*   121–6 Now . . . mire!!!] *not in the McMurdo
MS (Cunningham)*   122 native] dear-loved *Fintry Afton*   126 And] *corrected
to* To *in Fintry*: To *Afton*

On the Birth of a Posthumous Child. *Text from the Edinburgh edition, 1793,
collated with Glenriddell (pp. 104–5) and Victoria and Albert Museum MSS, and the
edition of 1794. The Museum text is headed* A Monsr Henri. *The Glenriddell MS is
headed:* Extempore nearly—On the birth of Monsr Henri, posthumous child to a
Monsr Henri, a Gentleman of family and fortune from Switzerland; who died in
three days illness, leaving his lady, a sister of Sir Thos Wallace, in her sixth month
of this her first child.—The Lady and her Family were particular friends of the
Author.—The child was born in November —90—

May HE, the friend of woe and want,
   Who heals life's various stounds,
Protect and guard the mother plant,   15
   And heal her cruel wounds.

But late she flourished, rooted fast,
   Fair on the summer morn:
Now, feebly bends she, in the blast,
   Unsheltered and forlorn.   20

Blest be thy bloom, thou lovely gem,
   Unscathed by ruffian hand!
And from thee many a parent stem
   Arise to deck our land.

320. Song—

Tune, Banks of Banna

Song. *Text from the Glenriddell MS (p. 19; ll. 17–24 on p. 26), collated with the Dalhousie MS (Dal; following letter to Thomson, 4 July 1796), MMC (pp. 9–10), and Stewart, 1802 (p. 213). See Commentary*

1

YESTREEN I had a pint o' wine,
   A place where body saw na;
Yestreen lay on this breast o' mine
   The gowden locks of Anna.—
The hungry Jew in wilderness   5
   Rejoicing o'er his manna,
Was naething to my hiney bliss
   Upon the lips of Anna.—

2

Ye Monarchs take the East and West,
   Frae Indus to Savannah!   10
Gie me within my straining grasp
   The melting form of Anna.—
There I'll despise Imperial charms,
   An Empress or Sultana,
While dying raptures in her arms   15
   I give and take with Anna!!!

3

Awa, thou flaunting god o' day!
   Awa, thou pale Diana!
Ilk star, gae hide thy twinkling ray!
   When I'm to meet my Anna.—   20
Come, in thy raven plumage, Night;
   Sun, moon and stars withdrawn a';
And bring an angel pen to write
   My transports wi' my Anna.—

1 had] got *Currie* (*MS variant*)   4 gowden] raven *MMC Stewart*
5 hungry Jew]Israelite *alternative in Glenriddell*   12 melting] lovely *Dal*
15 dying raptures] rapt, encircled *Dal*   16 give and take with] speechless, gaze
on *Dal*   24 Postscript by Another Hand *in MMC:*

> The kirk and state may join and tell;
>   To do sic things I manna:
> The kirk and state may gae to h–ll,
>   And I shall gae to Anna.
> She is the sunshine o' my e'e,
>   To live but her I canna:
> Had I on earth but wishes three,
>   The first should be my Anna.

321. Tam o' Shanter. A Tale

Of Brownyis and of Bogillis full is this buke.
GAWIN DOUGLAS.

WHEN chapman billies leave the street,
  And drouthy neebors, neebors meet,
As market-days are wearing late,
An' folk begin to tak the gate;
While we sit bousing at the nappy,   5
And getting fou and unco happy,
We think na on the lang Scots miles,
The mosses, waters, slaps, and styles,
That lie between us and our hame,
Whare sits our sulky sullen dame,   10
Gathering her brows like gathering storm,
Nursing her wrath to keep it warm.

  This truth fand honest *Tam o' Shanter*,
As he frae Ayr ae night did canter,
(Auld Ayr, wham ne'er a town surpasses,   15
For honest men and bonny lasses.)

Tam o' Shanter. *Text from the Edinburgh edition, 1793, collated with the Kilmarnock MS (Kil), the Lochryan MS (Loch; letter to Mrs. Dunlop, 6 December 1790), MSS Adam, Fintry, Afton Lodge, and Glenriddell (Glen), Grose's Antiquities of Scotland, 1791, the print of c. 1791 (91; title Aloway Kirk; or, Tam o' Shanter. A Tale. By Robert Burns the Ayrshire Poet), the Edinburgh Magazine, March 1791 (EM), the Edinburgh Herald, 18 March 1791 (EH), and the edition of 1794. Glen is a transcript corrected by Burns. See Commentary*

Epigraph lacking in MSS. 91 gives ll. 219–24 as epigraph. Introductory note in Afton Aloway-kirk, the scene of the following Poem, is an old Ruin in Ayr-shire, hard by the great road from Ayr to Maybole, on the banks of the river Doon, and near the old bridge of that name.—A Drawing of this Ruin will make its appearance in Grose's Antiquities of Scotland.—*In Fintry* Aloway-kirk . . . on the banks of the river Doon, in Ayrshire, and hard by the great road . . . to Maybole.— A Drawing . . . Antiquities of Scotland.—*In Loch as in Afton, ending* A Drawing of this old Ruin, accompanied perhaps with 'Tam o' Shanter', will make its appearance in Grose's Antiquities of Scotland. *In Glen* When Captain Grose was at Friars-Carse in Summer 1790 Collecting materials for his Scottish Antiquities he applied to M.ʳ Burns then living in the neighbourhood to write him an account of the Witches Meetings at Aloway Church near Ayr who complied with his request and wrote for him the following Poem.
  1 chapman] chapmen *MSS Grose*   8 mosses, waters] waters, mosses *Glen Grose*

O *Tam*! hadst thou but been sae wise,
As ta'en thy ain wife *Kate*'s advice!
She tauld thee weel thou was a skellum,
A blethering, blustering, drunken blellum;   20
That frae November till October,
Ae market-day thou was nae sober;
That ilka melder, wi' the miller,
Thou sat as lang as thou had siller;
That every naig was ca'd a shoe on,   25
The smith and thee gat roaring fou on;
That at the L—d's house, even on Sunday,
Thou drank wi' Kirkton Jean till Monday.
She prophesied that late or soon,
Thou would be found deep drown'd in Doon;   30
Or catch'd wi' warlocks in the mirk,
By *Alloway*'s auld haunted kirk.

Ah, gentle dames! it gars me greet,
To think how mony counsels sweet,
How mony lengthen'd sage advices,   35
The husband frae the wife despises!

But to our tale: Ae market-night,
Tam had got planted unco right;
Fast by an ingle, bleezing finely,
Wi' reaming swats, that drank divinely;   40
And at his elbow, Souter *Johnny*,
His ancient, trusty, drouthy crony;
Tam lo'ed him like a vera brither;
They had been fou for weeks thegither.
The night drave on wi' sangs and clatter;   45
And ay the ale was growing better:
The landlady and *Tam* grew gracious,
Wi' favours, secret, sweet, and precious:
The Souter tauld his queerest stories;
The landlord's laugh was ready chorus: 50
The storm without might rair and rustle,
Tam did na mind the storm a whistle.

22 was nae] was na *Kil Fintry Afton Glen Grose 91*: wastna *Adam*   27 L—d's]
L—s's *Kil*: Laird's *91*   house] *om. Adam EM EH*   30 would] wad *MSS 91*
EM EH   47 and *Tam* grew] grew unco *Loch*   48 favours, secret,] secret
favors, *Kil*   50 *See Commentary*   52 mind] *correcting* care *in Kil*

Care, mad to see a man sae happy,
E'en drown'd himsel amang the nappy:
As bees flee hame wi' lades o' treasure,   55
The minutes wing'd their way wi' pleasure:
Kings may be blest, but *Tam* was glorious,
O'er a' the ills o' life victorious!

But pleasures are like poppies spread,
You seize the flower, its bloom is shed;   60
Or like the snow falls in the river,
A moment white—then melts for ever;
Or like the borealis race,
That flit ere you can point their place;
Or like the rainbow's lovely form   65
Evanishing amid the storm.—
Nae man can tether time or tide;
The hour approaches *Tam* maun ride;
That hour, o' night's black arch the key-stane,
That dreary hour he mounts his beast in;   70
And sic a night he taks the road in,
As ne'er poor sinner was abroad in.

The wind blew as 'twad blawn its last;
The rattling showers rose on the blast;
The speedy gleams the darkness swallow'd;   75
Loud, deep, and lang, the thunder bellow'd:
That night, a child might understand,
The Deil had business on his hand.

Weel mounted on his gray mare, *Meg*,
A better never lifted leg,   80
Tam skelpit on thro' dub and mire,
Despising wind, and rain, and fire;

53-54 Care . . . nappy:] *om. Kil: added in the margin*   53 *No paragraph in*
Grose   54 himsel] himself *Grose* 94   55 wi' lades o'] *correcting* laden wi'
in Kil (o' *om.*)   56 The minutes . . . their] *correcting* Ilk minute . . . its *in Kil*
67 or] and *Loch*   70 hour] *om. Adam*   he mounts] Tam mounts *correcting*
Tam taks *in Kil*   71 he taks] ~~Tam~~ he took *Kil*   79 mare] meare *MSS Grose*
EM EH

Whiles holding fast his gude blue bonnet;
Whiles crooning o'er some auld Scots sonnet;
Whiles glowring round wi' prudent cares,   85
Lest bogles catch him unawares:
Kirk-Alloway was drawing nigh,
Whare ghaists and houlets nightly cry.—

By this time he was cross the ford,
Whare, in the snaw, the chapman smoor'd;   90
And past the birks and meikle stane,
Whare drunken *Charlie* brak 's neck-bane;
And thro' the whins, and by the cairn,
Whare hunters fand the murder'd bairn;
And near the thorn, aboon the well,   95
Whare *Mungo*'s mither hang'd hersel.—
Before him *Doon* pours all his floods;
The doubling storm roars thro' the woods;
The lightnings flash from pole to pole;
Near and more near the thunders roll: 100
When, glimmering thro' the groaning trees,
Kirk-Alloway seem'd in a bleeze;
Thro' ilka bore the beams were glancing;
And loud resounded mirth and dancing.—

Inspiring bold *John Barleycorn*!   105
What dangers thou canst make us scorn!
Wi' tippeny, we fear nae evil;
Wi' usquabae, we'll face the devil!—
The swats sae ream'd in *Tammie*'s noddle,
Fair play, he car'd na deils a boddle.   110
But *Maggie* stood right sair astonish'd,
Till, by the heel and hand admonish'd,
She ventured forward on the light;
And, vow! *Tam* saw an unco sight!
Warlocks and witches in a dance;   115
Nae cotillion brent new frae *France*,

83 holding] hadding 91 *EM EH*   84 some] an *MSS Grose*   85 prudent]
anxious *Kil*   91 thorn] *correcting* tree *in Kil Fintry Glen*: tree *Grose*
97 *Paragraph in Adam*   101 the] *om. Grose*   102 seem'd] seems *Loch*
107 fear] dread *Fintry*   113 on] to *EM EH*   114 vow] wow *Kil Loch*
Adam Afton Glen Grose   115 *Paragraph in MSS and Grose*   116 cotillion]
cotillon *MSS* 91 *Grose*

But hornpipes, jigs, strathspeys, and reels,
Put life and mettle in their heels.
A winnock-bunker in the east,
There sat auld Nick, in shape o' beast;   120
A towzie tyke, black, grim, and large,
To gie them music was his charge:
He screw'd the pipes and gart them skirl,
Till roof and rafters a' did dirl.—
Coffins stood round, like open presses,   125
That shaw'd the dead in their last dresses;
And by some devilish cantraip slight
Each in its cauld hand held a light.—
By which heroic *Tam* was able
To note upon the haly table,   130
A murderer's banes in gibbet airns;
Twa span-lang, wee, unchristen'd bairns;
A thief, new-cutted frae a rape,
Wi' his last gasp his gab did gape;
Five tomahawks, wi' blude red-rusted;   135
Five scymitars, wi' murder crusted;
A garter, which a babe had strangled;
A knife, a father's throat had mangled,
Whom his ain son o' life bereft,
The grey hairs yet stack to the heft;   140
Wi' mair o' horrible and awefu',
Which even to name wad be unlawfu'.

As *Tammie* glowr'd, amaz'd, and curious,
The mirth and fun grew fast and furious:

125–8 Coffins . . . light.] *Marginal correction in Kil of cancelled lines:*
> The torches climb around the wa',
> Infernal fires, blue-bleezing a';

132 unchristen'd] unchirsten'd *MSS Grose*   136 *Additional couplet cancelled in Kil:*
> Seven gallows pins, three hangman's whittles;
> A raw o' weel-seal'd Doctors' bottles

137 which] that *Afton*   142 Which] That *Grose*   142 *Additional lines in MSS 91 Grose EM EH:*
> Three Lawyers' tongues, turn'd inside out,
> Wi' lies seam'd like a beggar's clout;
> Three [And 91] Priests' hearts, rotten, black as muck,
> Lay stinking, vile, in every neuk.—

The piper loud and louder blew;   145
The dancers quick and quicker flew;
They reel'd, they set, they cross'd, they cleekit,
Till ilka carlin swat and reekit,
And coost her duddies to the wark,
And linket at it in her sark!   150

Now, *Tam*, O *Tam*! had thae been queans,
A' plump and strapping in their teens,
Their sarks, instead o' creeshie flannen,
Been snaw-white seventeen hunder linnen!
Thir breeks o' mine, my only pair,   155
That ance were plush, o' gude blue hair,
I wad hae gi'en them off my hurdies,
For ae blink o' the bonie burdies!

But wither'd beldams, auld and droll,
Rigwoodie hags wad spean a foal,   160
Lowping and flinging on a crummock,
I wonder didna turn thy stomach.

But *Tam* kend what was what fu' brawlie,
There was ae winsome wench and wawlie,
That night enlisted in the core,   165
(Lang after kend on *Carrick* shore;
For mony a beast to dead she shot,
And perish'd mony a bony boat,
And shook baith meikle corn and bear,
And kept the country-side in fear:)   170
Her cutty sark, o' Paisley harn,
That while a lassie she had worn,
In longitude tho' sorely scanty,
It was her best, and she was vauntie.—
Ah! little kend thy reverend grannie,   175
That sark she coft for her wee Nannie,

145 loud and louder] *correcting* quick and quicker *in Kil*   149 to] on *Kil
Adam Fintry Afton Glen Grose*   153 flannen] flainen *MSS Grose*   159 *No
paragraph in Kil*   beldams] Carlins *Fintry*   170 kept] *alternative* held *in
Kil*: held *Loch*   fear: *Kil Adam Afton*: fear. 93 *and other MSS*   175 kend]
thought *MSS* 91 *Grose EM EH*

Wi' twa pund Scots, ('twas a' her riches),
Wad ever grac'd a dance of witches!

But here my Muse her wing maun cour;
Sic flights are far beyond her pow'r;   180
To sing how Nannie lap and flang,
(A souple jade she was, and strang),
And how *Tam* stood, like ane bewitch'd,
And thought his very een enrich'd;
Even Satan glowr'd, and fidg'd fu' fain,   185
And hotch'd and blew wi' might and main:
Till first ae caper, syne anither,
Tam tint his reason a' thegither,
And roars out, 'Weel done, Cutty-sark!'
And in an instant all was dark: 190
And scarcely had he Maggie rallied,
When out the hellish legion sallied.

As bees bizz out wi' angry fyke,
When plundering herds assail their byke;
As open pussie's mortal foes,   195
When, pop! she starts before their nose;
As eager runs the market-crowd,
When 'Catch the thief!' resounds aloud;
So Maggie runs, the witches follow,
Wi' mony an eldritch skreech and hollow.   200

Ah, *Tam*! Ah, *Tam*! thou'll get thy fairin!
In hell they'll roast thee like a herrin!
In vain thy *Kate* awaits thy comin!
Kate soon will be a woefu' woman!
Now, do thy speedy utmost, Meg,   205
And win the key-stane* of the brig;

* It is a well known fact that witches, or any evil spirits, have no power to follow
a poor wight any farther than the middle of the next running stream.—It may be
proper likewise to mention to the benighted traveller, that when he falls in with
bogles, whatever danger may be in his going forward, there is much more hazard in
turning back.

177 her] their 91   178 Wad] Should *Kil Fintry Afton Glen* 91 *Grose*   188 tint]
lost *Kil Adam Glen* 91 *Grose*   189 And roars] Then roar'd 91   190 And . . .
was] Syne . . . grew 91   192 When] Till *Adam* 91   198 Catch] Haud
Loch   200 skreech] skriech *Kil:* shout *other MSS* 91 *Grose*   205 *Paragraph
in Afton*   206 *Foot-note lacking in MSS*

There at them thou thy tail may toss,
A running stream they dare na cross.
But ere the key-stane she could make,
The fient a tail she had to shake!   210
For Nannie, far before the rest,
Hard upon noble Maggie prest,
And flew at *Tam* wi' furious ettle;
But little wist she Maggie's mettle—
Ae spring brought off her master hale,   215
But left behind her ain gray tail:
The carlin claught her by the rump,
And left poor Maggie scarce a stump.

Now, wha this tale o' truth shall read,
Ilk man and mother's son, take heed: 220
Whene'er to drink you are inclin'd,
Or cutty-sarks run in your mind,
Think, ye may buy the joys o'er dear,
Remember Tam o' Shanter's mare.

322. [Ken ye ought o' Captain Grose?]

Written in a wrapper inclosing a letter to Capt.ⁿ Grose, to be left
with M.ʳ Cardonnel Antiquarian—

Tune, Sir John Malcolm—

Slow

2 14 wist] *alternative* kend *in Kil*: kend *Adam Fintry Glen 91 Grose*   220 Ilk]
Each *Kil Fintry Afton*   224 mare] meare *MSS Grose EM EH*

Ken ye ought o' Captain Grose. *Text from the Glenriddell MS (Glen; pp. 144–5),
collated with the Alloway MS (Al; letter to Findlater, (?) late 1790) and Currie (iv.
398–9)*

K EN ye ought o' Captain Grose?
    Igo and ago—
If he's amang his friends or foes?
    Iram coram dago.—

Is he South, or is he North?   5
    Igo and ago—
Or drowned in the river Forth?
    Iram coram dago.—

Is he slain by Highland bodies?
    Igo and ago—   10
And eaten like a wether-haggis?
    Iram coram dago.—

Is he to Abram's bosom gane?
    Igo and ago—
Or haudin Sarah by the wame?   15
    Iram coram dago.—

Whare'er he be, the Lord be near him!
    Igo and ago—
As for the deil, he daur na steer him,
    Iram coram dago.—   20

But please transmit th' inclosed letter,
    Igo and ago—
Which will oblidge your humble debtor,
    Iram coram dago.—

So may ye hae auld Stanes in store,   25
    Igo and ago—
The very Stanes that Adam bore;
    Iram coram dago.—

So may ye get in glad possession,
    Igo and ago—   30
The coins o' Satan's Coronation!
    Iram coram dago.—

3 foes ?] *correcting* foes, *in Glen*   11 wether-haggis *Al:* weather-haggis *Glen*
Currie

323. Epigram on Capt. Francis Grose, The Celebrated Antiquary

The following epigram, written in a moment of festivity by Burns, was so much relished by Grose, that he made it serve as an excuse for prolonging the convivial occasion that gave it birth to a very late hour.

THE Devil got notice that GROSE was a-dying,
So whip! at the summons, old Satan came flying;
But when he approach'd where poor FRANCIS lay moaning,
And saw each bed-post with its burden a-groaning,
Astonished! confounded! cry'd Satan, by G–d,   5
I'll want 'im, ere I take such a d——ble load.

Epigram on Capt. Francis Grose. *Text from Stewart, 1801 (p. 83). Stewart's note on line 4:* Mr. Grose was exceedingly corpulent, and used to rally himself, with the greatest good humour, on the singular rotundity of his figure. *Holograph in the Glenriddell MS (p. 26), headed* Epigram— On Captⁿ F. Grose—Antiquarian—, *with* damnable load *in l. 6. Variant in Magee's Belfast edition of Burns's Poems, 1793 (ii. 94):*

The Devil once heard that Old Grose was a-dying,
And whip! on the wings of the wind he came flying;
But when he beheld honest Francis a-moaning,
And mark'd each bed-post with its burthen a-groaning;
Confounded he roar'd, 'I shall leave him, by G—,
'Ere I carry to H–ll such a damnable load.'

VIII

POEMS
1791

❧

ELLISLAND AND DUMFRIES

324. A Fragment, which was meant for the beginning of an Elegy on the late Miss Burnet of Monboddo—

LIFE ne'er exulted in so rich a prize,
  As Burnet lovely from her native skies;
Nor envious Death so triumph'd in a blow,
  As that which laid th' accomplish'd Burnet low.—

Thy form and mind, sweet Maid! can I forget,   5
  In richest ore the brightest jewel set!
In thee, what Heaven above, was truest shown,
  For by his noblest work the Godhead best is known.—

In vain ye flaunt in summer's pride, ye groves;
  Thou crystal streamlet with thy flowery shore,   10
Ye woodland choir that chant your idle loves,
  Ye cease to charm, Eliza is no more.—

Ye heathy wastes immix'd with reedy fens,
  Ye mossy streams with sedge and rushes stor'd,
Ye rugged cliffs o'erhanging dreary glens,   15
  To you I fly, ye with my soul accord.—

Princes whose cumbrous pride was all their worth,
  Shall venal lays their pompous exit hail;
And thou, sweet Excellence! forsake our earth,
  And not a Muse in honest grief bewail!   20

We saw thee shine in youth and beauty's pride,
  And virtue's light that beams beyond the spheres;
But like the sun eclips'd at morning tide,
  Thou left'st us darkling in a world of tears.—

A Fragment. *Text from the Afton Lodge MS (ff. 32ᵛ–33ʳ), collated with the Rylands Library MS (RL; letter to Mrs. Dunlop, 7 February 1791), the Adam MS, and Currie (ii. 319–20; letter to Alexander Cunningham, 23 January 1791). Title in RL and Currie* Elegy on the late Miss Burnet of Monboddo. *Adam has ll. 9–24 only; Currie lacks ll. 25–28*
    7 what] high *Currie*   8 For] As *Currie*   work] works *RL*   16 To . . . ye] *alternative to* Your gloomy horrors *in RL*   18 hail;] hail? *Currie*

The Parent's heart that nestled fond in thee,   25
   That heart how sunk a prey to grief and care!
So deckt the woodbine sweet yon aged tree;
   So, rudely ravish'd, left it bleak and bare.—

325. To Terraughty, on his birth-day

HEALTH to the Maxwels' veteran Chief!
   Health, ay unsour'd by care or grief:
Inspired, I turn'd Fate's sybil leaf,
      This natal morn,
I see thy life is stuff o' prief,   5
      Scarce quite half-worn.—

This day thou metes threescore eleven,
And I can tell that bounteous Heaven
(The Second-sight, ye ken, is given
      To ilka Poet)   10
On thee a tack o' seven times seven
      Will yet bestow it.—

If envious buckies view wi' sorrow
Thy lengthen'd days on this blest morrow,
May DESOLATION's lang-teeth'd harrow,   15
      Nine miles an hour,
Rake them like Sodom and Gomorrah
      In brunstane stoure.—

But for thy friends, and they are mony,
Baith honest men and lasses bony,   20
May couthie fortune, kind and cany,
      In social glee,
Wi' mornings blythe and e'enings funny
      Bless them and thee:—

28 rudely ravish'd, left] from it ravish'd, leaves RL

To Terraughty, on his birth-day. *Text from the MS at Lady Stair's House, Edinburgh* (LSH), *collated with Cromek*, Reliques, *1808 (p. 402). H–H. record a MS dated Dumfries, 10 February 1792 (not traced), with these variants:* 2 by] wi' MS
8 tell] see MS   29 If] Gif MS

Fareweel, auld birkie! Lord be near ye,   25
And then the deil he daur na steer ye:
Your friends ay love, your faes ay fear ye!
                For me, Shame fa' me,
If neist my heart I dinna wear ye,
                While Burns they ca' me.   30

326. There'll never be peace till Jamie comes hame—

Slowish

30 Burns *Cromek:* — *LSH*

There'll never be peace. *Text from the Hastie MS, f. 65, collated with the Cunningham MS (letter to Cunningham, 11 March 1791), and SMM, 1792 (315; unsigned). Title in Cunningham MS Song; set in four-line stanzas. A MS formerly owned by the Earl of Lincoln (collated Dewar), set in four-line stanzas with both Song and l. 4 as title, has* moment *in l. 15*

B Y yon castle wa' at the close of the day,
I heard a man sing tho' his head it was grey;
And as he was singing the tears down came,
There'll never be peace till Jamie comes hame.—
The Church is in ruins, the State is in jars,   5
Delusions, oppressions, and murderous wars:
We dare na weel say't, but we ken wha's to blame,
There'll never be peace till Jamie comes hame.—

My seven braw sons for Jamie drew sword,
And now I greet round their green beds in the yerd; 10
It brak the sweet heart of my faithfu' auld Dame,
There'll never be peace till Jamie comes hame.—
Now life is a burden that bows me down,
Sin I tint my bairns, and he tint his crown;
But till my last moments my words are the same,   15
There'll never be peace till Jamie comes hame.—

327. I look to the North—

Slow

I look to the North. *Text from the Hastie MS, f. 123, collated with SMM, 1796 (421; unsigned). Lines 5–8 are quoted in Burns's letter to Cunningham, 11 March 1791, omitting the initial* But. *First-line title in SMM*

O<small>UT</small> over the Forth, I look to the North,
But what is the North and its Highlands to me;
The South, nor the East, gie ease to my breast,
The far foreign land, or the wide rolling sea:
But I look to the West, when I gae to rest,　　　5
That happy my dreams and my slumbers may be;
For far in the West lives he I lo'e best,
The man that is dear to my babie and me.—

*　　*　　*　　*　　*　　*

328. The Banks o' Doon (A)

Cambdelmore

Y<small>E</small> flowery banks o' bonie Doon,
How can ye blume sae fair;
How can ye chant, ye little birds,
And I sae fu' o' care!

The Banks o' Doon. (A). *Text from Cromek,* Reliques, *1808, p. 17, completed from the Cunningham MS (letter to Cunningham, 11 March 1791). Cromek's text is a letter to Ballantine (? March 1791). Tune in MS* Ballendalloch's reel; *title in MS* Song— 1–4 Ye . . . care!] *MS has*

Sweet are the banks, the banks o' Doon,
The spreading flowers are fair,
And every thing is blythe and glad
But I am fu' o' care—

Thou'll break my heart, thou bonie bird   5
　　That sings upon the bough;
Thou minds me o' the happy days
　　When my fause luve was true.

Thou'll break my heart, thou bonie bird
　　That sings beside thy mate;   10
For sae I sat, and sae I sang,
　　And wist na o' my fate.

Aft hae I rov'd by bonie Doon,
　　To see the wood-bine twine,
And ilka bird sang o' its love,   15
　　And sae did I o' mine.

Wi' lightsome heart I pu'd a rose
　　Frae aff its thorny tree,
And my fause luver staw the rose,
　　But left the thorn wi' me.   20

Wi' lightsome heart I pu'd a rose,
　　Upon a morn in June:
And sae I flourish'd on the morn,
　　And sae was pu'd or noon!

18 Frae aff] Upon MS   19 And . . . the] But . . . my *MS*   21–24 *not in*
Cromek. Text from MS

The Banks o' Doon (B)

The Caledonian Hunt's Delight

Slow and tender

Y E banks and braes o' bonie Doon,
   How can ye bloom sae fresh and fair;
How can ye chant, ye little birds,
   And I sae weary, fu' o' care!
Thou'll break my heart, thou warbling bird,   5
   That wantons thro' the flowering thorn:
Thou minds me o' departed joys,
   Departed, never to return.—

Oft hae I rov'd by bonie Doon,
   To see the rose and woodbine twine;   10
And ilka bird sang o' its Luve,
   And fondly sae did I o' mine.—

The Banks o' Doon. (B). *Text from the Hastie MS, f. 97, collated with SMM, 1792
(374; signed B), and SC, 1798 (43). Cancelled title of air in MS* Caledonian Hunt's
delight—
   5 Thou'll] Thou'lt *SC*   6 flowering] flowery *SC*

Wi' lightsome heart I pu'd a rose,
    Fu' sweet upon its thorny tree;
And my fause Luver staw my rose,   15
    But, ah! he left the thorn wi' me.—

329. On Mr. James Gracie

GRACIE, thou art a man of worth,
    O be thou Dean for ever!
May he be damn'd to hell henceforth,
    Who fauts thy weight or measure!

330. Orananaoig, or, The Song of death

A Gaelic Air

Very slow

On Mr. James Gracie. *Text from McDowall*, Burns in Dumfriesshire, *1870 (p. 59)*

Orananaoig. *Text from SMM, 1792 (385; Written for this Work by Robert Burns),
collated with SC, 1799 (76) and Currie, i. 212–13 and ii. 381 (letter to Mrs Dunlop,
? May 1791). First-line title in SC; set in four-line stanzas to the air My Lodging is on
the Cold Ground. Note in SC* SCENE—A Field of Battle—Evening—The Wounded

F̲AREWELL, thou fair day; thou green earth; and ye skies,
   Now gay with the broad setting sun!
Farewell, loves and friendships, ye dear tender ties!
   Our race of existence is run.
Thou grim king of terrors, thou life's gloomy foe,   5
   Go frighten the coward and slave!
Go teach them to tremble, fell tyrant! but know,
   No terrors hast thou to the Brave.

Thou strik'st the dull peasant, he sinks in the dark,
   Nor saves e'en the wreck of a name: 10
Thou strik'st the young hero, a glorious mark!
   He falls in the blaze of his fame.
In the field of proud honor, our swords in our hands,
   Our King and our Country to save,
While victory shines on life's last ebbing sands,   15
   O, who would not die with the Brave!

331. Address, To the Shade of Thomson, on crowning his Bust, at *Ednam, Roxburgh-shire*, with Bays

W̲HILE virgin Spring, by Eden's flood,
   Unfolds her tender mantle green,
Or pranks the sod in frolic mood,
   Or tunes Eolian strains between.

and Dying of the Victorious Army are supposed to join in the following Song.
Similar note in letter to Mrs. Dunlop; title Song of Death
   2 broad] bright *Currie i.*   16 die] rest *Currie i.*

Address. *Text from the Edinburgh edition, 1793, collated with the* Edinburgh Advertiser, *13 September 1791, the* Gentleman's Magazine, *November 1791, the Earl of
Buchan's* Essay on the Life of Thomson, *1792, the Cowie, Watson and Adam MSS,
a MS in the possession of Mrs Otto Manley* (M), *and the edition of 1794. The variants
given by H–H. and Currie from early drafts agree with the cancellations in M. An
undated print without significant variation (not recorded by Egerer) has the title* Verses /
to the Memory / of / James Thomson, / Author of the Seasons, / by Robert
Burns / the Ayrshire Poet, / to which is added, / A Poem, / written in Carse
Hermitage, by Nithside; / By / the Same Author. / And an Epitaph / on / Sir
Isaac Newton. *Title in Adam* Lines sent to the Earl of Buchan on being requested
by him to send him some lines on the occasion of his Lordship inaugurating a bust
to the Poet Thomson at Ednam, Sept 1791
   1 While . . . flood,] *correcting* While cold-eyed Spring, a virgin coy, *in M*
2 tender . . . green] *correcting* verdant . . . sweet *in M*   3 mood] *correcting*
joy *in M*   4 Or . . . between.] *correcting* A carpet for her youthful feet, *in M*

While Summer with a matron grace   5
　　Retreats to Dryburgh's cooling shade,
Yet oft, delighted, stops to trace
　　The progress of the spiky blade.

While Autumn, benefactor kind,
　　By Tweed erects his aged head,   10
And sees, with self-approving mind,
　　Each creature on his bounty fed.

While maniac Winter rages o'er
　　The hills whence classic Yarrow flows,
Rousing the turbid torrent's roar,   15
　　Or sweeping, wild, a waste of snows.

So long, sweet Poet of the Year,
　　Shall bloom that wreath thou well hast won;
While Scotia, with exulting tear,
　　Proclaims that *Thomson* was her son.   20

332. Extempore—on some Commemorations of Thomson

DOST thou not rise, indignant Shade,
　　　And smile wi' spurning scorn,
When they wha wad hae starv'd thy life,
　　Thy senseless turf adorn.—

6 Retreats to Dryburgh's] *correcting* Walks stately in the *in* M   7 Yet . . .
stops] *correcting* And . . . loves *in* M   8 the] a *Adam*   9–12 While . . .
fed] *following, as alternative verses, these lines in Cowie:*
　　　　　　While Autumn on Tweed's fruitful side,
　　　　　　　　With sober pace and hoary head,
　　　　　　Surveys in self-approving pride
　　　　　　　　Each creature on his bounty fed.
9 benefactor kind,] *corrected to* by Tweed's fruitful side *in* M   10 By Tweed
. . . head,] With age's hoary honors clad, *corrected to* With sober pace and hoary
head *in* M   11 And sees] Surveys M   with . . . mind,] *corrected to* in . . .
pride *in* M   12 on] *correcting* by *in* M   17–20 *not in* M   18 hast] has
94

Extempore. *Text from the Fintry MS (letter to Graham of Fintry, 5 January 1793),
collated with Chambers (1856, iv. 335)*

They wha about thee mak sic fuss   5
  Now thou art but a name,
Wad seen thee d–mn'd ere they had spar'd
  Ae plack to fill thy wame.—

Helpless, alane, thou clamb the brae,
  Wi' meikle, meikle toil,   10
And claught th' unfading garland there,
  Thy sair-won, rightful spoil.—

And wear it there! and call aloud,
  This axiom undoubted—
'Wouldst thou hae Nobles' patronage,   15
  First learn to live without it!'

To whom hae much, shall yet be given,
  Is every Great man's faith;
But he, the helpless, needful wretch,
  Shall lose the mite he hath.—   20

10 meikle toil] honest toil *Chambers*   17 shall yet] more shall *Chambers*
19 needful] needless *Fintry*

333. Lovely Davies

Tune, Miss Muir

Slow

Lovely Davies. *Text from the Hastie MS, f. 79, collated with SMM, 1792 (349; un-signed). SMM sets in two sixteen-line stanzas*

O H O W shall I, unskilfu', try
    The Poet's occupation?
The tunefu' Powers, in happy hours,
    That whisper, inspiration,
Even they maun dare an effort mair   5
    Than aught they ever gave us,
Or they rehearse in equal verse
    The charms o' lovely DAVIES.—

Each eye it chears when she appears,
    Like Phebus in the morning,   10
When past the shower, and every flower
    The garden is adorning:
As the wretch looks o'er Siberia's shore,
    When winter-bound the wave is;
Sae droops our heart when we maun part   15
    Frae charming, lovely DAVIES.—

Her smile's a gift frae boon the lift,
    That maks us mair than princes;
A scepter'd hand, a king's command,
    Is in her darting glances: 20
The man in arms 'gainst female charms,
    Even he her willing slave is;
He hugs his chain, and owns the reign
    Of conquering lovely DAVIES.—

My Muse to dream of such a theme,   25
    Her feeble powers surrender;
The eagle's gaze alane surveys
    The sun's meridian splendor:
I wad in vain essay the strain,
    The deed too daring brave is;   30
I'll drap the lyre, and, mute, admire
    The charms o' lovely DAVIES.—

---

9 Each eye it] *correcting* Ilk ane she *in MS*   17 lift, *SMM:* lift; *MS*
22 willing] *correcting* humble *in MS*

334. Lament for James, Earl of Glencairn

THE wind blew hollow frae the hills,
    By fits the sun's departing beam
Look'd on the fading yellow woods
    That wav'd o'er Lugar's winding stream:
Beneath a craigy steep, a Bard,   5
    Laden with years and meikle pain,
In loud lament bewail'd his lord,
    Whom death had all untimely taen.

He lean'd him to an ancient aik,
    Whose trunk was mould'ring down with years;   10
His locks were bleached white with time,
    His hoary cheek was wet wi' tears;
And as he touch'd his trembling harp,
    And as he tuned his doleful sang,
The winds, lamenting thro' their caves,   15
    To echo bore the notes alang.

'Ye scatter'd birds that faintly sing,
    'The reliques of the vernal quire;
'Ye woods that shed on a' the winds
    'The honours of the aged year: 20
'A few short months, and glad and gay,
    'Again ye'll charm the ear and e'e;
'But nocht in all-revolving time
    'Can gladness bring again to me.

'I am a bending aged tree,   25
    'That long has stood the wind and rain;
'But now has come a cruel blast,
    'And my last hald of earth is gane:

Lament for James, Earl of Glencairn. *Text from the Edinburgh edition, 1793,
collated with MSS Fintry, Huntington Library (HL), Glenriddell (pp. 150–3; Glen),
Don, and Lochryan (Loch; copy with autograph corrections), and the edition of 1794. HL
begins at l. 17*
    1 frae] from *Don*   2 departing] descending *Fintry Glen Don Loch*   4 o'er]
on *Loch*   11 with] by *Fintry Glen Don Loch*   12 hoary] aged *Don*   17 *HL
begins*   18 vernal] *correcting* tunef *in HL*   quire] queire *MSS*   19 a']
correcting all *in HL*   20 aged] *correcting* bluming *in HL*   21 months]
correcting years *in Glen*   25 bending aged] aged, bending *HL*   26 long]
lang *HL*   27 But] And *Glen*   28 hald *MSS 93*: hold *94*

'Nae leaf o' mine shall greet the spring,
 'Nae simmer sun exalt my bloom;   30
'But I maun lie before the storm,
 'And ithers plant them in my room.

'I've seen sae mony changefu' years,
 'On earth I am a stranger grown;
'I wander in the ways of men,   35
 'Alike unknowing and unknown:
'Unheard, unpitied, unreliev'd,
 'I bear alane my lade o' care,
'For silent, low, on beds of dust,
 'Lie a' that would my sorrows share.   40

'And last, (the sum of a' my griefs!)
 'My noble master lies in clay;
'The flower amang our barons bold,
 'His country's pride, his country's stay:
'In weary being now I pine,   45
 'For all the life of life is dead,
'And hope has left my aged ken,
 'On forward wing for ever fled.

'Awake thy last sad voice, my harp!
 'The voice of woe and wild despair!   50
'Awake, resound thy latest lay,
 'Then sleep in silence evermair!
'And thou, my last, best, only friend,
 'That fillest an untimely tomb,

---

31 maun] *correcting* am *in HL Glen*   38 alane . . . care] my lade o' care
alane *HL*   39–40 For . . . share.] *HL has*

    For ilka friend of early days,
    And ilka dear companion's gane.

Fintry has

    For low lie a' in silent dust,
    That wad my pains and sorrows share.

39 silent . . . of] *correcting* low lie a' in silent *in Glen*   41 Now joy is dead,
and hope is flown *deleted in HL*   43 amang] *correcting* of a' *in HL*   46 life
of life] joy of life *HL*   51 thy] my *MSS*   lay] *corrected to* song *in HL*

'Accept this tribute from the Bard   55
'Thou brought from fortune's mirkest gloom.

'In Poverty's low barren vale,
  'Thick mists, obscure, involv'd me round;
'Though oft I turned the wistful eye,
  'Nae ray of fame was to be found: 60
'Thou found'st me, like the morning sun
  'That melts the fogs in limpid air,
'The friendless Bard and rustic song,
  'Became alike thy fostering care.

'O! why has Worth so short a date?   65
  'While villains ripen grey with time!
'Must thou, the noble, generous, great,
  'Fall in bold manhood's hardy prime!
'Why did I live to see that day?
  'A day to me so full of woe?   70
'O! had I met the mortal shaft
  'Which laid my benefactor low!

'The bridegroom may forget the bride,
  'Was made his wedded wife yestreen;
'The monarch may forget the crown   75
  'That on his head an hour has been;
'The mother may forget the child
  'That smiles sae sweetly on her knee;
'But I'll remember thee, Glencairn,
  'And a' that thou hast done for me!'   80

55–56 Accept . . . gloom.] *HL has*
          Accept this lay from him thou brought'st
          Frae hapless fortune's mirkest gloom.

56 brought] brought'st *MSS*   57 low] lone *MSS*   59 oft . . . wistful eye]
aft . . . wistfu' e'e *HL*   60 of] o' *HL*   63 song] sang *HL*   67 generous,]
good and *HL*   72 Which] That *HL Fintry Glen Don Loch*   75 the] *correcting*
his *in HL*   77 the child] her bairn *HL*: the bairn *Fintry Glen Don Loch*
79 thee,] good *Fintry HL Glen Loch*   80 thou hast] he has *HL Fintry Glen Loch*

334A. Lines, sent to Sir John Whiteford, of Whiteford, Bart. with the foregoing Poem

THOU, who thy honour as thy God rever'st,
Who, save thy *mind's reproach*, nought earthly fear'st,
To thee this votive off'ring I impart,
The tearful tribute of a broken heart.
The *Friend* thou valued'st, I, the *Patron*, lov'd;   5
His worth, his honour, all the world approv'd.
We'll mourn till we too go as he has gone,
And tread the shadowy path to that dark world unknown.

335. To R***** G***** of F*****, Esq.

LATE crippled of an arm, and now a leg,
About to beg a *pass* for leave to beg;
Dull, listless, teased, dejected, and deprest,
(Nature is adverse to a cripple's rest);
Will generous G***** list to his Poet's wail?   5
(It soothes poor Misery, heark'ning to her tale),
And hear him curse the light he first surveyed,
And doubly curse the luckless rhyming trade?

Lines, Sent to Sir John Whiteford. *Text from the Edinburgh edition, 1793, collated
with the Glenriddell MS (p. 158) and the edition of 1794. Title in MS* Lines . . . with
the Poem to the memory of Lord Glencairn
   3–4 To thee . . . heart.] *MS has*
> Witness the ardour of this votive lay,
> With streaming eyes and throbbing heart I pay.

8 shadowy *MS*: dreary *93 94. See Commentary*

To R***** G***** of F*****, Esq. *Text from the Edinburgh edition, 1793, collated
with the Alloway MS (Al; dated* Ellisland 5ᵗʰ Octʳ *1791 and signed), the Glenriddell
MS (Glen; pp. 154–7; dated 5 October 1791), the Adam MSS (A, lines 9–75, with
additions, headed* The Poet's Progress—A Poem in Embryo—; B, *undated draft;
C, letter to Mrs. Dunlop, dated* Ellisland New-year-day morning 1789, *including
lines 56–75 as an* Apostrophe to Dulness *for* The Poet's Progress), *the Lochryan
MSS (Loch A, letter to Mrs. Dunlop, dated* Mauchline, 29ᵗʰ Oct. 1788, *including
lines 9–55 as* The Poet's Progress, *an embryotic Poem in the womb of Futurity;
B, letter to Mrs. Dunlop, 23–26 October 1788, including lines on Creech and Smellie),
and the edition of 1794. See Commentary*
   3 dejected] *correcting* neglected *in Adam B*   5 G*****] Graham *MSS*   his]
correcting a *in Glen*   6 heark'ning *94*: hearkening *MSS 93*   8 trade?]
trade. *MSS 93 94*

Thou, Nature, partial Nature, I arraign,
Of thy caprice maternal I complain.   10
The lion and the bull thy care have found,
One shakes the forest, and one spurns the ground:
Thou giv'st the ass his hide, the snail his shell,
Th' envenomed wasp, victorious, guards his cell.—
Thy minions, kings, defend, controul, devour,   15
In all th' omnipotence of rule and power.—
Foxes and statesmen, subtile wiles ensure;
The cit and polecat stink, and are secure.
Toads with their poison, doctors with their drug,
The priest and hedgehog in their robes, are snug.   20
Even silly woman has her warlike arts,
Her tongue and eyes, her dreaded spear and darts.

But O! thou bitter step-mother and hard,
To thy poor, fenceless, naked child—the Bard!
A thing unteachable in world's skill,   25
And half an idiot too, more helpless still.
No heels to bear him from the opening dun;
No claws to dig, his hated sight to shun;
No horns, but those by luckless Hymen worn,
And those, alas! not Amalthea's horn: 30

9 *Adam A and Loch A begin*   11–12 The lion . . . ground:] *Adam A–B and Loch A have*

> The peopled fold thy kindly care have found,
> The horned bull tremendous spurns the ground;
> The lordly lion has enough and more,
> The forest trembles at his very roar:

Adam B corrects the first couplet as in 93, 94, and deletes the second couplet
12 forest] forests 94   14 envenomed] *correcting* pois'nous *in Adam B*: puny
Adam A: poisonous *Loch A   After 14 Adam A has 19–24 (deleted)*   15–20 Thy
. . . snug.] *Loch A has*

> Thy minion Man, exulting in his powers,
> In fields, courts, camps, by altars, bars devours.
> Kings bear the civil, Priests the sacred blade;
> Soldiers and hangmen murder by their trade:

15 kings, *MSS*: kings 93 94   21–22 Even . . . darts.] *MSS have*

> Even silly women have defensive arts,
> Their eyes, their tongues, and nameless other parts.

23 *No paragraph in Adam A*   bitter] cruel *Adam A Loch A*   24 thy . . .
child—the] that . . . thing—a *Loch A*   25 world's] worldly *MSS*   28 hated]
alternative dreaded *in Adam A*

No nerves olfact'ry, Mammon's trusty cur,
Clad in rich Dulness' comfortable fur.
In naked feeling, and in aching pride,
He bears the unbroken blast from every side:
Vampyre booksellers drain him to the heart,   35
And scorpion Critics cureless venom dart.

Critics—appalled, I venture on the name,
Those cut-throat bandits in the paths of fame:
Bloody dissectors, worse than ten Monroes;
He hacks to teach, they mangle to expose.   40

His heart by causeless wanton malice wrung,
By blockheads' daring into madness stung;
His well-won bays, than life itself more dear,
By miscreants torn, who ne'er one sprig must wear:
Foiled, bleeding, tortured, in the unequal strife,   45
The hapless Poet flounders on thro' life.
Till fled each hope that once his bosom fired,
And fled each Muse that glorious once inspired,
Low-sunk in squalid, unprotected age,
Dead, even resentment, for his injured page,   } 50
He heeds or feels no more the ruthless Critic's rage!)

31–32 No . . . fur.] *Adam A has*
               No nerves olfactory, true to Mammon's foot,
               Or grunting, grub sagacious-Evil's-root:
Loch A has
               His dart satyric, his unheeded sting;
               And idle fancy's pinion all his wing;
32 rich] *corrected to* fat *in Adam B:* fat *Al Glen*   33 In . . . pride] The silly
sheep that wanders wild astray *Adam A Loch A*   34 He . . . side:] Is not more
friendless, is not more a prey: *Adam A:* Not more unfriended, and not more a
prey. *Loch A*   36 scorpion] viper *Adam A-B:* butcher *Loch A*   cureless venom dart]
cut him up by art *Loch A*   venom] *alternative to* malice *in Adam A*   38 Those
. . . in] Those bandits that infest *Loch A*   40 hacks] cuts *Loch A*   41 *No
paragraph in Adam A*   causeless wanton] wanton, causeless *Al Glen Adam A–B*
41, 42 *transposed in Adam A*   42 blockheads' *MSS:* blockhead's 93 94   into]
even to *Loch A*   43 bays] *correcting* wreath *in Adam A*   43–44 His . . .
wear:] *Not in Loch A*   44 miscreants] *correcting* wretches *in Adam B*
45 Foiled] Torn *Loch A*   46 flounders] flounces *MSS*   47–48 Till . . .
inspired,] *Loch A has*
               Till fled each Muse that glorious once inspir'd,
               Extinct each ray that once his bosom fir'd.
47 hope] *correcting* Muse *in Al*   49 squalid] feeble *Loch A*   50 resentment]
resentments *Loch A*   51 he heeds or feels] He heeds *Adam A:* He feels *Loch A*

So, by some hedge, the generous steed deceased,
For half-starved snarling curs a dainty feast;
By toil and famine wore to skin and bone,
Lies, senseless of each tugging bitch's son.   55

O Dulness! portion of the truly blest!
Calm sheltered haven of eternal rest!
Thy sons ne'er madden in the fierce extremes
Of Fortune's polar frost, or torrid beams.
If mantling high she fills the golden cup,   60
With sober selfish ease they sip it up:
Conscious the bounteous meed they well deserve,
They only wonder 'some folks' do not starve.

55 *Loch A ends. Additional lines, included as fragments in Loch B, follow in Adam A:*

A little, upright, pert, tart, tripping wight,
And still his precious Self his dear delight;
Who loves his own smart shadow in the streets
Better than e'er the fairest ^{fair}/_{she} he meets.

Much specious lore, but little understood,   5
Fineering oft outshines the solid wood:
A man of fashion too, he made his tour,
Learn'd vive la bagatelle et vive l'amour;
So travell'd monkies their grimace improve,
Polish their grin, nay sigh for ladies' love: 10
His meddling Vanity, a busy fiend,
Still making work his Selfish-craft must mend—

Crochallan came;
The old cock'd hat, the brown surtout the same;
His grisly beard just bristling in its might,   15
'Twas four long nights and days from shaving-night;
His uncomb'd, hoary locks, wild-staring, thatch'd,
A head for thought profound and clear unmatch'd:
Yet, tho' his caustic wit was biting rude,
His heart was warm, benevolent and good.   20

In Loch B the sequence is lines 1–4, 7–10, 5–6, an additional couplet—

His solid sense by inches you must tell,
But mete his subtle cunning by the ell;

and 11–20, with these variants: 2 dear] vast *Loch B*   15 grisly . . . its] rising
. . . his *Loch B*   16 four. . . from] five . . . to *Loch B*   17 uncomb'd,
hoary locks] grisly, uncomb'd hair *Loch B.*

Scott Douglas records a manuscript variant in the additional couplet, But mete his
cunning by the Scottish ell!

56 *Adam C begins*   62 the bounteous meed] *correcting* their high desert *in
Al Adam B:* their great success *Adam A. C*

The grave sage hern thus easy picks his frog,
And thinks the Mallard a sad worthless dog.   65
When disappointment snaps the clue of hope,
And thro' disastrous night they darkling grope,
With deaf endurance sluggishly they bear,
And just conclude that 'fools are fortune's care.'
So, heavy, passive to the tempest's shocks,   70
Strong on the sign-post stands the stupid ox.

Not so the idle Muses' mad-cap train,
Nor such the workings of their moon-struck brain;
In equanimity they never dwell,
By turns in soaring heaven, or vaulted hell.   75

I dread thee, Fate, relentless and severe,
With all a poet's, husband's, father's fear!
Already one strong hold of hope is lost,
Glencairn, the truly noble, lies in dust;
(Fled, like the sun eclips'd as noon appears,   80
And left us darkling in a world of tears:)
O! hear my ardent, grateful, selfish prayer!
F*****, my other stay, long bless and spare!
Thro' a long life his hopes and wishes crown;
And bright in cloudless skies his sun go down!   85
May *bliss domestic* smooth his private path;   ⎫
Give energy to life; and soothe his latest breath,   ⎬
With many a filial tear circling the bed of death!   ⎭

---

64 grave sage] sage, grave *Glen Adam C*   66 clue] thread *Adam A, C*
67 And] *corrected to* When *in Adam A*: When *Adam C*   71 stupid] *alternative
seeming in Adam A*   72 *No paragraph in Al Adam A*   73 moon-struck]
correcting distempered *in Adam A*   75 *Adam A and C end*   76 I dread
thee] *correcting* And thou too *in Adam B*   77 With . . . father's] *correcting*
I with a husband's, father's feelings *in Adam B*   80–81 (Fled . . . tears:)]
Not in Glen Adam B   83 F*****] Fintry *correcting* My Friend *in Adam B*
86 his] *corrected to* life's *in Adam B*

336. Gloomy December

Thro' the lang muir

A<small>NCE</small> mair I hail thee, thou gloomy December!
Ance mair I hail thee, wi' sorrow and care;
Sad was the parting thou makes me remember,
Parting wi' Nancy, Oh, ne'er to meet mair!

Gloomy December. Text from the Hastie MS, f. 162 (Ha), collated with the Watson MSS (1134, f. 2ʳ) and SMM, 1796 (499; signed R). Title from SMM. Ha is headed Tune, Thro' the lang muir I follow'd him home. *Title in Watson Song, to a charming plaintive Scots air—. The Watson MS (letter to Clarinda, 27 December 1791) has ll. 1–8 only, with the note* The rest of this song is on the wheels. *Lines 9–16 were apparently added later in Ha*

Fond lovers' parting is sweet, painful pleasure,   5
   Hope beaming mild on the soft parting hour,
But the dire feeling, 'O, farewell for ever!'
   Anguish unmingl'd and agony pure.—

Wild as the winter now tearing the forest,
   Till the last leaf o' the summer is flown,   10
Such is the tempest has shaken my bosom
   Till my last hope and last comfort is gone:
Still as I hail thee, thou gloomy December,
   Still shall I hail thee wi' sorrow and care;
For sad was the parting thou makes me remember,   15
   Parting wi' Nancy, Oh, ne'er to meet mair.—

337. Song—

Tune, Rory Dall's port

Slow and tender

AE fond kiss, and then we sever;
   Ae fareweel, and then for ever!
Deep in heart-wrung tears I'll pledge thee,
   Warring sighs and groans I'll wage thee.—

10 flown] *correcting* gone *in Ha*   15 For] *added in Ha*

Song. *Text from the Watson MSS, 1134 (letter to Clarinda, 27 December 1791),
collated with SMM, 1792 (347; signed X). Title in SMM Rory Dall's Port; set in
three eight-line stanzas*

Who shall say that Fortune grieves him,   5
While the star of hope she leaves him:
Me, nae chearful twinkle lights me;
Dark despair around benights me.—

I'll ne'er blame my partial fancy,
Naething could resist my Nancy: 10
But to see her, was to love her;
Love but her, and love for ever.—

Had we never lov'd sae kindly,
Had we never lov'd sae blindly!
Never met—or never parted,   15
We had ne'er been broken-hearted.—

Fare-thee-weel, thou first and fairest!
Fare-thee-weel, thou best and dearest!
Thine be ilka joy and treasure,
Peace, Enjoyment, Love and Pleasure!—   20

Ae fond kiss, and then we sever!
Ae fareweel, Alas, for ever!
Deep in heart-wrung tears I'll pledge thee,
Warring sighs and groans I'll wage thee.—

IX

POEMS
1792

DUMFRIES

338. [There was twa Wives]

Tak your auld cloak about you

THERE was twa wives, and twa witty wives,
  As e'er play'd houghmagandie,
And they coost oot, upon a time,
  Out o'er a drink o' brandy;
Up Maggy rose, and forth she goes,   5
  And she leaves auld Mary flytin,
And she f—rted by the byre-en'
  For she was gaun a sh—ten.

She f—rted by the byre-en',
  She f—rted by the stable;   10
And thick and nimble were her steps
  As fast as she was able:
Till at yon dyke-back the hurly brak,
  But raxin for some dockins,
The beans and pease cam down her thighs,   15
  And she cackit a' her stockins.

There was twa Wives. *Text from the Law MS (letter to Cleghorn, ?January 1792; transcript from Davidson Cook)*

339. O saw ye bonie Lesley

The collier's dochter

O SAW ye bonie Lesley,
　　As she gaed o'er the Border?
She's gane, like Alexander,
　　To spread her conquests farther.

To see her is to love her,　　　　　　　　5
　　And love but her for ever;
For Nature made her what she is
　　And never made anither.

Thou art a queen, fair Lesley,
　　Thy subjects we, before thee:　　　　10

O saw ye bonie Lesley. *Text from the Dalhousie MS (Dal; letter to Thomson, 8 November 1792), collated with the Law MS (letter to Mrs. Dunlop, 22 August 1792), the Alloway MS (Al; letter to Alexander Cunningham, 10 September 1792; transcribed in the Glenriddell MS), and SC, 1798 (33). The Law MS, 'literally the first copy,' has an additional stanza after l. 12, and lines 13–16, 17–20, transposed. The Alloway MS has ll. 9–16 only. A MS in private hands in Edinburgh (photostat supplied by Mr. John McVie) has the readings of the Law MS, but lacks the additional stanza and follows the order in the Dalhousie MS. It is headed* Lesley Bailie—A Scots Ballad—Tune, My bonie Lizie Bailie—*and ends with a note:* The foregoing Ballad was composed as I galloped from Cumbertrees to town, after spending the day with the Family of Mayfield—. *Set in 8-line stanzas in SC to the air* The Collier's bonie Lassie, *with Thomson's note:* This song was written on Miss LESLEY BAILLIE of Ayrshire, now Mrs CUMMING of Logie.

1 O . . . Lesley] The bonie Lesley Bailie *Law*　　2 As she gaed] O she's gaen *Law*　　8 never made] ne'er made sic *Thomson's alteration in Dal, SC*　　9 art a . . . Lesley] bonie Lesley, art a queen *Law Al*

Thou art divine, fair Lesley,
   The hearts o' men adore thee.

The deil he could na scaith thee,
   Or aught that wad belang thee:
He'd look into thy bonie face,   15
   And say, 'I canna wrang thee!'

The Powers aboon will tent thee,
   Misfortune sha'na steer thee;
Thou'rt like themsels sae lovely,
   That ill they'll ne'er let near thee.   20

Return again, fair Lesley,
   Return to Caledonie!
That we may brag, we hae a lass
   There's nane again sae bonie.

---

11 art . . . Lesley] bonie Lesley, art divine *Law Al*   12 *Additional stanza in Law:*

      O could a body be sae blest,
        As add unto thy pleasure!
      The dearest life o' mortal man
        Were ill-worth sic a treasure.

13 The deil . . . thee,] The very deil, he could na scaithe *Law Al*   14 Or aught that] Whatever *Law Al*   17 tent thee,] ay tak care *Law*   19 Thou'rt . . . lovely] Thou art sae fair & like them sels *Law*   21 Return . . . Lesley] My bonie Lesley Bailie *Law*

340. Craigieburn-wood—A Song—

Slow

I

SWEET closes the evening on Craigieburn-wood,
  And blythely awaukens the morrow;
But the pride o' the spring in the Craigieburn-wood
  Can yield me nought but sorrow.—

2

I see the spreading leaves and flowers,   5
  I hear the wild birds singing;
But pleasure they hae nane for me
  While care my heart is wringing.

Craigieburn-wood. *Text from the Hastie MS, f. 58 (Ha), collated with the Afton Lodge MS, ff. 30ᵛ–31ʳ (1791), the Alloway MS (letter to Gillespie, ?1791), SMM, 1792 (301; signed B). For a later version, see 483. Title in Alloway MS* Craigieburn-wood—Scots Song—

3

I can na tell, I maun na tell,
  I dare na for your anger: 10
But secret love will break my heart,
  If I conceal it langer.

4

I see thee gracefu', straight and tall,
  I see thee sweet and bonie;
But Oh, what will my torments be,   15
  If thou refuse thy Johnie!

5

To see thee in another's arms,
  In love to lie and languish:
'Twad be my dead, that will be seen,
  My heart wad brust wi' anguish!   20

6

But Jeanie, say thou wilt be mine,
  Say thou locs nane before me;
And a' my days o' life to come
  I'll gratefully adore thee.

Old Chorus

Beyond thee, Dearie, beyond thee, Dearie,   25
  And Oh to be lying beyond thee!
O sweetly, soundly, weel may he sleep,
  That's laid in the bed beyond thee.——

10 na] na, *Al*   11 love] loove *Afton Al*   19 'Twad] 'Twill *Afton Al*
25 Old Chorus *om. Afton*   27 O sweetly *SMM*: Sweetly *Ha: Al defective*
may he *Al SMM*: wad I *Ha*   28 That's *SMM*: Were I *Ha: Al defective*

341. Frae the friends and Land I love

Tune, Carron Side

Plentive

FRAE the friends and Land I love,
　　Driven by Fortune's felly spite,
Frae my best Beloved I rove,
　　Never mair to taste delight.—
Never mair maun hope to find　　　　　　5
　　Ease frae toil, relief frae care:
When Remembrance wracks the mind,
　　Pleasures but unveil Despair.—

Brightest climes shall mirk appear,
　　Desart ilka blooming shore;　　　　　　10
Till the Fates, nae mair severe,
　　Friendship, Love and Peace restore.—
Till Revenge, wi' laurell'd head,
　　Bring our Banished hame again;
And ilk loyal, bonie lad　　　　　　　　15
　　Cross the seas and win his ain.—

Frae the friends and Land I love. *Text from the Hastie MS, f. 59, collated with SMM,
1792 (302; unsigned). Title from SMM*

342. Hughie Graham

Slow

O U R lords are to the mountains gane,
    A hunting o' the fallow deer;
And they hae gripet Hughie Graham
    For stealing o' the bishop's mare.—

And they hae tied him hand and foot,   5
    And led him up thro' Stirling town;
The lads and lasses met him there,
    Cried, Hughie Graham thou art a loun.—

O lowse my right hand free, he says,
    And put my braid sword in the same;   10
He's no in Stirling town this day,
    Daur tell the tale to Hughie Graham.—

Up then bespake the brave Whitefoord,
    As he sat by the bishop's knee;
Five hundred white stots I'll gie you,   15
    If ye'll let Hughie Graham gae free.—

Hughie Graham. *Text from the Hastie MS, f. 60, collated with SMM, 1792 (303; unsigned)*

O haud your tongue, the bishop says,
    And wi' your pleading let me be;
For tho' ten Grahams were in his coat,
    Hughie Graham this day shall die.—   20

Up then bespake the fair Whitefoord,
    As she sat by the bishop's knee;
Five hundred white pence I'll gie you,
    If ye'll gie Hughie Graham to me.—

O haud your tongue now lady fair,   25
    And wi' your pleading let me be;
Altho' ten Grahams were in his coat,
    Its for my honor he maun die.—

They've taen him to the gallows knowe,
    He looked to the gallows tree,   30
Yet never color left his cheek,
    Nor ever did he blin' his e'e.—

At length he looked round about,
    To see whatever he could spy;
And there he saw his auld father,   35
    And he was weeping bitterly.—

O haud your tongue, my father dear,
    And wi' your weeping let it be;
Thy weeping's sairer on my heart,
    Than a' that they can do to me.—   40

And ye may gie my brother John
    My sword that's bent in the middle clear,
And let him come at twelve o'clock
    And see me pay the bishop's mare.—

And ye may gie my brother James   45
    My sword that's bent in the middle brown;
And bid him come at four o'clock,
    And see his brother Hugh cut down.—

39–40 Thy . . . me. *SMM: the MS has*
        For tho' they rob me o' my life,
          They cannot o' the Heaven high.
42 clear] *correcting* brown *in MS*

Remember me to Maggy my wife,
    The niest time ye gang o'er the moor;   50
Tell her, she staw the bishop's mare,
    Tell her, she was the bishop's whore.

And ye may tell my kith and kin,
    I never did disgrace their blood;
And when they meet the bishop's cloak,   55
    To mak it shorter by the hood.—

343. John come kiss me now—

Lively

Chorus

O JOHN, come kiss me now, now, now;
    O John, my luve, come kiss me now;
O John, come kiss me by and by,
    For weel ye ken the way to woo.—

John come kiss me now. *Text from the Hastie MS, f. 62, collated with SMM, 1792*
(*305; unsigned*)

O some will court and compliment,   5
    And ither some will kiss and daut;
But I will mak o' my gudeman,
    My ain gudeman, it is nae faute.—
      O John &c.

O some will court and compliment,
    And ither some will prie their mou,   10
And some will hause in ithers arms,
    And that's the way I like to do.—
      O John &c.

344. Cock up your Beaver

Slowish

Cock up your Beaver. *Text from SMM, 1792 (309; unsigned), collated with the Hastie MS, f. 113ᵛ (torn; ll. 4–8 only). The Hastie MS has also (f. 171) a transcript in another hand. Both MSS have* thy *for* your *in ll. 4, 5 (correcting* your *in autograph), and 8*

W HEN first my brave Johnie lad came to this town,
He had a blue bonnet that wanted the crown,
But now he has gotten a hat and a feather,
Hey, brave Johnie lad, cock up your beaver.

Cock up your beaver, and cock it fu' sprush;   5
We'll over the border and gie them a brush;
There's somebody there we'll teach better behaviour,
Hey, brave Johnie lad, cock up your beaver.

345. My Tochers the Jewel

Slow

O MEIKLE thinks my Luve o' my beauty,
And meikle thinks my Luve o' my kin;
But little thinks my Luve, I ken brawlie,
My tocher's the jewel has charms for him.
It's a' for the apple he'll nourish the tree;   5
It's a' for the hiney he'll cherish the bee;
My laddie's sae meikle in love wi' the siller,
He canna hae luve to spare for me.

My Tochers the Jewel. *Text from SMM, 1792 (312; signed B), collated with SC,
1799 (73). Lines 13–16 are in the Watson MSS (1143). First-line title in SC*
6 bee;] bee, *SMM*

Your proffer o' luve's an airle-penny,
　　My tocher's the bargain ye wad buy;　　　　10
But an ye be crafty, I am cunnin,
　　Sae ye wi' anither your fortune maun try.
Ye're like to the timmer o' yon rotten wood,
　　Ye're like to the bark o' yon rotten tree,
Ye'll slip frae me like a knotless thread,　　　15
　　And ye'll crack your credit wi' mae nor me.

346. Then Guidwife count the lawin

Lively

G̲ANE is the day and mirk's the night,
　But we'll ne'er stray for faute o' light,
For ale and brandy's stars and moon,
And blude-red wine's the rysin Sun.

Chorus

Then guidwife count the lawin, the lawin, the lawin,　　5
Then guidwife count the lawin, and bring a coggie mair.

There's wealth and ease for gentlemen,
And semple-folk maun fecht and fen;
But here we're a' in ae accord,
For ilka man that's drunk's a lord.　　　　10
　　Cho.ˢ Then goodwife count &c.

11 an] gin SC

Then Guidwife count the lawin. *Text from SMM, 1792 (313; signed B), collated with the Hastie MS, f. 64. For* Then guidwife *in title and chorus the MS has* Landlady. *Burns inscribed ll. 11–14 on a window of the Globe Tavern, Dumfries*

My coggie is a haly pool,
That heals the wounds o' care and dool;
And pleasure is a wanton trout,
An' ye drink it a', ye'll find him out.
    Cho: Then goodwife count &c.

347. What can a young lassie do wi' an auld man

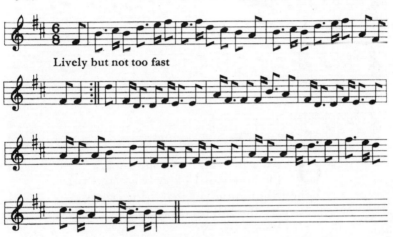

Lively but not too fast

W HAT can a young lassie, what shall a young lassie,
    What can a young lassie do wi' an auld man?
Bad luck on the pennie, that tempted my Minnie
    To sell her poor Jenny for siller and lan'!

He's always compleenin frae mornin to e'enin,   5
    He hosts and he hirpls the weary day lang:
He's doyl't and he's dozin, his blude it is frozen,
    O, dreary's the night wi' a crazy auld man!

He hums and he hankers, he frets and he cankers,
    I never can please him, do a' that I can;   10
He's peevish, and jealous of a' the young fallows,
    O, dool on the day I met wi' an auld man!

What can a young lassie do. *Text from the Hastie MS. f. 66, collated with SMM,
1792 (316; signed R). Title from SMM*

My auld auntie Katie upon me taks pity,
    I'll do my endeavour to follow her plan;
I'll cross him, and wrack him untill I heartbreak him,   15
    And then his auld brass will buy me a new pan.—

348. The bonie lad that's far awa

Slowish

O ʜ o w can I be blythe and glad,
    Or how can I gang brisk and braw,
When the bonie lad that I loe best,
    Is o'er the hills and far awa.—
        [When the &c.]

[It's no the frosty winter wind,   5
    It's no the driving drift and snaw;
But ay the tear comes in my e'e,
    To think on him that's far awa.—
        But the &c.]

My father pat me frae his door,
    My friends they hae disown'd me a';   10
But there is ane will tak my part,
    The bonie lad that's far awa.—
        [But there &c.]

The bonie lad that's far awa. *Text from the Hastie MS, f. 67, collated with SMM,
1792 (317; signed X), SC, 1818 (212), and Cromek, Reliques, (p. 432). Title from
SMM; first-line title in SC. Tune in SC Miss Forbes's farewell. The last line of each
stanza is repeated as chorus in the MS, and cancelled. The two-line chorus in the text
is added in another hand, and printed in SMM. SC has no chorus*
    1 O] *added to MS in another hand*   5-8 It's . . . awa. *SC Cromek; not in MS
SMM*   11 there is] I hae *SC Cromek*

A pair o' gloves he bought to me,
  And silken snoods he gae me twa,
And I will wear them for his sake,   15
  The bonie lad that's far awa.—
    [And I will &c.]

O weary winter soon will pass,
  And spring will cleed the birken shaw:
And my young babie will be born,
  And he'll be hame that's far awa.—   20
    [And my &c.]

349. I do confess thou art sae fair—

Slowish

I DO confess thou art sae fair,
  I wad been o'er the lugs in luve;
Had I na found, the slightest prayer
  That lips could speak, thy heart could muve.—

13–16 A pair . . . awa.] *om. SC*   17 O] The *SC Cromek*   19–20 And . . .
awa.] *SC has*

  And a' my tears be tears of joy,
    When he comes hame that's far awa.

20 be] come *Cromek*

I do confess thou art sae fair. *Text from the Hastie MS, f. 69, collated with SMM,
1792 (321; signed Z)*

I do confess thee sweet, but find,   5
  Thou art sae thriftless o' thy sweets,
Thy favors are the silly wind
  That kisseth ilka thing it meets.—

See yonder rose-bud, rich in dew,
  Amang its native briers sae coy,   10
How sune it tines its scent and hue,
  When pu'd and worn a common toy!

Sic fate ere lang shall thee betide;
  Tho' thou may gayly bloom a while,
Yet sune thou shalt be thrown aside,   15
  Like ony common weed and vile.—

350. Galloway Tam

Lively

8 kisseth] kisses *SMM*   9 See . . . in] *correcting* See yonder rose that droops
in *in MS*

Galloway Tam. *Text from SMM, 1792 (325; unsigned)*

O GALLOWAY Tam came here to woo,
    I'd rather we'd gin him the brawnit cow;
For our lass Bess may curse and ban
    The wanton wit o' Galloway Tam.

O Galloway Tam came here to shear,   5
    I'd rather we'd gin him the gude gray mare;
He kist the gudewife and strack the gudeman,
    And that's the tricks o' Galloway Tam.

351. Song—

Very slow

As I cam down by yon castle wa',
    And in by yon garden green,
O there I spied a bony bony lass,
    But the flower-borders were us between.

A bony bony lassie she was,   5
    As ever mine eyes did see:
O five hundred pounds would I give,
    For to have such a pretty bride as thee.

To have such a pretty bride as me,
    Young man ye are sairly mista'en;   10
Tho' ye were king o' fair Scotland,
    I wad disdain to be your queen.

3 ban] ban, *SMM*   6 mare;] mare, *SMM*   8 that's] thats *SMM*

Song. *Text from the Hastie MS, f. 68ᵛ, collated with SMM, 1792 (326; unsigned).*
First-line title in SMM

Talk not so very high, bony lass,
    O talk not so very, very high:
The man at the fair that wad sell,   5
    He maun learn at the man that wad buy.

I trust to climb a far higher tree,
    And herry a far richer nest:
Tak this advice o' me, bony lass,
    Humility wad set thee best.   20

352. Lord Ronald my Son—

Very slow

O WHERE hae ye been, Lord Ronald, my son?
    O where hae ye been, Lord Ronald, my son?
I hae been wi' my sweetheart, mother, make my bed soon;
For I'm weary wi' the hunting, and fain wad lie down.—

What got ye frae your sweetheart, Lord Ronald, my son? 5
What got ye frae your sweetheart, Lord Ronald, my son?
I hae got deadly poison, mother, make my bed soon;
For life is a burden that soon I'll lay down.—

            *   *   *   *   *   *

Lord Ronald my Son. *Text from the Hastie MS, f. 129ᵛ, collated with SMM,* 1792
(327; unsigned)

353. Bonie laddie, Highland laddie

Tune, The old Highland laddie

Lively.

I HAE been at Crookieden,
   My bonie laddie, Highland laddie,
Viewing Willie and his men,
   My bonie laddie, Highland laddie.—
There our faes that brunt and slew,   5
   My bonie laddie, Highland laddie,
There, at last, they get their due,
   My bonie laddie, Highland laddie.—

Satan sits in his black neuk,
   My bonie &c.   10
Breaking sticks to roast the Duke,
   My bonie &c.
The bloody monster gae a yell,
   My bonie &c.
And loud the laugh gaed round a' hell!   15
   My bonie &c.

Bonie laddie, Highland laddie. *Text from the Hastie MS, f. 71, collated with SMM,*
1792 (332; unsigned)
  3 Viewing . . . men] *correcting* There I saw some folk I ken *in MS*

354. It is na, Jean, thy bonie face

The maid's complaint

Slow

I T is na, Jean, thy bonie face,
Nor shape that I admire,
Altho' thy beauty and thy grace
    Might weel awauk desire.—

Something in ilka part o' thee   5
    To praise, to love, I find,
But dear as is thy form to me,
    Still dearer is thy mind.—

Nae mair ungen'rous wish I hae,
    Nor stronger in my breast,   10
Than, if I canna mak thee sae,
    At least to see thee blest.

Content am I, if Heaven shall give
    But happiness to thee:
And as wi' thee I'd wish to live,   15
    For thee I'd bear to die.

It is na, Jean, thy bonie face. *Text from the Hastie MS, f. 72, collated with SMM,
1792 (333; unsigned). Title from SMM, which sets the song in two eight-line stanzas*

355. Eppie McNab—

Slow

O SAW ye my dearie, my Eppie McNab?
O saw ye my dearie, my Eppie McNab?
She's down in the yard, she's kissin the Laird,
She winna come hame to her ain Jock Rab.—

O come thy ways to me, my Eppie McNab;   5
O come thy ways to me, my Eppie McNab;
What-e'er thou has done, be it late, be it soon,
Thou's welcome again to thy ain Jock Rab.—

Eppie McNab. *Text from the Hastie MS, f. 73, collated with SMM, 1792 (336; signed X). SMM sets in two eight-line stanzas*
  8 Thou's] *correcting* Thou art *in MS*

What says she, my dearie, my Eppie M^cnab?
What says she, my dearie, my Eppie M^cnab?   10
She lets thee to wit, that she has thee forgot,
And for ever disowns thee, her ain Jock Rab.—

O had I ne'er seen thee, my Eppie M^cnab!
O had I ne'er seen thee, my Eppie M^cnab!
As light as the air, and fause as thou's fair,   15
Thou's broken the heart o' thy ain Jock Rab!

356. Wha is that at my bower door?

Lively

W H A is that at my bower-door?
       O wha is it but Findlay;
Then gae your gate, ye'se nae be here!
    Indeed maun I, quo' Findlay.—

What mak ye, sae like a thief?   5
    O come and see, quo' Findlay;
Before the morn ye'll work mischief;
    Indeed will I, quo' Findlay.—

Gif I rise and let you in,
    Let me in, quo' Findlay;   10
Ye'll keep me waukin wi' your din;
    Indeed will I, quo' Findlay.—

Wha is that at my bower door. *Text from the Hastie MS, f. 74, collated with SMM,*
1792 (337; Written for this Work [by] Robert Burns)
    3 Then gae] *correcting* Gae *in MS*   10 Let] *correcting* And let *in MS*

In my bower if ye should stay,
   Let me stay, quo' Findlay;
I fear ye'll bide till break o' day;   15
   Indeed will I, quo' Findlay.—

Here this night if ye remain,
   I'll remain, quo' Findlay;
I dread ye'll learn the gate again;
   Indeed will I, quo' Findlay.—   20

What may pass within this bower,
   Let it pass, quo' Findlay;
Ye maun conceal till your last hour;
   Indeed will I, quo' Findlay.—

357. The bonny wee thing

15 bide] *correcting* stay *in MS*

The bonny wee thing. *Text from the Hastie MS, f. 77, collated with SMM, 1792*
(*341; signed R*). *Subscription in MS* Note the first part of the music is repeated, for the
Chorus—

Chorus

BONIE wee thing, canie wee thing,
Lovely wee thing, was thou mine;
I wad wear thee in my bosom,
Least my Jewel I should tine.—

Wishfully I look and languish   5
In that bonie face o' thine;
And my heart it stounds wi' anguish,
Least my wee thing be na mine.—
Bonie wee &c.

Wit, and Grace, and Love, and Beauty,
In ae constellation shine;   10
To adore thee is my duty,
Goddess o' this soul o' mine!

358. Geordie—An old Ballad

Very slow

THERE was a battle in the north,
And nobles there was many,
And they hae kill'd Sir Charlie Hay,
And they laid the wyte on Geordie.

O he has written a lang letter,   5
He sent it to his lady;
Ye maun cum up to Enbrugh town
To see what words o' Geordie.

4 I *SMM*: it *MS*

Geordie. *Text from SMM, 1792 (346; unsigned)*

When first she look'd the letter on,
   She was baith red and rosy;   10
But she had na read a word but twa,
   Till she wallow't like a lily.

Gar get to me my gude grey steed,
   My menzie a' gae wi' me;
For I shall neither eat nor drink,   15
   Till Enbrugh town shall see me.

And she has mountit her gude grey steed,
   Her menzie a' gaed wi' her;
And she did neither eat nor drink
   Till Enbrugh town did see her.   20

And first appear'd the fatal block,
   And syne the aix to head him;
And Geordie cumin down the stair,
   And bands o' airn upon him.

But tho' he was chain'd in fetters strang,   25
   O' airn and steel sae heavy,
There was na ane in a' the court,
   Sae bra' a man as Geordie.

O she's down on her bended knee,
   I wat she's pale and weary,   30
O pardon, pardon, noble king,
   And gie me back my Dearie!

I hae born seven sons to my Geordie dear,
   The seventh ne'er saw his daddie:
O pardon, pardon, noble king,   35
   Pity a waefu' lady!

Gar bid the headin-man mak haste!
   Our king reply'd fu' lordly:
O noble king, tak a' that's mine,
   But gie me back my Geordie.   40

The Gordons cam and the Gordons ran,
  And they were stark and steady;
And ay the word amang them a'
  Was, Gordons keep you ready.

An aged lord at the king's right hand   45
  Says, noble king, but hear me;
Gar her tell down five thousand pound
  And gie her back her Dearie.

Some gae her marks, some gae her crowns,
  Some gae her dollars many;   50
And she's tell'd down five thousand pound,
  And she's gotten again her Dearie.

She blinkit blythe in her Geordie's face,
  Says, dear I've bought thee, Geordie:
But there sud been bluidy bouks on the green, 55
  Or I had tint my laddie.

He claspit her by the middle sma',
  And he kist her lips sae rosy:
The fairest flower o' woman-kind
  Is my sweet, bonie Lady!   60

46 Says,] Says *SMM*   49 marks,] marks *SMM*

359. As I was a wand'ring

Tune, Rinn m'eudial mo mhealladh.—
A Gaelic air—

Plaintive

As I was a wand'ring ae midsummer e'enin,
   The pipers and youngsters were makin their game,
Amang them I spyed my faithless fause luver,
   Which bled a' the wounds o' my dolour again.—

As I was a wand'ring. *Text from the Hastie MS, f. 78, collated with SMM, 1792
(348; unsigned). Title from SMM*

Chorus

Weel, since he has left me, may pleasure gae wi'
  him;   5
 I may be distress'd, but I winna complain:
I'll flatter my fancy I may get anither,
 My heart it shall never be broken for ane.—

I could na get sleepin till dawin, for greetin;
 The tears trickl'd down like the hail and the rain: 10
Had I na got greetin, my heart wad a broken,
 For Oh, luve forsaken's a tormenting pain!
  Weel since he has &c.

Although he has left me for greed o' the siller,
 I dinna envy him the gains he can win:
I rather wad bear a' the lade o' my sorrow, 15
 Than ever hae acted sae faithless to him.—
  Weel, since he has &c.

360. The weary Pund o' Tow

The weary Pund o' Tow. *Text from the Hastie MS, f. 80, collated with SMM, 1792*
(350; unsigned). Title from SMM. In SMM the chorus precedes and follows the stanza

Chorus

THE weary pund, the weary pund,
　　The weary pund o' tow;
I think my wife will end her life,
　　Before she spin her tow.—

I bought my wife a stane o' lint,   5
　　As gude as e'er did grow;
And a' that she has made o' that
　　Is ae poor pund o' tow.—
　　　　The weary &c.

There sat a bottle in a bole,
　　Beyont the ingle low;   10
And ay she took the tither souk,
　　To drouk the stourie tow.—
　　　　The weary &c.

Quoth I, for shame, ye dirty dame,
　　Gae spin your tap o' tow!
She took the rock, and wi' a knock,   15
　　She brak it o'er my pow.—
　　　　The weary &c.

At last her feet, I sang to see 't,
　　Gaed foremost o'er the knowe;
And or I wad anither jad,
　　I'll wallop in a tow.—   20
　　　　The weary &c.

11 souk] *correcting* suck *in MS*

361. I hae a wife o' my ain

I HAE a wife o' my ain,
    I'll partake wi' naebody;
I'll tak Cuckold frae nane,
    I'll gie Cuckold to naebody.—

I hae a penny to spend,   5
    There, thanks to naebody;
I hae naething to lend,
    I'll borrow frae naebody.—

I am naebody's lord,
    I'll be slave to naebody;   10
I hae a gude braid sword,
    I'll tak dunts frae naebody.—

I'll be merry and free,
    I'll be sad for naebody;
Naebody cares for me,   15
    I care for naebody.—

I hae a wife o' my ain. *Text from the Hastie MS, f. 82, collated with SMM, 1792* (*352; signed B*). *Title from SMM*
  2 partake] *correcting* share *in MS*

362. When she cam ben she bobbed

Lively but not too fast

O WHEN she cam ben she bobbed fu' law,
  O when she cam ben she bobbed fu' law;
And when she cam ben she kiss'd Cockpen,
  And syne deny'd she did it at a'.—

And was na Cockpen right saucy witha',   5
And was na Cockpen right saucy witha',
In leaving the dochter of a lord,
  And kissin a Collier-lassie an' a'.—

O never look down, my lassie at a',
O never look down, my lassie at a';   10
Thy lips are as sweet and thy figure compleat,
  As the finest dame in castle or ha'.—

Tho' thou has nae silk and holland sae sma,
Tho' thou has nae silk and holland sae sma,
Thy coat and thy sark are thy ain handywark   15
  And Lady Jean was never sae braw.—

When she cam ben she bobbed. Text from the Hastie MS, f. 83, collated with SMM 1792 (353; unsigned)
  11 lips] *correcting* purse *in MS*   13 silk] *correcting* silks *in MS*

363. O, for ane and twenty Tam

Tune, The Moudiewort

Aɴ O, for ane and twenty Tam!
    An hey, sweet ane and twenty, Tam!
I'll learn my kin a rattlin sang,
    An I saw ane and twenty, Tam.

They snool me sair, and haud me down,   5
    And gar me look like bluntie, Tam;
But three short years will soon wheel roun',
    And then comes ane and twenty, Tam.
      An O, for &c.

A gleib o' lan', a claut o' gear,
    Was left me by my Auntie, Tam;   10
At kith or kin I need na spier,
    An I saw ane and twenty, Tam.
      An O, for &c.

O, for ane and twenty Tam. *Text from SMM, 1792 (355; signed B), collated with SC,*
1799 (59). Air in SC Up in the morning early. *SC has a final* Tam *only in l. 1*
4, 12 An] Gin *SC*

They'll hae me wed a wealthy coof,
  Tho' I mysel hae plenty, Tam;
But hearst thou, laddie, there's my loof,   15
  I'm thine at ane and twenty, Tam!
    An O, for &c.

364. O Kenmure's on and awa, Willie

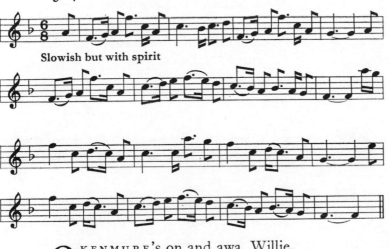

Slowish but with spirit

O KENMURE'S on and awa, Willie,
  O Kenmure's on and awa;
An Kenmure's Lord's the bravest Lord
  That ever Galloway saw.

Success to Kenmure's band, Willie!   5
  Success to Kenmure's band,
There's no a heart that fears a Whig
  That rides by Kenmure's hand.

Here's Kenmure's health in wine, Willie,
  Here's Kenmure's health in wine,   10
There ne'er was a coward o' Kenmure's blude,
  Nor yet o' Gordon's Line.

O Kenmure's on and awa, Willie. *Text from SMM, 1792 (359; unsigned), collated with the Alloway MS. Title from SMM. The MS adds* Willie *to all but the third line of each stanza, and has the spelling* Kenmore
  3 bravest] *correcting* ae best *in MS*   5–7 *follow cancelled lines in MS* O Kenmore's rais'd a band, Willie, &c.   7 no] *correcting* ne'er *in MS*

O Kenmure's lads are men, Willie,
  O Kenmure's lads are men,
Their hearts and swords are metal true,   15
  And that their faes shall ken.

They'll live, or die wi' fame, Willie,
  They'll live, or die wi' fame,
But soon wi' sounding victorie
  May Kenmure's Lord come hame.   20

Here's Him that's far awa, Willie,
  Here's Him that's far awa,
And here's the flower that I lo'e best,
  The rose that's like the snaw.

365. Bessy and her spinning wheel

Slow

23 that I lo'e best] the bony, sweet flower *MS*

Bessy and her spinning wheel. *Text from the Hastie MS, f. 85, collated with SMM, 1792 (360; Written for this Work by Robert Burns)*

O LEEZE me on my spinnin-wheel,
　And leeze me on my rock and reel;
Frae tap to tae that cleeds me bien,
And haps me fiel and warm at e'en!
I'll set me down and sing and spin,   5
While laigh descends the simmer sun,
Blest wi' content, and milk and meal,
O leeze me on my spinnin-wheel.——

On ilka hand the burnies trot,
And meet below my theekit cot;   10
The scented birk and hawthorn white
Across the pool their arms unite,
Alike to screen the birdie's nest,
And little fishes' callor rest:
The sun blinks kindly in the biel'   15
Where, blythe I turn my spinnin wheel.——

On lofty aiks the cushats wail,
And Echo cons the doolfu' tale;
The lintwhites in the hazel braes,
Delighted, rival ithers lays: 20
The craik amang the claver hay,
The pairtrick whirrin o'er the ley,
The swallow jinkin round my shiel,
Amuse me at my spinnin wheel.——

Wi' sma' to sell, and less to buy,   25
Aboon distress, below envy,
O wha wad leave this humble state,
For a' the pride of a' the Great?
Amid their flairing, idle toys,
Amid their cumbrous, dinsome joys,   30
Can they the peace and pleasure feel
Of Bessy at her spinnin wheel!

29-30 follow cancellation in MS:

　　　Can they, amid their flairing toys,
　　　Amid their cumbrous empty joys,
　　　Cam

366. My Collier laddie—

Slowish

WHARE live ye, my bonie lass,
    And tell me how they ca' ye?
My name, she says, is Mistress Jean,
    And I follow my Collier laddie.
My name, she says, is Mistress Jean,   5
    And I follow my Collier laddie.

See you not yon hills and dales
    The sun shines on sae brawlie?
They a' are mine and they shall be thine,
    Gin ye'll leave your Collier laddie.   10
They a' are &c.

Ye shall gang in gay attire,
    Weel buskit up sae gaudy;
And ane to wait on every hand,
    Gin ye'll leave your Collier laddie.
And ane to wait on every &c.

Tho' ye had a' the sun shines on,   15
    And the earth conceals sae lowly;
I wad turn my back on you and it a',
    And embrace my Collier laddie.
I wad turn &c.

My Collier laddie. *Text from the Hastie MS, f. 86, collated with the Liverpool City Library MS (L) and SMM, 1792 (361; unsigned). Title in L* Song—
    1 Whare] O Whare *L*   5–6 *No repetitions in L*   7 See you] O see ye *L*
10 Gin] If *L*   11 Ye] An ye *L*   gay] rich *L*   12 sae] fu' *L*   13 on] at *L*
14 Gin] If *L*

I can win my five pennies in a day
   And spen't at night fu' brawlie;   20
And make my bed in the Collier's neuk,
   And lie down wi' my Collier laddie.
And make my bed &c.

Loove for loove is the bargain for me,
   Tho' the wee Cot-house should haud me;
And the warld before me to win my bread,   25
   And fair fa' my Collier laddie!
And the warld before me to win my bread,
   And fair fa' my Collier laddie!

367. The Shepherd's Wife

Canty

T HE Shepherd's wife cries o'er the knowe,
   Will ye come hame, will ye come hame;
The Shepherd's wife cries o'er the knowe,
   Will ye come hame again een, jo?

21 And make] I can mak *L*   26 fair] fare *L*

The Shepherd's Wife. *Text from the Hastie MS, f. 87, collated with SMM, 1792
(362; unsigned)*
   4, 8, 12 again] *correcting* gin *in MS*

What will I get to my supper,   5
   Gin I come hame, gin I come hame?
What will I get to my supper,
   Gin I come hame again een, jo?

Ye'se get a panfu' o' plumpin parridge,
   And butter in them, and butter in them,   10
Ye'se get a panfu' o' plumpin parridge,
   Gin ye'll come hame again een, jo.—

Ha, ha, how! that's naething that dow,
   I winna come hame, I canna come hame;
Ha, ha, how! that's naething that dow,   15
   I winna come hame gin een, jo.—

The Shepherd's wife &c.
What will I get &c.

A reekin fat hen, weel fryth'd i' the pan,
   Gin ye'll come hame, gin ye'll come hame,   20
A reekin fat hen weel fryth'd i' the pan,
   Gin ye'll come hame again een jo.—

Ha, ha, how! &c.
The Shepherd's wife &c.
What will I get &c.   25

A weel made bed and a pair o' clean sheets,
   Gin ye'll come hame, gin ye'll come hame,
A weel made bed and a pair o' clean sheets,
   Gin ye'll come hame again een jo.—

Ha, ha, how! &c.   30
The Shepherd's wife &c.
What will I get &c.

A luving wife in lily-white linens,
   Gin ye'll come hame, gin ye'll come hame,
A luving wife in lily-white linens,   35
   Gin ye'll come hame again een, jo.—

18, 25, 32 *Editor*: (the 1st & 2d verses sung here—*MS SMM*   19 reekin fat]
correction over erasure in MS   23, 30 (the 4th verse here) *added in MS SMM*

Ha, ha, how! that's something that dow,
I will come hame, I will come hame;
Ha, ha, how! that's something that dow,
I will come hame again een, jo.——   40

368. Johnie Blunt—

Recitative

THERE liv'd a man in yonder glen,
    And John Blunt was his name, O;
He maks gude maut, and he brews gude ale,
    And he bears a wondrous fame, O.——

The wind blew in the hallan ae night,   5
    Fu' snell out o'er the moor, O;
'Rise up, rise up, auld Luckie,' he says,
    'Rise up and bar the door, O.'——

They made a paction tween them twa,
    They made it firm and sure, O,   10
Whae'er sud speak the foremost word,
    Should rise and bar the door, O.——

Three travellers that had tint their gate,
    As thro' the hills they foor, O,
They airted by the line o' light   15
    Fu' straught to Johnie Blunt's door, O.——

They haurl'd auld Luckie out o' her bed,
    And laid her on the floor, O;
But never a word auld Luckie wad say,
    For barrin o' the door, O.——   20

Johnie Blunt. *Text from the Hastie MS, f. 89, collated with SMM, 1792 (365; unsigned)*
   2 John *SMM*: Johnie *MS*   5 the *SMM*: his *MS*

'Ye've eaten my bread, ye hae druken my ale,
   'And ye'll mak my auld wife a whore, O—'
Aha, Johnie Blunt! ye hae spoke the first word,
   Get up and bar the door, O.—

369. Country Lassie—

I n simmer when the hay was mawn,
   And corn wav'd green in ilka field,
While claver blooms white o'er the lea,
   And roses blaw in ilka bield;
Blythe Bessie, in the milkin-shiel,   5
   Says, I'll be wed come o't what will;
Outspak a dame in wrinkled eild,
   O' gude advisement comes nae ill.—

Its ye hae wooers mony ane,
   And lassie ye're but young ye ken;   10
Then wait a wee, and canie wale,
   A routhie butt, a routhie ben:

Country Lassie. *Text from the Hastie MS (Ha), f. 90, collated with the Alloway MS (Al) and SMM, 1792 (366; signed R). No title in Al, which ends at l. 24*

There's Johnie o' the Buskieglen,
　　Fu' is his barn, fu' is his byre;
Tak this frae me, my bonie hen,   15
　　It's plenty beets the luver's fire.—

For Johnie o' the Buskieglen,
　　I dinna care a single flie;
He loes sae weel his craps and kye,
　　He has nae loove to spare for me: 20
But blythe's the blink o' Robie's e'e,
　　And weel I wat he loes me dear;
Ae blink o' him I wad na gie
　　For Buskieglen and a' his gear.—

O thoughtless lassie, life's a faught,   25
　　The canniest gate, the strife is sair;
But ay fu'-han't is fechtin best,
　　A hungry care's an unco care:
But some will spend, and some will spare,
　　An' wilfu' folk maun hae their will;   30
Syne as ye brew, my maiden fair,
　　Keep mind that ye maun drink the yill.—

O gear will buy me rigs o' land,
　　And gear will buy me sheep and kye;
But the tender heart o' leesome loove,   35
　　The gowd and siller canna buy:
We may be poor, Robie and I,
　　Light is the burden Loove lays on;
Content and Loove brings peace and joy,
　　What mair hae queens upon a throne.—   40

21 Robie's] *correcting* Robin's *in Ha*   21–24 But . . . gear.] *Al has*
　　　　But Robie's heart is frank and free,
　　　　　　Fu' weel I wat he lo'es me dear,
　　　　And loove blinks bonie in his e'e,
　　　　　　For loove I'll wed, and work for gear.—
26 the strife is] *correcting* we fecht it *in Ha*

370. Fair Eliza

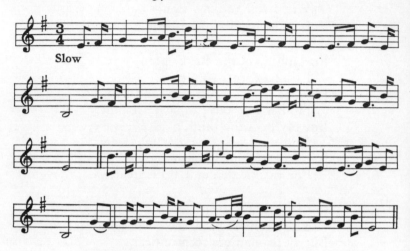

Slow

TURN again, thou fair Eliza,
  Ae kind blink before we part;
Rew on thy despairing Lover,
  Canst thou break his faithfu' heart!
Turn again, thou fair Eliza,   5
  If to love thy heart denies,
For pity hide the cruel sentence
  Under friendship's kind disguise!

Thee, sweet maid, hae I offended?
  The offence is loving thee: 10
Canst thou wreck his peace for ever,
  Wha for thine wad gladly die!
While the life beats in my bosom,
  Thou shalt mix in ilka throe:
Turn again, thou lovely maiden,   15
  Ae sweet smile on me bestow.—

Turn again, thou fair Eliza. *Text from the Hastie MS, f. 92, collated with f. 91*
(Ha 1), SMM, 1792 (367, 368; signed B), and SC, 1798 (42). SMM repeats the song
to accompany two airs. Air in SC The Bonny Brucket Lassie. Title in Ha 1 Rabina.—
  1, 5 Eliza] Rabina *Ha 1*   4 Canst] Can *Ha 1*   5 Turn] O turn *Ha 1*
9 sweet] dear *SC Ha 1*   13 While] O, while *Ha 1*   15 lovely maiden] fair
Rabina *Ha 1*

Not the bee upon the blossom,
  In the pride o' sinny noon;
Not the little sporting fairy,
  All beneath the simmer moon;   20
Not the Poet in the moment
  Fancy lightens in his e'e,
Kens the pleasure, feels the rapture,
  That thy presence gies to me.—

371. Ye Jacobites by name—

Slowish

Ye Jacobites by name, give an ear, give an ear;
  Ye Jacobites by name, give an ear;
    Ye Jacobites by name
      Your fautes I will proclaim,
        Your doctrines I maun blame,   5
          You shall hear.—

What is Right, and what is Wrang, by the law, by the law?
  What is Right, and what is Wrang, by the law?
    What is Right, and what is Wrang?
      A short Sword, and a lang,   10
        A weak arm, and a strang
          For to draw.—

23 the . . . the] sic . . . sic *Ha 1*   24 That] As *Ha 1*

Ye Jacobites by name. *Text from the Hastie MS, f. 93, collated with SMM, 1792*
(371; unsigned). Lines 19–24 were added later in the MS

What makes heroic strife, fam'd afar, fam'd afar?
What makes heroic strife, fam'd afar?
     What makes heroic strife?   15
          To whet th' Assassin's knife,
          Or hunt a Parent's life
               Wi' bludie war.—

Then let your schemes alone, in the State, in the State,
     Then let your schemes alone in the State,   20
          Then let your schemes alone,
               Adore the rising sun,
               And leave a Man undone
                    To his fate.—

372. The Posie

Slow

tr

O LUVE will venture in where it daur na weel be seen,
     O luve will venture in where wisdom ance has been;
But I will down yon river rove, amang the woods sae green,
     And a' to pu' a posie to my ain dear May.—

The primrose I will pu', the firstling o' the year;   5
And I will pu' the pink, the emblem o' my Dear,
For she is the pink o' womankind, and blooms without a
          peer;
     And a' to be a posie to my ain dear May.—

The Posie. *Text from the Hastie MS, f. 96, collated with the Lochryan (Loch) and
Alloway (Al) MSS, and SMM, 1792 (373; signed B). Title in Loch Ballad. The last
two verses of each stanza are marked for repetition in Al*
     1 it daur] he dare *Loch*

I'll pu' the budding rose when Phebus peeps in view,
For it's like a baumy kiss o' her sweet, bonie mou;   10
The hyacinth's for constancy, wi' its unchanging blue,
    And a' to be a posie to my ain dear May.—

The lily it is pure, and the lily it is fair,
    And in her lovely bosom I'll place the lily there;
The daisy's for simplicity and unaffected air,   15
    And a' to be a posy to my ain dear May.—

The hawthorn I will pu', wi' its locks o' siller grey,
Where like an aged man it stands at break o' day;
But the songster's nest within the bush I winna tak away;
    And a' to be a posie to my ain dear May.—   20

The woodbine I will pu' when the e'ening star is near,
And the diamond draps o' dew shall be her een sae clear;
The violet's for modesty which weel she fa's to wear,
    And a' to be a posie to my ain dear May.—

I'll tie the posie round wi' the silken band o' luve,   25
And I'll place it in her breast, and I'll swear by a' abuve,
That to my latest draught o' life the band shall ne'er remuve,
    And this will be a posie to my ain dear May.—

9 budding] morning- *Al*   10 For . . . mou;] *follows cancellation in Al* I will
pu' the rose, where its budding in the dew   11 hyacinth's for] hyacinth is *Al*
blue] hue *Loch*   14 in] on *Al*   25 tie] *correcting* wind *in Al*
25, 27 band] *correcting* tie *in Al*   28 this] that *Loch Al*

373. Song—Sic a wife as Willie's wife—

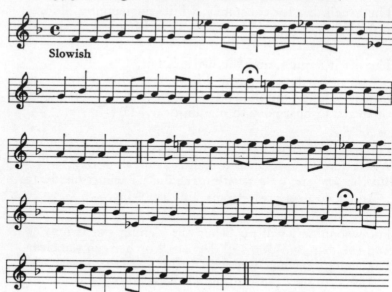

Slowish

WILLIE Wastle dwalls on Tweed,
   The spot they ca' it Linkumdoddie;
A creeshie wabster till his trade,
   Can steal a clue wi' ony body:
He has a wife that's dour and din,   5
   Tinkler Madgie was her mither;
Sic a wife as Willie's wife,
   I wadna gie a button for her.—

She has an e'e, she has but ane,
   Our cat has twa, the very colour;   10
Five rusty teeth, forbye a stump,
   A clapper-tongue wad deave a miller:

Sic a wife as Willie's wife. *Text from the MS in the possession of Mr. Clark Hunter,
Paisley, collated with the Hastie MS, f. 98 (Ha), SMM, 1792 (376; signed B), and
SC, 1805 (192). Title in Ha and SMM* Sic a wife as Willie had—; *in SC* Willie
Wastle's Wife (*alternative words to the song and air* Tibbie Fowler)
   1 dwalls] dwalt *Ha SMM SC*   2 ca'] ca'd *Ha SMM SC*   3 A . . . trade]
Willie was a wabster gude *Ha SMM SC*   4 Can steal] Cou'd stown *Ha SMM
SC*   5 has . . . that's] had . . . was *Ha SMM SC*   7, 15, 23, 31 Willie's
wife] Willie had *Ha SMM SC*   10 Our] The *Ha SMM SC*

A whiskin beard about her mou,
  Her nose and chin they threaten ither;
Sic a wife as Willie's wife,   15
  I wad na gie a button for her.—

She's bow-hough'd, she's hem-shin'd,
  Ae limpin leg a hand-bread shorter;
She's twisted right, she's twisted left,
  To balance fair in ilka quarter: 20
She has a hump upon her breast,
  The twin o' that upon her shouther;
Sic a wife as Willie's wife,
  I wad na gie a button for her.—

Auld baudrans by the ingle sits,   25
  An wi' her loof her face a washin;
But Willie's wife is nae sae trig,
  She dights her grunzie wi' a hushian:
Her waly nieves like midden-creels,
  Her feet wad fyle the Logan-water;   30
Sic a wife as Willie's wife,
  I wad na gie a button for her.—

17 hem-shin'd] hein-shinn'd *SC*   23–24 Sic . . . her.] Sic a wife &c. *Hunter MS*

374. My bonie laddie's young but he's growin yet—

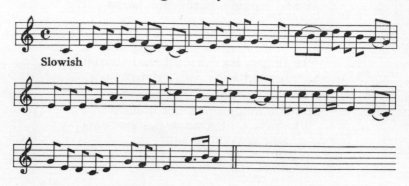

Slowish

O LADY Mary Ann looks o'er the castle-wa',
She saw three bonie boys playin at the ba',
The youngest he was the flower amang them a',
My bonie laddie's young but he's growin yet.—

O Father, O Father, an ye think it fit,　　　　　5
We'll send him a year to the College yet,
We'll sew a green ribban round about his hat,
And that will let them ken he's to marry yet.—

Lady Mary Ann was a flower in the dew,
Sweet was its smell and bonie was its hue,　　　　10
And the langer it blossom'd, the sweeter it grew,
For the lily in the bud will be bonier yet.—

Young Charlie Cochran was the sprout of an aik,
Bonie, and bloomin and straught was its make,
The sun took delight to shine for its sake,　　　　15
And it will be the brag o' the forest yet.—

The Simmer is gane when the leaves they were green,
And the days are awa that we hae seen,
But far better days I trust will come again,
For my bonie laddie's young but he's growin yet.—　20

My bonie laddie's young. *Text from the Hastie MS, f. 99, collated with SMM, 1792*
(377; unsigned). Title in SMM Lady Mary Ann

375. Such a parcel of rogues in a nation—

Slow

FAREWEEL to a' our Scotish fame,
    Fareweel our ancient glory;
Fareweel even to the Scotish name,
    Sae fam'd in martial story!
Now Sark rins o'er the Solway sands,   5
    And Tweed rins to the ocean,
To mark whare England's province stands,
    Such a parcel of rogues in a nation!

What force or guile could not subdue,
    Thro' many warlike ages,   10
Is wrought now by a coward few,
    For hireling traitors' wages.

Such a parcel of rogues. *Text from the Hastie MS, f. 100, collated with SMM, 1792* (*378; unsigned*). *Dewar collated a MS headed* Such a . . . nation—A Song—*with these variants:* 4 fam'd] ken'd *MS*   9 force or guile] guile or force *MS*
17 or] ere *MS*   21 till] to *MS*   22 mak this declaration] breathe this exclamation *MS*
    9 or] *correcting* nor *in MS*

The English steel we could disdain,
  Secure in valor's station;
But English gold has been our bane,   15
  Such a parcel of rogues in a nation!

O would, or I had seen the day
  That treason thus could sell us,
My auld grey head had lien in clay,
  Wi' Bruce and loyal Wallace!   20
But pith and power, till my last hour,
  I'll mak this declaration;
We're bought and sold for English gold,
  Such a parcel of rogues in a nation!

376. Kellyburnbraes—

Lively

There lived a carl in Kellyburnbraes,
  Hey and the rue grows bonie wi' thyme;
And he had a wife was the plague o' his days,
  And the thyme it is wither'd and rue is in prime;
And he had a wife was the plague o' his days,   5
  And the thyme it is wither'd and rue is in prime.—

Ae day as the carl gaed up the lang-glen,
  Hey &c.
He met wi' the d–v–l, says, how do ye fen?
  And &c.

Kellyburnbraes. Text from the Hastie MS, f. 101, collated with SMM, 1792 (379; unsigned). SMM does not adopt the repetition of the second part of the stanza

I've got a bad wife, Sir, that's a' my complaint,
 Hey &c.
For, saving your presence, to her ye're a saint, 10
 And &c.

It's neither your stot nor your staig I shall crave,
 Hey &c.
But gie me your wife, man, for her I must have,
 And &c.

O, welcome most kindly! the blythe carl said;
 Hey &c.
But if ye can match her—ye're waur than ye're ca'd,
 And &c.

The d–v–l has got the auld wife on his back, 15
 Hey &c.
And like a poor pedlar he's carried his pack,
 And &c.

He's carried her hame to his ain hallan-door,
 Hey &c.
Syne bade her gae in for a b——ch and a wh——,
 And &c.

Then straight he makes fifty, the pick o' his band,
 Hey &c.
Turn out on her guard in the clap of a hand, 20
 And &c.

The carlin gaed thro' them like onie wud bear,
 Hey &c.
Whae'er she gat hands on, cam near her nae mair,
 And &c.

A reekit, wee devil looks over the wa',
 Hey &c.
O help, Master, help! or she'll ruin us a',
 And &c.

The d–v–l he swore by the edge o' his knife,   25
  Hey &c.
He pitied the man that was ty'd to a wife,
  And &c.

The d–v–l he swore by the kirk and the bell,
  Hey &c.
He was not in wedlock, thank Heaven, but in h—,
  And &c.

Then Satan has travell'd again wi' his pack,
  Hey &c.
And to her auld husband he's carried her back,   30
  And &c.

I hae been a d–v–l the feck o' my life,
  Hey and the rue grows bonie wi' thyme;
But ne'er was in h–ll till I met wi' a wife,
  An' the thyme it is wither'd, and rue is in prime.
But ne'er was in h–ll till I met wi' a wife,   35
  An' the thyme it is wither'd and rue is in prime.

377. [Jockey fou and Jenny fain]

Lively

Jockey fou. *Text from the Hastie MS (f. 103), collated with SMM, 1792 (381).*
Lines 5–8 are Burns's addition to the old words

[—Ithers seek they kenna what,
   Features, carriage, and a' that,
Gie me loove in her I court;
Loove to loove maks a' the sport.—]
Let loove sparkle in her e'e;   5
Let her loe nae man but me;
That's the tocher gude I prize,
There the Luver's treasure lies.—

378. The Slave's Lament—

Slow

It was in sweet Senegal that my foes did me enthrall
   For the lands of Virginia-ginia O;
Torn from that lovely shore, and must never see it more,
   And alas! I am weary, weary O!
     Torn from &c.

All on that charming coast is no bitter snow and frost,   5
   Like the lands of Virginia-ginia O;
There streams for ever flow, and there flowers for ever blow,
   And alas! I am weary, weary O!
     There streams &c.

The Slave's Lament. *Text from the Hastie MS, f. 105, collated with SMM, 1792
(384; unsigned)*
   7 there] *correcting* the *in MS*

The burden I must bear, while the cruel scourge I fear,
   In the lands of Virginia-ginia O;   10
And I think on friends most dear with the bitter, bitter tear,
   And Alas! I am weary, weary O!
     And I think &c.

379. Bonie Bell

Slow

THE smiling spring comes in rejoicing,
   And surly winter grimly flies;
Now crystal clear are the falling waters,
   And bonny blue are the sunny skies.
Fresh o'er the mountains breaks forth the morning, 5
   The ev'ning gilds the Ocean's swell;
All Creatures joy in the sun's returning,
   And I rejoice in my Bonie Bell.

The flowery Spring leads sunny Summer,
   And yellow Autumn presses near,   10
Then in his turn comes gloomy Winter,
   Till smiling Spring again appear.
Thus seasons dancing, life advancing,
   Old Time and Nature their changes tell,
But never ranging, still unchanging,   15
   I adore my Bonie Bell.

Bonie Bell. *Text from SMM, 1792 (387; signed B), collated with the transcript in the Hastie MS, f. 174*

380. The gallant Weaver

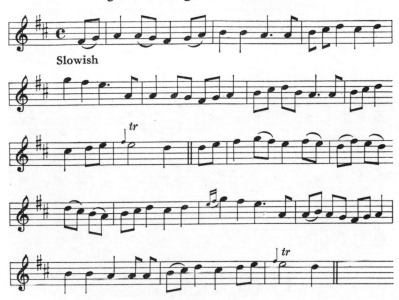

Slowish

WHERE Cart rins rowin to the sea,
By mony a flower and spreading tree,
There lives a lad, the lad for me,
He is a gallant Weaver.—

Oh I had wooers aught or nine,   5
They gied me rings and ribbans fine;
And I was fear'd my heart wad tine
And I gied it to the Weaver.—

My daddie sign'd my tocher-band
To gie the lad that has the land,   10
But to my heart I'll add my hand
And give it to the Weaver.—

The Gallant Weaver. *Text from the Hastie MS, f. 106, collated with SMM, 1792
(389; signed R), and SC, 1798 (39). Title from SMM; the MS adds* or the Weaver's
March—. *SMM sets in two eight-line stanzas. First-line title in SC, set to the air* The
Auld Wife ayont the Fire
   4, 8, 12, 16 Weaver] Sailor *SC*   5 Oh *SMM: not in MS, but probably cut
away*

While birds rejoice in leafy bowers,
While bees delight in opening flowers,
While corn grows green in simmer showers   15
I love my gallant Weaver.—

381. Hey Ca' thro'

With spirit

Up wi' the carls of Dysart,
   And the lads o' Buckhiven,
And the Kimmers o' Largo,
   And the lasses o' Leven.
     Hey ca' thro' ca' thro'   5
       For we hae mickle a do,
     Hey ca' thro' ca' thro'
       For we hae mickle a do.

We hae tales to tell,
   And we hae sangs to sing;   10
We hae pennies to spend,
   And we hae pints to bring.
     Hey ca' thro' &c.

We'll live a' our days,
   And them that comes behin',
Let them do the like,   15
   And spend the gear they win.
     Hey ca' thro' &c.

14 opening flowers] *correcting* simmer showers *in MS*
Hey Ca' thro'. *Text from SMM, 1792 (392; unsigned)*

382. Can ye labor lea—

Chorus

Slow

Chorus

O CAN ye labor lea, young man,
　　O can ye labor lea;
Gae back the gate ye came again,
　Ye'se never scorn me.—

I fee'd a man at martinmass,　　　　　　　5
　Wi' airle-pennies three;
But a' the faute I had to him,
　He could na labor lea.—
　　O can ye &c.

O clappin's gude in Febarwar,
　An kissin's sweet in May;　　　　　　　10
But what signifies a young man's love,
　An 't dinna last for ay.—
　　O can ye &c.

Can ye labor lea. *Text from the Hastie MS, f. 107, collated with SMM, 1792 (394; unsigned). First-line title in SMM*
　1 O can] *correcting* Can *in MS*　　3-4 Gae . . . me. *SMM: MS has*
　　　　　　It's fee, na bountith shall us twin,
　　　　　　　Gin ye can labor lea.
11-12 But . . . ay. *SMM: MS has*
　　　　　　But my delight's the Ploughman-lad
　　　　　　　That weel can labor lay.

O kissin is the key o' luve,
    An clappin is the lock,
An makin-of 's the best thing,   15
    That e'er a young Thing got.—
        O can ye &c.

383. The deuks dang o'er my daddie—

Lively

T H E bairns gat out wi' an unco shout,
    The deuks dang o'er my daddie, O,
The fien-ma-care, quo' the feirrie auld wife,
    He was but a paidlin body, O.—
He paidles out, an' he paidles in,   5
    An' he paidles late and early, O;
This seven lang year I hae lien by his side,
    An he is but a fusionless carlie, O.—

O had your tongue, my feirrie auld wife,
    O had your tongue, now Nansie, O: 10
I've seen the day, and sae hae ye,
    Ye wad na been sae donsie, O.—

15 makin-of 's] *correcting* makin-o 's *in MS*

The deuks dang o'er my daddie. Text from the Hastie MS, f. 108, collated with
SMM, 1792 (396; signed B)
    3, 9 feirrie] *correcting* ferrie *in MS*

I've seen the day ye butter'd my brose,
And cuddled me late and early, O;
But downa do's come o'er me now, 15
And, Oh, I find it sairly, O!

384. As I went out ae May morning

Lively

As I went out ae may morning,
A may morning it chanc'd to be;
There I was aware of a weelfar'd Maid
Cam linkin' o'er the lea to me.—

O but she was a weelfar'd maid, 5
The boniest lass that's under the sun;
I spier'd gin she could fancy me,
But her answer was, I am too young.—

To be your bride I am too young,
To be your loun wad shame my kin, 10
So therefore pray young man begone,
For you never, never shall my favor win.—

But amang yon birks and hawthorns green,
Where roses blaw and woodbines hing,
O there I learn'd my bonie lass 15
That she was not a single hour too young.—

As I went out ae May morning. *Text from the Hastie MS, f. 109, collated with SMM,*
1792 (397; unsigned). Title from SMM

The lassie blush'd, the lassie sigh'd,
    And the tear stood twinklin in her e'e;
O kind Sir, since ye hae done me this wrang,
    It's pray when will ye marry me.—   20

It's of that day tak ye nae heed,
    For that's ae day ye ne'er shall see;
For ought that pass'd between us twa,
    Ye had your share as weel as me.—

She wrang her hands, she tore her hair,   25
    She cried out most bitterlie,
O what will I say to my mammie,
    When I gae hame wi' my big bellie!

O as ye maut, so maun ye brew,
    And as ye brew, so maun ye tun;   30
But come to my arms, my ae bonie lass,
    For ye never shall rue what ye now hae done!—

385. She's fair and fause &c.

The lads of Leith

S HE's fair and fause that causes my smart,
    I lo'ed her meikle and lang;
She's broken her vow, she's broken my heart,
    And I may e'en gae hang.—

She's fair and fause &c. *Text from the Hastie MS, f. 110, collated with SMM, 1792 (398; signed R), and SC, 1798 (40). Title from SMM, SC*

A coof cam in wi' routh o' gear,   5
And I hae tint my dearest dear;
But woman is but warld's gear,
    Sae let the bonie lass gang.—

Whae'er ye be that woman love,
    To this be never blind;   10
Nae ferlie 'tis tho' fickle she prove,
    A woman has't by kind:
O woman, lovely woman fair!
An angel form's faun to thy share;
'Twad been o'er meikle to gien thee mair,   15
    I mean an angel mind.

386. The De'il's awa wi' th' Exciseman

With spirit

THE deil cam fiddlin thro' the town,
   And danc'd awa wi' th' Exciseman;
And ilka wife cries, auld Mahoun,
   I wish you luck o' the prize, man.

13 woman, lovely] woman lovely, *SC*   15 to gien] to 've gi'en *SC*

The De'il's awa wi' th' Exciseman. *Text from SMM, 1792 (399; unsigned), collated with the Arbroath MS and Stewart, 1802 (p. 202; S)*
   3 wife cries] auld wife cry'd *S*   4 I] We *S*

Chorus

The deil's awa the deil's awa   5
  The deil's awa wi' th' Exciseman,
He's danc'd awa he's danc'd awa
  He's danc'd awa wi' th' Exciseman.

We'll mak our maut and we'll brew our drink,
  We'll laugh, sing, and rejoice, man;   10
And mony braw thanks to the meikle black deil,
  That danc'd awa wi' th' Exciseman.
    The deil's awa &c.

There's threesome reels, there's foursome reels,
  There's hornpipes and strathspeys, man,
But the ae best dance e'er cam to the Land   15
  Was, the deil's awa wi' th' Exciseman.
    The deil's awa &c.

387. Song

Tune, Ewe bughts Marion

5 awa the] awa & the *MS*   7 awa he's] awa & he's *MS*   5–8 *om. Stewart,*
who marks ll. 9–12 as chorus   9 we'll] *om. S*   10 laugh, sing] dance and
sing *S:* & *deleted in MS*   11 braw *om. S*   13 there's] and *S*   15 the Land]
our lan' *S*

Song. *Text from the Dalhousie MS (Dal; letter to Thomson, 27 October 1792)*

1

WILL ye go to the Indies, my Mary,
 And leave auld Scotia's shore;
Will ye go to the Indies, my Mary,
 Across th' Atlantic roar.

2

O sweet grows the lime and the orange   5
 And the apple on the pine;
But a' the charms o' the Indies
 Can never equal thine.

3

I hae sworn by the Heavens to my Mary,
 I hae sworn by the Heavens to be true;   10
And sae may the Heavens forget me,
 When I forget my vow!

4

O plight me your faith, my Mary,
 And plight me your lily-white hand;
O plight me your faith, my Mary,   15
 Before I leave Scotia's strand.

5

We hae plighted our truth, my Mary,
 In mutual affection to join:
And curst be the cause that shall part us,
 The hour, and the moment o' time!!!   20

collated with the Second Commonplace Book (2CPB; p. 34) and Currie (iv. 12).
Title from 2CPB
    2 auld] old 2CPB   4 Atlantic] Atlantic's Currie   10 I hae] I've 2CPB
16 I] correcting we in Dal   17 truth] troth Currie

388. My wife's a winsome wee thing

Lively

S HE is a winsome wee thing,
   She is a handsome wee thing,
She is a lo'esome wee thing,
    This sweet wee wife o' mine.

2

I never saw a fairer,   5
I never lo'ed a dearer;
And neist my heart I'll wear her,
   For fear my jewel tine.

My wife's a winsome wee thing. Text from the Dalhousie MS (letter to Thomson, 8 November 1792). Burns (letter to Thomson, 1 December 1792) accepted Thomson's attempt to spin a stanza to replace ll. 9–16 (Currie, iv. 21–22):

        O leeze me on my wee thing,
        My bonnie blythsome wee thing;
        Sae lang's I hae my wee thing,
           I'll think my lot divine.

        Tho' warld's care we share o't,
        And may see meikle mair o't,
        Wi' her I'll blythly bear it,
           And ne'er a word repine.

Title winsome] *correcting* wanton *in MS*
   3 lo'esome] bonie *Thomson's alteration in MS*   4 sweet] *correcting* dear *in MS*

3

She is a winsome wee thing,
She is a handsome wee thing,   10
She is a lo'esome wee thing,
    This dear wee wife o' mine.

4

The warld's wrack we share o't,
The warstle and the care o't;
Wi' her I'll blythely bear it,   15
    And think my lot divine.

389. Highland Mary—

Tune, Katharine Ogie—

13 o't] *correcting* on't *in MS*

Highland Mary. *Text from the Dalhousie MS (letter to Thomson, 14 November 1792), collated with SC, 1799 (83). First-line title in SC*

Y E banks, and braes, and streams around
    The castle o' Montgomery,
Green be your woods, and fair your flowers,
    Your waters never drumlie!
There Simmer first unfald her robes,   5
    And there the langest tarry:
For there I took the last Fareweel
    O' my sweet Highland Mary.

How sweetly bloom'd the gay, green birk,
    How rich the hawthorn's blossom;   10
As underneath their fragrant shade,
    I clasp'd her to my bosom!
The golden Hours, on angel wings,
    Flew o'er me and my Dearie;
For dear to me as light and life   15
    Was my sweet Highland Mary.

Wi' mony a vow, and lock'd embrace,
    Our parting was fu' tender;
And pledging aft to meet again,
    We tore oursels asunder: 20
But Oh, fell Death's untimely frost,
    That nipt my Flower sae early!
Now green's the sod, and cauld's the clay,
    That wraps my Highland Mary!

O pale, pale now, those rosy lips   25
    I aft hae kiss'd sae fondly!
And clos'd for ay, the sparkling glance,
    That dwalt on me sae kindly!
And mouldering now in silent dust,
    That heart that lo'ed me dearly!   30
But still within my bosom's core
    Shall live my Highland Mary.

7 Fareweel] farewel *SC*   25 those] *correcting* the *in MS*

390. The Rights of Woman—Spoken by Miss Fontenelle on her benefit night

WHILE Europe's eye is fixed on mighty things,
The fate of Empires, and the fall of Kings;
While quacks of State must each produce his plan,
And even children lisp The Rights of Man;
Amid this mighty fuss, just let me mention,   5
The Rights of Woman merit some attention.—

First, in the Sexes' intermixed connection,
One sacred Right of Woman is, Protection.
The tender flower that lifts its head, elate,
Helpless, must fall before the blasts of Fate,   10
Sunk on the earth, defaced its lovely form,
Unless *your Shelter* ward th' impending storm.

Our second Right—but needless here is caution,
To keep that Right inviolate's the fashion.
Each man of sense has it so full before him   15
He'd die before he'd wrong it—'tis Decorum.—
There was, indeed, in far less polished days,
A time when rough, rude man had naughty ways:
Would swagger, swear, get drunk, kick up a riot,
Nay even thus invade a lady's quiet.—   20
Now, thank our Stars! these Gothic times are fled,
Now well-bred men (and you are all well-bred)
Most justly think (and we are much the gainers)
Such conduct neither spirit, wit, nor manners.—

The Rights of Woman. *Text from the Fintry MS (letter to Mrs. Graham of Fintry, 5 January 1793), collated with the Rosenbach MS (R; letter to Miss Fontenelle, November 1792; collated Dewar) and Currie (ii. 413–14; letter to Mrs. Dunlop, 6 December 1792). Title in R* The Rights of Woman—A Prologue—. *Subscription in Fintry:* To M͞r͞s Graham of Fintry, this little poem, written in haste on the spur of the occasion, and therefore inaccurate; but a sincere Compliment to that Sex, the most amiable of THE WORKS OF GOD—is most respectfully presented by—THE AUTHOR
 3 must each produce] *correcting* produces each *in R*   5 this] the *R*
 6 merit some] claim some small *R*   13 needless] idle *R*   19 Would . . .
 drunk,] Got drunk, would swagger, swear, *R*   21 these] those *R*

For Right the third, our last, our best, our dearest, 25
That Right to fluttering Female hearts the nearest,
Which even the Rights of Kings, in low prostration,
Most humbly own—'tis dear, dear Admiration!
[In that blest sphere alone we live and move;
There taste that life of life—immortal love.—] 30
Smiles, glances, sighs, tears, fits, flirtations, airs;
'Gainst such an host, what flinty savage dares.—
When aweful Beauty joins in all her charms,
Who is so rash as rise in rebel arms?

But truce with kings, and truce with Constitutions, 35
With bloody armaments, and Revolutions;
Let MAJESTY your first attention summon,
Ah, ça ira! THE MAJESTY OF WOMAN!!!

391. Here's a Health to them that's awa

Slow

28 humbly own] fall before *R*   29–30 In . . . love.] *Text from Currie: om.*
Fintry   30 There taste] And thence *R*   31 Smiles . . . tears,] Sighs, tears,
smiles, glances, *R*   33 in] with *R Currie*   35 But] Then *R*

Here's a health to them that's awa. *Text from the* Edinburgh Gazeteer, *1792*
(reprinted in the Edinburgh Magazine, *January 1818; EM), collated with B.M.*
MS Egerton 1656 (f. 27). The MS has ll. 1–24 and 33–36 only, but is not defective.
Title in MS Song.—

Here's a health to them that's awa,
Here's a health to them that's awa;
And wha winna wish gude luck to our cause,
May never gude luck be their fa'!
It's gude to be merry and wise,   5
It's gude to be honest and true,
It's gude to support Caledonia's cause,
And bide by the Buff and the Blue.

Here's a health to them that's awa,
Here's a health to them that's awa;   10
Here's a health to Charlie, the chief o' the clan,
Altho' that his band be sma'.
May Liberty meet wi' success!
May Prudence protect her frae evil!
May Tyrants and Tyranny tine i' the mist,   15
And wander their way to the devil!

Here's a health to them that's awa,
Here's a health to them that's awa;
Here's a health to Tammie, the Norland laddie,
That lives at the lug o' the law!   20
Here's freedom to him that wad read,
Here's freedom to him that wad write!
There's nane ever fear'd that the Truth should be heard,
But they whom the Truth wad indite.

Here's a health to them that's awa,   25
An' here's to them that's awa!
Here's to Maitland and Wycombe! Let wha does na like 'em
Be built in a hole in the wa'!
Here's timmer that's red at the heart,
Here's fruit that is sound at the core;   30
And may he that wad turn the buff and blue coat
Be turn'd to the back o' the door!

Here's a health to them that's awa,
Here's a health to them that's awa;
Here's Chieftan M^cleod, a chieftan worth gowd,   35
Tho' bred amang mountains o' snaw!

2, 10, 18, 34 Here's a health] An' here's *EM*   15 i'] in *MS*   16 their
the *MS EM*   way] road *EM*   24 whom] wham *MS*

811843.2   M

Here's friends on baith sides o' the Forth,
And friends on baith sides o' the Tweed;
And wha wad betray old Albion's right,
May they never eat of her bread!   40

392. The lea-rig—

Slow

WHEN o'er the hill the eastern star
     Tells bughtin-time is near, my jo,
And owsen frae the furrowed field
     Return sae dowf and weary O:
Down by the burn where scented birks   5
     Wi' dew are hanging clear, my jo,
I'll meet thee on the lea-rig,
     My ain kind Dearie O.

The lea-rig. *Text from the Dalhousie MS (Dal B; letter to Thomson, 1 December 1792),
collated with MS Dal A (ll. 1–16; letter to Thomson, 26 October 1792), Currie (iv. 8,
24), and SC, 1805 (195). First-line title in SC. Lines 17–24 added in Dal B*
    1 eastern star *Dal A SC*: e'enin star *alternative* parting sun *Dal B. See Commentary*
4 O: *Dal A*: O, *Dal B*   5 scented birks] *alternative to* birken buds *in Dal B*:
birken bobs *Dal A*

At midnight hour, in mirkest glen,
   I'd rove and ne'er be irie O,   10
If thro' that glen I gaed to thee,
   My ain kind Dearie O:
Altho' the night were ne'er sae wet,
   And I were ne'er sae weary O,
I'd meet thee on the lea-rig,   15
   My ain kind Dearie O.

The hunter lo'es the morning sun,
   To rouse the mountain deer, my jo,
At noon the fisher takes the glen,
   Adown the burn to steer, my jo;   20
Gie me the hour o' gloamin grey,
   It maks my heart sae cheary O
To meet thee on the lea-rig
   My ain kind Dearie O.

393. Auld Rob Morris

9 At . . . glen,] In mirkest glen, at midnight hour, *Dal A*   13 wet *MSS:*
wild *Currie SC. See Commentary*   15 I'd *Dal A SC*: I'll *Dal B*   19 takes]
alternative to seeks *in Dal B*: seeks *SC*   20 Adown] Along *Currie. See*
Commentary   22 maks] makes *SC*

Auld Rob Morris. *Text from the Dalhousie MS (letter to Thomson, 4 December 1792),*
collated with SC, 1793 (17). See Commentary. Title in SC There 's auld Rob Morris

T HERE's auld Rob Morris that wons in yon glen,
    He's the king o' gude fellows, and wale of auld men;
He has gowd in his coffers, he has owsen and kine,
And ae bonie lassie, his dawtie and mine.

She's fresh as the morning, the fairest in May;   5
She's sweet as the e'enin amang the new hay;
As blythe and as artless as the lambs on the lea,
And dear to my heart as the light to my e'e.

But oh, she's an Heiress, auld Robin's a laird;
And my daddie has nocht but a cot-house and yard: 10
A wooer like me maunna hope to come speed;
The wounds I must hide that will soon be my dead.

The day comes to me, but delight brings me nane;
The night comes to me, but my rest it is gane:
I wander my lane like a night-troubled ghaist,   15
And I sigh as my heart it wad burst in my breast.

O had she but been of a laigher degree,
I then might hae hop'd she wad smil'd upon me!
O, how past descriving had then been my bliss,
As now my distraction no words can express!   20

394. Duncan Gray

Brisk

3 owsen and] sheep, he has *SC*   4 dawtie] darling *Thomson's alteration in
MS, SC*   6 e'enin] ev'ning *Thomson in MS, SC*   10 nocht] nought *Thomson
in MS, SC*   12 must . . . that] maun . . . which *SC*   17 laigher] lower
Thomson in MS, SC   18 hop'd] *follows a cancellation* been of a *in MS*
19 descriving] all telling *Thomson in MS*

Duncan Gray. *Text from the Dalhousie MS (letter to Thomson, 4 December 1792),
collated with SC, 1798 (48)*

Duncan Gray cam here to woo,
  Ha, ha, the wooing o't,
On blythe Yule night when we were fu',
  Ha, ha, the wooing o't.
Maggie coost her head fu' high,   5
Look'd asklent and unco skiegh,
Gart poor Duncan stand abiegh;
  Ha, ha, the wooing o't.

Duncan fleech'd, and Duncan pray'd;
  Ha, ha, the wooing o't.   10
Meg was deaf as Ailsa craig,
  Ha, ha, the wooing o't.
Duncan sigh'd baith out and in,
Grat his een baith bleer't an' blin',
Spak o' lowpin o'er a linn;   15
  Ha, ha, the wooing o't.

Time and Chance are but a tide,
  Ha, ha, the wooing o't.
Slighted love is sair to bide,
  Ha, ha, the wooing o't.   20
Shall I, like a fool, quoth he,
For a haughty hizzie die?
She may gae to —— France for me!
  Ha, ha, the wooing o't.

How it comes let Doctors tell,   25
  Ha, ha, the wooing o't.
Meg grew sick as he grew heal,
  Ha, ha, the wooing o't.
Something in her bosom wrings,
For relief a sigh she brings;   30
And O her een, they spak sic things!
  Ha, ha, the wooing o't.

---

3 On blythe Yule] *correcting* Ae feast *in MS*: On new-year's *SC*   4 *et passim*
Ha . . . o't.] Ha, &c. *MS*   6–7 skiegh . . . abiegh] skeigh . . . abeigh *SC*
11 *Note in SC* A great insulated Rock to the south of the Island of Arran
15 lowpin] louping *SC*   27 Meg] *correcting* She *in MS*   he] *correcting* she *in*
MS   31 spak] spake *SC*

Duncan was a lad o' grace,
    Ha, ha, the wooing o't.
Maggie's was a piteous case,   35
    Ha, ha, the wooing o't.
Duncan could na be her death,
Swelling Pity smoor'd his Wrath;
Now they're crouse and canty baith,
    Ha, ha, the wooing o't.   40

395. [Why should na poor folk mowe]

WHEN Princes and Prelates and het-headed zealots
    All Europe hae set in a lowe,
The poor man lies down, nor envies a crown,
And comforts himsel with a mowe.—

Chorus

And why shouldna poor folk mowe, mowe, mowe,   5
    And why shouldna poor folk mowe:
The great folk hae siller, and houses and lands,
    Poor bodies hae naething but mowe.—

2

When Br—nsw—ck's great Prince cam a cruising to Fr—nce
    Republican billies to cowe,   10
Bauld Br—nsw—c's great Prince wad hae shawn better sense,
    At hame with his Princess to mowe.—
    And why should na &c.—

Why should na poor folk mowe. *Text from the Dalhousie MS (Dal; letter to Thomson, July 1794), collated with the Huntington Library MS (HL; letter to Cleghorn, 12 December 1792) and MMC (pp. 80–82). Title in HL* Why should na poor people mow: *in MMC* Poor Bodies do Naething but M—w: *no title in Dal. See Commentary*   3 nor] *correcting* not *in Dal*   5, 6 folk] people *HL*: bodies *MMC*   8 hae] *correcting* dow *in Dal*   9 cam] gade *MMC*   11 Bauld . . . great] Great . . . strang *MMC*   12 *Followed by ll. 17–20 and additional stanza in MMC:*

    When the brave duke of Y—k
    The Rhine first did pass,
    Republican armies to cow, cow, cow,
    They bade him gae hame,
    To his P—ss—n dame,
    An' gie her a kiss an' a m—w, a m—w.

3

Out over the Rhine proud Pr—ss—a wad shine,
   To *spend* his best blood he did vow;
But Frederic had better ne'er forded the water,   15
   But *spent* as he docht in a mowe.—
     And why &c.—

4

By sea and by shore! the Emp—r—r swore,
   In Paris he'd kick up a row;
But Paris sae ready just leugh at the laddie
   And bade him gae tak him a mowe.—   20
     And why &c.—

5

Auld Kate laid her claws on poor Stanislaus,
   And Poland has bent like a bow:
May the deil in her a— ram a huge pr—ck o' brass!
   And damn her in h—ll with a mowe!
     And why &c.—

6

But truce with commotions and new-fangled notions,   25
    A bumper I trust you'll allow:
Here's George our gude king and Charlotte his queen,
   And lang may they tak a gude mowe!

13 wad] did *MMC*   14 best] last *MMC*   16 in] at *MMC*   *Additional stanza in MMC:*

           The black-headed eagle,
           As keen as a beagle,
   He hunted o'er height an' o'er howe, howe, howe,
           In the braes of Gemap,
           He fell in a trap,
   E'en let him come out as he dow, dow, dow.

24 in] to *MMC*   25–28 But truce . . . mowe.] *om. MMC*   26 I . . . allow] *correcting* I'll fill it I vow *in HL*   27 Charlotte his queen] lang may he ring *HL*   28 lang . . . gude] Charlotte and he tak a *HL*

396. Here awa', there awa'

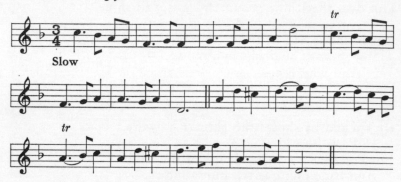

H ERE awa', there awa' wandering, Willie,
    Here awa', there awa', haud awa' hame;
Come to my bosom, my ae only deary,
    Tell me thou bring'st me my Willie the same.

Loud tho' the winter blew cauld on our parting,   5
    'Twas na the blast brought the tear in my e'e:
Welcome now Simmer, and welcome my Willie;
    The Simmer to Nature, my Willie to me.

Rest, ye wild storms, in the cave o' your slumbers,
    How your dread howling a lover alarms!   10
Wauken, ye breezes! row gently, ye billows!
    And waft my dear Laddie ance mair to my arms.

Here awa', there awa'. Text from SC, 1793 (2; copy presented to Miss Graham of Fintry, with holograph corrections), collated with the Alloway MS (Al; letter to John MᶜMurdo, 1792) and the Dalhousie MS (Dal; letter to Thomson, 27 March 1793). See Commentary. Title in MSS: Song—
  1 Here] ~~Lang~~ here *MSS*   awa' wandering, *Dal*: awa' wandering *Al*: awa', wandering *SC* 2 Here awa', there awa',] Now tired wi' wandering *MSS*   3 ae *MSS: holograph correction of* ain *in SC*   4 Tell] And tell *MSS*   5 Loud . . . on] *holograph correction of* Winter winds blew, loud and cauld, at *in SC*: Loud blew the cauld winter wind at *MSS*   6 'Twas . . . tear] *holograph correction of* Fears for my Willie brought tears *in SC*: But 'twas . . . tear *Al*: It was na the blast . . . tear *Dal (altered by Thomson to first SC reading)*   7 Welcome now] Now welcome the *MSS*   9 Rest, ye wild storms,] Ye hurricanes rest *MSS* o' *MSS:* of *SC*   10 How . . . howling] O how your wild horrors *MSS* 11 Wauken] Awaken *altered by Thomson to* Blow gently *in Dal*   row gently] *altered by Thomson to* roll softly *in Dal*   12 waft] *correcting* bring *in Al*

But oh, if he's faithless, and minds na his Nanie,
   Flow still between us, thou wide roaring main:
May I never see it, may I never trow it,   15
   But, dying, believe that my Willie's my ain!

13 oh . . . his] if he's forgotten his faithfullest *MSS*   14 Flow still] O still flow
MSS   15 see] hear *Al*

X

POEMS

1793

DUMFRIES

397. Galla Water

Very slow

Braw, braw lads on Yarrow braes,
    Rove among the blooming heather;
But Yarrow braes, nor Ettrick shaws,
    Can match the lads o' Galla water.

But there is ane, a secret ane,   5
    Aboon them a' I loe him better;
And I'll be his, and he'll be mine,
    The bonie lad o' Galla water.

Altho' his daddie was nae laird,
    And tho' I hae na meikle tocher,   10
Yet rich in kindest, truest love,
    We'll tent our flocks by Galla water.

Galla Water. *Text from SC, 1793 (11), collated with the Dalhousie MS (Dal; letter to Thomson, January 1793). Title from MS: first-line title in SC*
    1–3 *Cancelled opening in MS:*

> Braw, braw lads o' Galla-water,
>   O braw lads o' Galla-water;
> I'll kilt my coats aboon

1 Braw] *Thomson's correction of* There's braw *in Dal*   2 Rove among] *Burns's correction (see Commentary):* That wander thro' *altered by Thomson to* Ye wander thro' *in Dal*   10 na] *Thomson's alteration of* a *in Dal (see Commentary)*
11 Yet] *Thomson's alteration of* He's *in Dal*   12 We'll . . . by] *Thomson's alteration of* The bonie lad o' *in Dal*

It ne'er was wealth, it ne'er was wealth,
That coft contentment, peace, or pleasure;
The bands and bliss o' mutual love,   15
O that's the chiefest warld's treasure!

398. Song—

Tune, Cauld kail in Aberdeem

Lively

O POORTITH cauld, and restless love,
  Ye wrack my peace between ye;
Yet poortith a' I could forgive
An 'twere na for my Jeanie.

Chorus

O why should Fate sic pleasure have,   5
Life's dearest bands untwining?
Or why sae sweet a flower as love,
Depend on Fortune's shining?

14 coft *Dal SC*: brought *Thomson's rejected alteration in Dal*

Song. *Text from the Dalhousie MS (Dal B; letter to Thomson, August 1793), collated
with the Alloway MS (Al) and the Dalhousie MS (Dal A; letter to Thomson, January
1793), and SC, 1798 (49). Title in Dal A* Weel loe I my Jeanie*; in Al* I canna want
my Jeanie
  3 could] *correcting* would *in Dal B*   4 An 'twere na for] But tynin o' *Al
Dal A*   5–8 *Al and Dal A have*
                    For weel loe I my Jeanie, Sirs,
                       I canna want my Jeanie;
                    How happy I, were she my ain,
                       Tho' I had ne'er a guinea.
In Dal A Thomson alters canna want *to* doat upon

This warld's wealth when I think on,
    Its pride, and a' the lave o't;   10
My curse on silly coward man,
    That he should be the slave o't.
      O why &c.

Her een sae bonie blue betray,
    How she repays my passion;
But Prudence is her o'erword ay,   15
    She talks o' rank and fashion.
      O why &c.

O wha can prudence think upon,
    And sic a lassie by him:
O wha can prudence think upon,
    And sae in love as I am?   20
      O why &c.

How blest the wild-wood Indian's fate,
    He wooes his simple Dearie:
The silly bogles, Wealth and State,
    Did never make them eerie.
      O why &c.

---

11 My curse] *Thomson alters to* O fy (*Dal A*), Fy Fy (*Dal B*)   17–22 *Al defective*   21 wild-wood Indian's] simple Lover's *Thomson's alteration in Dal A:* humble cotter's *SC*   22 simple] *corrected to* artless *in Dal A*   23 Wealth] Rank *Al Dal A*   24 Did] Can *SC*

399. Lord Gregory—

Adagio

O MIRK, mirk is this midnight hour,
   And loud the tempest's roar:
A waefu' wanderer seeks thy tower,
   Lord Gregory ope thy door.

An exile frae her father's ha',   5
   And a' for loving thee;
At least some pity on me shaw,
   If love it may na be.

Lord Gregory, mind'st thou not the grove,
   By bonie Irwine-side,   10
Where first I own'd that virgin-love
   I lang, lang had denied.

Lord Gregory. *Text from the Dalhousie MS (letter to Thomson, 26 January 1793),
collated with the Hanley MS (University of Texas), the Alloway MS (Al), and SC,
1798 (38). Title from the MSS; first-line title in SC*
  1 O . . . hour] O bitter drives the northern shower *Hanley*   3 A . . . tower]
And mirk, mirk is this midnight hour *Hanley*   6 loving] sake o' *Al*

How aften didst thou pledge and vow,
  Thou wad for ay be mine;
And my fond heart, itsel sae true,   15
  It ne'er mistrusted thine.

Hard is thy heart, Lord Gregory,
  And flinty is thy breast:
Thou dart of Heaven that flashest by,
  O wilt thou give me rest!   20

Ye mustering thunders from above
  Your willing victim see!
But spare, and pardon my fause Love,
  His wrangs to Heaven and me!

400. Sonnet—On hearing a thrush sing on a morning walk in January

SING on, sweet thrush, upon the leafless bough,
  Sing on, sweet bird, I'll listen to thy strain;
See aged Winter 'mid his surly reign
At thy blythe carol clears his furrowed brow.—

Thus in bleak Poverty's dominion drear   5
Sits meek Content, with light, unanxious heart,
Welcomes the rapid moments, bids them part,
Nor asks if they bring aught to hope, or fear.—

I thank thee, Author of this opening day,
Thou whose bright sun now gilds yon orient skies.   10
Riches denied, thy boon was purer joys,
What Wealth could never give, nor take away!—

14 wad] wouldst *SC*   17 Hard is thy heart] Then fare thee weel *alternative in Hanley*   19 dart] bolt *Al*   20 give] bring *Al*   21–24 *not in Hanley*

Sonnet. *Text from the Adam MS (subscribed* To Mrs Riddel of Woodley park, A small, but sincere mark of respect from— The Author), *collated with the Cunningham MS (Cun; letter to Alexander Cunningham, 20 February 1793), the Bliss MS (transcript from R. T. Fitzhugh), and Currie (iv. 382). Title in Currie* Sonnet, Written on the 25th January, 1793, the birth-day of the Author, on hearing a thrush sing in a morning walk.
   Title thrush sing on] thrush in *Cun*   2 I'll] I *Currie*   5 Thus] So *Cun Currie*   bleak *Bliss (correcting* lone): lone *Adam Cun Currie*

But come, thou child of Poverty and Care,
The mite high Heaven bestowed, that mite with thee I'll
share.

401. Address to General Dumourier

Y OU'RE welcome to Despots, Dumourier;
You're welcome to Despots, Dumourier.—
How does Dampiere do?
Aye, and Bournonville too?
Why did they not come along with you, Dumourier?   5

I will fight France with you, Dumourier,—
I will fight France with you, Dumourier:—
I will fight France with you,
I will take my chance with you;
By my soul I'll dance a dance with you, Dumourier.   10

Then let us fight about, Dumourier;
Then let us fight about, Dumourier;
Then let us fight about,
'Till freedom's spark is out,
Then we'll be d–mned no doubt—Dumourier.   15

402. [A Toast]

A T a meeting of the Dumfriesshire Volunteers, held to com-
memorate the anniversary of Rodney's Victory, April 12th, 1782,
BURNS was called upon for a Song, instead of which he delivered
the following lines extempore.

13 But *Bliss*: Yet *Adam Cun Currie*

Address to General Dumourier. *Text from Cromek*, Reliques, *1808 (p. 421). Cromek*
gives a sub-title (A Parody on Robin Adair), *and a note:* It is almost needless to
observe that the song of *Robin Adair*, begins thus:—

> You're welcome to Paxton, Robin Adair;
> You're welcome to Paxton, Robin Adair.—
> How does Johnny Mackerell do?
> Aye, and Luke Gardener too?
> Why did they not come along with you, Robin Adair?

A Toast. *Text from Stewart, 1801 (p. 61), collated with the* Edinburgh Advertiser,
19 April 1793 (entitled On the Occasion of the Anniversary of the Late Admiral
Rodney's Glorious Victory: on Friday last, at King's Arms, Dumfries. Extempore
by Burns).

INSTEAD of a song, boys, I'll give you a toast,
Here's the memory of those on the twelfth that we lost;
That we lost, did I say, nay, by heav'n that we found,
For their fame it shall last while the world goes round.
The next in succession, I'll give you the King,   5
Whoe'er wou'd betray him, on high may he swing;
And here's the grand fabric, our free Constitution,
As built on the base of the great Revolution;
And longer with Politics, not to be cramm'd,
Be Anarchy curs'd, and be Tyranny damn'd;   10
And who wou'd to Liberty e'er prove disloyal,
May his son be a hangman, and he his first trial.

403. Open the door to me Oh

OH, open the door, some pity to shew,
    If love it may na be, Oh;
Tho' thou hast been false, I'll ever prove true,
    Oh, open the door to me, Oh.

Cauld is the blast upon my pale cheek,   5
    But caulder thy love for me, Oh:
The frost that freezes the life at my heart,
    Is nought to my pains frae thee, Oh.

3 That] *om. Advertiser*   4 last] live *Advertiser*   6 Whoe'er] And who
Advertiser

Open the door to me Oh. *Text from the Dalhousie MS (letter to Thomson, April 1793),
collated with SC, 1793 (21). First-line title in SC*
    2 If . . . be] Oh, open the door to me *Thomson's alteration in MS, SC*   7 frost]
following cancellation freeze *in MS*   heart] breast *SC*   8 frae] from *SC*

The wan moon sets behind the white wave,
　And time is setting with me, Oh: 10
False friends, false love, farewell! for mair
　I'll ne'er trouble them, nor thee, Oh.

She has open'd the door, she has open'd it wide,
　She sees his pale corse on the plain, Oh:
My true love! she cried, and sank down by his side, 15
　Never to rise again, Oh.

404. Jessie—A new Scots song

To the tune—Bonie Dundee

TRUE-HEARTED was he, the sad swain o' the Yarrow,
　And fair are the maids on the banks o' the Ayr;
But by the sweet side o' the Nith's winding river,
　Are lovers as faithful, and maidens as fair:
To equal young Jessie, seek Scotia all over;   5
　To equal young Jessie, you seek it in vain:
Grace, Beauty and Elegance fetter her lover,
　And maidenly modesty fixes the chain.

Fresh is the rose in the gay, dewy morning,
　And sweet is the lily at evening close;   10
But in the fair presence o' lovely, young Jessie,
　Unseen is the lily, unheeded the rose.
Love sits in her smile, a wizard ensnaring;
　Enthron'd in her een he delivers his law:
And still to her charms she alone is a stranger,   15
　Her modest demeanor's the jewel of a'.

9 sets] is setting *Thomson's alteration in MS, SC*   10 time] *autograph correction of* life *in MS*   11 mair] more *SC*   15 sank] sunk *SC*

Jessie. *Text from the Dalhousie MS (Dal; letter to Thomson, April 1793), collated with the Alloway MS (Al) and SC, 1798 (46). Title from superscription on Dal; title in MSS* Song—Tune, Bonie Dundee; *Al adds* Composed on Miss Jessie Staig, Dumfries. *First-line title in SC*
    5 Scotia] Scotland *Thomson's alteration in Dal; SC*   7 Grace] Truth *Al*
9 Fresh] Fair *Al:* Oh! fresh *SC*

405. Song—

Nansy 's to the green-wood gane

FAREWELL, thou stream that winding flows
  Around Eliza's dwelling;
O mem'ry, spare the cruel throes
  Within my bosom swelling:

Song. Text from the Dalhousie MS (Dal C; letter to Thomson, November 1794), collated with the Huntington Library MS (HL), the Adam MS (letter to Mrs. Riddell, April 1793), MS Dal A (letter to Thomson, 26 April 1793), the Esty MS (letter to Mrs. Riddell, ? November 1793), the Lochryan MS (Loch; letter to Mrs. Dunlop, 15 December 1793), MS Dal B (letter to Thomson, July 1794), and SC, 1799 (80). Title in Dal B Loch Song—; *first-line titles elsewhere. MSS Dal B and Esty contain only the corrected version of the opening lines*
  1–4 Farewell . . . swelling:] *HL Adam Dal A have*

> The last time I came o'er the moor,
>   And left Maria's dwelling,
> What throes, what tortures, passing cure,
>   Were in my bosom swelling.

2 Eliza's] Maria'   *Loch*   3 O . . . cruel] O cruel Mem'ry, spare the *Esty Loch*

Condemn'd to drag a hopeless chain,   5
    And yet in secret languish;
To feel a fire in every vein,
    Nor dare disclose my anguish.—

Love's veriest wretch, unseen, unknown
    I fain my griefs would cover;   10
The bursting sigh, th' unweeting groan,
    Betray the hapless lover:
I know thou doom'st me to despair,
    Nor wilt, nor canst relieve me;
But, Oh Eliza, hear one prayer,   15
    For pity's sake forgive me!

The music of thy voice I heard,
    Nor wist while it enslav'd me;
I saw thine eyes, yet nothing fear'd,
    Till fears no more had sav'd me: 20
Th' unwary Sailor thus, aghast,
    The wheeling torrent viewing,
Mid circling horrors sinks at last
    In overwhelming ruin.—

5 drag a hopeless chain] see my rival's reign *HL*   6 And yet] While I *HL*:
yet *corrected to* still *in Adam*   8 Nor dare disclose] Yet dare not speak *HL
Adam Dal A*   9 Love's veriest wretch . . . unknown] Love's veriest wretch,
despairing, I *HL*: The wretch of love . . . unknown *Adam Dal A*   10 I] Fain,
HL   griefs] crime *HL Adam Dal A Loch*   11 The . . . groan] Th' unweeting
groan, the bursting sigh *HL*   12 hapless] guilty *HL Adam Dal A Loch*
13 thou doom'st me to] my doom must be *HL* (*correcting* No dawn my fate),
Adam Dal A Loch   14 Nor] Thou *HL Adam Dal A Loch*   15 Eliza]
Maria *HL Adam Dal A Loch*   hear] *correcting* grant *in HL*   17 voice]
tongue *HL Adam Dal A*   18 while it enslav'd] *correcting* it would enslave *in
HL*   23 Mid] In *HL* sinks] *corrected to* yields *in HL*: yields *Adam Dal A*
24 In overwhelming] To overwhelming *HL* (*correcting* In everlasting), *Adam Dal A*

406. When wild War's deadly Blast was blawn

The Mill, Mill O

Slow

WHEN wild War's deadly blast was blawn,
    And gentle Peace returning,
Wi' mony a sweet babe fatherless,
    And mony a widow mourning:
I left the lines, and tented field,   5
    Where lang I'd been a lodger,
My humble knapsack a' my wealth,
    A poor and honest sodger.

When wild War's deadly Blast. *Text from SC, 1793 (22; copy presented to Miss Graham of Fintry, with autograph corrections; at Alloway). The Aldine editor records (1839) a MS with these variants*   21 maid] lass *MS*   25 alter'd] fremit *MS*   34 was] look'd *MS*   42 pale like ony] wallow't like a *MS*   '51 poor in gear] wealth be sma' *MS*   53 gowd] gear *MS*   55 faithful] ain dear *MS*. *See Commentary*

3–4 Wi' . . . mourning:] SC (*1793 printing*) *has*

      And eyes again with pleasure beam'd,
      That had been blear'd with mourning.

In Miss Graham's copy Burns first altered eyes *to* een *and then replaced the two lines as in the text.* 8, 32, 35, 55, 59, 60, 61 sodger] soldier *SC. The rhymes in ll. 6–8, 30–32, suggest that Thomson has anglicized*

A leal, light heart was in my breast,
   My hand unstain'd wi' plunder;   10
And for fair Scotia, hame again
   I cheery on did wander.
I thought upon the banks of Coil,
   I thought upon my Nancy,
And ay I mind't the witching smile   15
   That caught my youthful fancy.

At length I reach'd the bonny glen,
   Where early life I sported;
I pass'd the mill and trysting thorn,
   Where Nancy aft I courted: 20
Wha spied I but my ain dear maid,
   Down by her mother's dwelling!
And turn'd me round to hide the flood
   That in my een was swelling.

Wi' alter'd voice, quoth I, sweet lass,
   Sweet as yon hawthorn's blossom,   25
O! happy, happy may he be
   That's dearest to thy bosom:
My purse is light, I've far to gang,
   And fain wad be thy lodger;   30
I've serv'd my king and country lang,
   Take pity on a sodger!

Sae wistfully she gaz'd on me,
   And lovelier was than ever;
Quo' she, a sodger ance I lo'ed,
   Forget him shall I never: 35
Our humble cot, and hamely fare,
   Ye freely shall partake it,
That gallant badge, the dear cockade,
   Ye're welcome for the sake o't.   40

She gaz'd—she redden'd like a rose,—
   Syne pale like ony lily,
She sank within my arms, and cried,
   Art thou my ain dear Willie?—

15 And ay I mind't] *autograph correction of* I thought upon *in SC*

By Him who made yon sun and sky, 45
    By whom true love's regarded,
I am the man—and thus may still
    True lovers be rewarded!

The wars are o'er, and I'm come hame,
    And find thee still true-hearted; 50
Tho' poor in gear, we're rich in love,
    And mair,—we'se ne'er be parted!
Quo' she, my grandsire left me gowd,
    A mailin plenish'd fairly;
And come, my faithful sodger lad, 55
    Thou'rt welcome to it dearly!

For gold the merchant ploughs the main,
    The farmer ploughs the manor;
But glory is the sodger's prize,
    The sodger's wealth is honour; 60
The brave poor sodger ne'er despise,
    Nor count him as a stranger;
Remember, he's his country's stay
    In day and hour of danger.

407 A. O ken ye what Meg o' the mill has gotten

A little lively

O KEN ye what Meg o' the mill has gotten,
An' ken ye what Meg o' the mill has gotten;
A braw new naig wi' the tail o' a rottan,
And that's what Meg o' the mill has gotten.

O ken ye what Meg o' the mill loes dearly,   5
An' ken ye what Meg o' the mill loes dearly;
A dram o' gude strunt in a morning early,
And that's what Meg o' the mill loes dearly.

O ken ye how Meg o' the mill was married,
An' ken ye how Meg o' the mill was married;   10
The Priest he was oxter'd, the Clerk he was carried,
And that's how Meg o' the mill was married.

O ken ye how Meg o' the mill was bedded,
An' ken ye how Meg o' the mill was bedded;
The groom gat sae fu' he fell awald beside it,   15
And that's how Meg o' the mill was bedded.

O ken ye. *Text from SMM, 1803 (566; unsigned)*

407B. Ken ye what Meg o' the mill has gotten—

O KEN ye what Meg o' the mill has gotten,
An ken ye what Meg o' the mill has gotten?
She's gotten a coof wi' a claut o' siller,
And broken the heart o' the barley Miller.—

The Miller was strappin, the Miller was ruddy,   5
A heart like a lord, and a hue like a lady;
The Laird was a widdefu', bleerit knurl;
She's left the gude-fallow and taen the churl.—

The Miller he hecht her, a heart leal and luving,
The Laird did address her wi' matter mair muving, 10
A fine pacing horse wi' a clear chainet bridle,
A whip by her side, and a bony side-sadle.

O wae on the siller, it is sae prevailing,
And wae on the luve that's fix'd on a mailin!
A tocher's nae word in a true luver's parle,   15
But, gie me my luve, and a fig for the warl!

408. Song—

Tune, Liggeram cosh—

Allegretto

Ken ye what Meg o' the mill has gotten. *Text from the Alloway MS (Al) collated with
the Dalhousie MS (letter to Thomson, April 1793) and Currie (iv. 54–55)*
   6 hue] *correcting* skin *in Al*   16 me] *om. Al*

Song. *Text from the Dalhousie MS (letter to Thomson, 30 June 1793), collated with
SC, 1799 (58), where the air is entitled* The Quaker's Wife

B LYTHE hae I been on yon hill,
    As the lambs before me;
Careless ilka thought and free,
    As the breeze flew o'er me:
Now nae langer sport and play,   5
    Mirth or sang can please me;
Lesley is sae fair and coy,
    Care and anguish seize me.

Heavy, heavy is the task,
    Hopeless love declaring: 10
Trembling, I dow nocht but glowr,
    Sighing, dumb, despairing!
If she winna ease the thraws,
    In my bosom swelling;
Underneath the grass-green sod   15
    Soon maun be my dwelling.

409. Song—

Tune Logan Water—

Song. *Text from the Dalhousie MS (Dal; letter to Thomson, ? 25 June 1793), collated*

O, LOGAN, sweetly didst thou glide,
 The day I was my Willie's bride;
And years sinsyne hae o'er us run,
Like Logan to the simmer sun.
But now thy flowery banks appear   5
Like drumlie Winter, dark and drear,
While my dear lad maun face his faes,
Far, far frae me and Logan braes.—

Again the merry month o' May
Has made our hills and vallies gay;   10
The birds rejoice in leafy bowers,
The bees hum round the breathing flowers:
Blythe Morning lifts his rosy eye,
And Evening's tears are tears of joy:
My soul, delightless, a' surveys,   15
While Willie's far frae Logan braes.—

Within yon milkwhite hawthorn bush,
Amang her nestlings sits the thrush;
Her faithfu' Mate will share her toil,
Or wi' his song her cares beguile: 20
But I, wi' my sweet nurslings here,
Nae Mate to help, nae Mate to cheer,
Pass widowed nights and joyless days,
While Willie's far frae Logan braes.—

O wae upon you, Men o' State,   25
That brethren rouse in deadly hate!
As ye make mony a fond heart mourn,
Sae may it on your heads return!
How can your flinty hearts enjoy
The widow's tears, the orphan's cry: 30
But soon may Peace bring happy days
And Willie, hame to Logan braes!

*with the Lochryan MS (Loch; letter to Mrs. Dunlop, ? December 1793) and SC, 1803
(116). First-line title in SC*
 29–30 How . . . cry. *Burns wrote in Dal* Ye mind na, mid your cruel joys . . .
cries. *Thomson commented on the MS* cruel not good *and altered as above. SC has
the amended text*

410. On being asked why God had made Miss D—— so little and M^rs A—— so big—

A s k why God made the GEM so small,
    And why so huge the granite?
Because God meant, mankind should set
    That higher value on it.—

411 A. [On] Maxwell of Cardoness—

B LESS J–s–s Ch———, O Cardoness,
    With grateful lifted eyes;
Who taught that not the soul alone,
    But body too shall rise.

For had he said, the soul alone   5
    From death I will deliver:
Alas, alas, O Cardoness!
    Then hadst thou lain forever!

411 B. Extempore—On being shown a beautiful Country seat belonging to the same—

W E grant they're thine, those beauties all,
    So lovely in our eye:
Keep them, thou eunuch, C———ss,
    For others to enjoy!

On being asked. *Text from the Huntington Library MS (with letter to Creech, 30 May 1795), collated with the Lochryan MS (letter to Mrs. Dunlop, June 1793), the Glenriddell MS (p. 160), and Stewart, 1801 (p. 62). Sub-title in Stewart* Written on a pane of glass in the Inn at Moffat

On Maxwell of Cardoness. *Text from the Lochryan MS (letter to Mrs. Dunlop, June 1793), collated with the Huntington Library MS (with letter to Creech, 30 May 1795), and the Glenriddell MS (p. 162). Title in these two MSS* On the laird of C–rd–nn–ss

Extempore. *Text from the Huntington Library MS (letter to Creech, 30 May 1795)*

412. [Annotations in Verse]

[A] WISDOM and Science—honor'd Powers!
     Pardon the truth a sinner tells;
I owe my dearest, raptured hours
     To FOLLY with her cap and bells.—

[B] GRANT me, indulgent Heaven, that I may live
To see the miscreants feel the pains they give:
Deal Freedom's sacred treasures free as air,
Till SLAVE and DESPOT be but *things which were!*

[C] PERISH their names, however great or brave,
Who in the DESPOT's cursed errands bleed!
But who for FREEDOM fills a hero's grave,
Fame with a Seraph-pen, record the glorious deed!

[D] LOVE's records, written on a heart like mine,
Not Time's last effort can efface a line.
                                        R. B.

413. O were my Love yon Lilack fair

Slow

O WERE my Love yon Lilack fair,
     Wi' purple blossoms to the Spring;
And I, a bird to shelter there,
     When wearied on my little wing.

Annotations in Verse. *Text from Syme's copy of* The British Album: Containing the
Poems of Della Crusca . . . , *1790 (i. 18, i. 21, i. 28, ii. 115);* Burns Chronicle,
1940, pp. 15–16. [B] *was published in Stewart, 1801, p. 74, as* Lines written extempore in a Lady's Pocket-Book. By R. Burns. *See Commentary*

O were my Love yon Lilack fair. *Text from the Dalhousie MS (letter to Thomson, ?25*
June 1793), collated with SC, 1805 (154). Set in three 8-line stanzas in SC (the second
interpolated), with the note The first and second Stanzas written for this work by
BURNS *and* J. RICHARDSON.—The last Stanza is old. *See Commentary*

How I wad mourn, when it was torn   5
  By Autumn wild, and Winter rude!
But I wad sing on wanton wing,
  When youthfu' May its bloom renew'd.

[O gin my love were yon red rose,
  That grows upon the castle wa'!   10
And I mysel' a drap o' dew,
  Into her bonnie breast to fa'!

Oh, there beyond expression blesst
  I'd feast on beauty a' the night;
Seal'd on her silk-saft faulds to rest,   15
  Till fley'd awa by Phebus' light!]

414. A Ballad

THERE was a lass and she was fair,
  At kirk and market to be seen;
When a' our fairest maids were met,
  The fairest maid was bonie Jean.

And ay she wrought her Mammie's wark,   5
  And ay she sang sae merrilie;
The blythest bird upon the bush
  Had ne'er a lighter heart than she.

But hawks will rob the tender joys
  That bless the little lintwhite's nest;   10
And frost will blight the fairest flowers,
  And love will break the soundest rest.

  5, 7 wad] would *SC*   8 youthfu'] *alternative to* gallant *and* merry *in MS*
bloom] *alternative leaf in MS*

A Ballad. *Text from the Dalhousie MS (Dal B; letter to Thomson, 2 July? 1793),
collated with the Adam MS, MS Dal A (letter to Thomson, April 1793; ll. 1–12 only),
the Alloway MS (Al; letter to Miss McMurdo, July 1793), and SC, 1805 (152). Title
from Al; first-line title in SC and Adam*
  5 wrought . . . wark] ?kept . . . ?cot *Thomson's alternative in Dal B*   Mammie's]
country *Dal A Adam*: mother's *Al*

Young Robie was the brawest lad,
  The flower and pride of a' the glen;
And he had owsen, sheep and kye,   15
  And wanton naigies nine or ten.

He gaed wi' Jeanie to the tryste,
  He danc'd wi' Jeanie on the down;
And lang e'er witless Jeanie wist,
  Her heart was tint, her peace was stown.   20

As in the bosom o' the stream
  The moon-beam dwells at dewy e'en;
So, trembling, pure, was tender love
  Within the breast o' bonie Jean.

And now she works her Mammie's wark,   25
  And ay she sighs wi' care and pain;
Yet wist na what her ail might be,
  Or what wad mak her weel again.

But did na Jeanie's heart lowp light,
  And did na joy blink in her e'e;   30
As Robie tauld a tale o' love,
  Ae e'enin on the lily lea.

The sun was sinking in the west,
  The birds sang sweet in ilka grove:
His cheek to hers he fondly laid,   35
  And whisper'd thus his tale o' love.

14 The . . . glen;] That turn'd the maute in yon toun-en', *Adam*   21–24 *Autograph note in Dal B* Is not this original: *stanza not in Adam*   23 trembling, pure,] trembling pure *Al*   25 now . . . Mammie's] as she wrought her country *Adam*   25, 39 Mammie's] mother's *Al*   26 And . . . wi'] Her life was nought but *Adam*   27 wist] *corrected to* kend *in Adam*   might] could *Adam* 28 mak her weel] *corrected to* ease her heart *in Adam*   31 As] When *Adam* tauld] tell'd *SC*   33–36 The . . . love.] *Adam has*

> While mony a bird sang sweet o' love,
>   And mony a flower bloom'd o'er the dale;
> His cheek to hers he aft did lay,
>   And whisper'd thus his tender tale.—

35 laid] prest *Currie*

O Jeanie fair, I loe thee dear;
   O canst thou think to fancy me!
Or wilt thou leave thy Mammie's cot,
   And learn to tent the farms wi' me.   40

At barn or byre thou shalt na drudge,
   Or naething else to trouble thee;
But stray amang the heather-bells,
   And tent the waving corn wi' me.

Now what could artless Jeanie do?   45
   She had na will to say him na:
At length she blush'd a sweet consent,
   And love was ay between them twa.

415. [Epigrams on Lord Galloway]

[A] On seeing the beautiful country-seat of lord G——

WHAT dost thou in that mansion fair,
     Flit, G——! and find
Some narrow, dirty, dungeon cave,
   The picture of thy mind.——

[B] On the same n–blem–n——

No St–w–rt art thou, G——,
   The St——ts all were brave:
Besides, the St——ts were but *fools*,
   Not one of them a *knave*.——

38 O] And *Adam*   39 Or] And *Adam*   Mammie's cot] country wark
Adam   40 tent the farms] turn the maute *Adam*   41–44 At . . . me.]
Adam has
                Thy handsome foot thou shalt na set
                   In barn or byre, to trouble thee;
                But sit on a cushion and sew at thy seam,
                   And learn to turn the maute wi' me.
45 what . . . do?] Jeanie wist na what to say, *Adam*   47 sweet] kind *Adam*
48 love] bliss *Adam*

Epigrams on Lord Galloway. *Text from the Huntington Library MS (letter to Creech, 30 May 1795), collated with Cromek*, Reliques, *1808 (p. 415)*

[C] on the same—

BRIGHT ran thy LINE, O G——,
    Thro' many a far-fam'd sire:
So ran the far-fam'd ROMAN WAY,
    So ended in a MIRE.——

[D] To the same, on the Author being threatened with his
resentment—

SPARE me thy vengeance, G——,
    In quiet let me live:
I ask no kindness at thy hand,
    —For thou hast none to give.——

416. [On the death of Echo, a Lap-dog]

[A]

IN wood and wild, ye warbling throng,
    Your heavy loss deplore;
Now half extinct your powers of song,
    Sweet Echo is no more.

Ye jarring, screeching things around,   5
    Scream your discordant joys;
Now half your din of tuneless sound
    With Echo silent lies.

[B]

YE warblers of the vocal grove,
    Your heavy loss deplore;
Now half your melody is lost,
    Sweet Echo is no more.

Each shrieking, screaming bird and beast,   5
    Exalt your tuneless voice;
Half your deformity is hid,
    Here Echo silent lies.

On the death of Echo, a Lap-dog. *Text of A from Currie, 1800 (i. 208). Text of B
from the Rosenbach MS (Dewar's transcript; cf. Rosenbach catalogue, Robert Burns,
1948, p. 54)*

417. On J–hn M–r–ne, laird of L–gg–n—

WHEN M–r–ne, deceased, to the devil went down,
'Twas nothing would serve him but Satan's own crown:
Thy fool's head, quoth Satan, that crown shall wear never;
I grant thou'rt as wicked—but not quite so clever.—

418. Phillis the fair—

Tune Robin Adair—

Slow

WHILE larks with little wing
Fann'd the pure air,
Viewing the breathing spring,
Forth I did fare:

On J–hn M–r–ne. *Text from the Glenriddell MS (p. 162), collated with the Hunting-ton Library MS (HL; letter to Creech, 30 May 1795) and Currie, 1800 (i. 210). Title in HL* On J— M–r–ne, Esq: of L——n —

Phillis the fair. *Text from the Dalhousie MS (letter to Thomson, 13 August 1793), collated with Currie (iv. 88)*
4 Viewing] Tasting *Thomson's alteration in MS, Currie*

Gay the sun's golden eye   5
Peep'd o'er the mountains high;
Such thy morn! did I cry,
    Phillis the fair.

In each bird's careless song,
    Glad, I did share;   10
While yon wild flowers among
    Chance led me there:
Sweet to the opening day,
Rosebuds bent the dewy spray;
Such thy bloom, did I say,   15
    Phillis the fair.

Down in a shady walk,
    Doves cooing were;
I mark'd the cruel hawk,
    Caught in a snare: 20
So kind may Fortune be,
Such make his destiny!
He who would injure thee,
    Phillis the fair.

419. Song

Had I a cave on some wild, distant shore,
Where the winds howl to the waves' dashing roar:
There would I weep my woes,
There seek my lost repose,
Till Grief my eyes should close,   5
    Ne'er to wake more.

Falsest of womankind, canst thou declare,
All thy fond plighted vows—fleeting as air!
To thy new lover hie,
Laugh o'er thy perjury—   10
Then in thy bosom try,
    What peace is there!

7 morn!] *correcting* bloom, *in MS*

Song. *Text from the Dalhousie MS (letter to Thomson, August 1793), collated with SC, 1799 (92). First-line title in SC*

420. Song—

O WHISTLE, and I'll come to ye, my lad,
  O whistle, and I'll come to ye, my lad;
Tho' father, and mother, and a' should gae mad,
  Thy JEANIE will venture wi' ye, my lad.

But warily tent, when ye come to court me,   5
  And come nae unless the back-yett be a-jee;
Syne up the back-style and let naebody see,
  And come as ye were na comin to me—
  And come as ye were na comin to me.—
    O whistle &c.

Song. *Text from the Dalhousie MSS (letter to Thomson, August 1793; 'improvement' of ll. 1–4 in letter to Thomson, 3 August 1795), collated with SC, 1799 (94). A short version was printed in SMM, 1788 (106) from Burns's holograph in the Hastie MS, f. 26ʳ:*

    O whistle, an' I'll come to you, my lad;
    O whistle, an' I'll come to you, my lad:
    Though father and mither should baith gae mad,
    O whistle, an' I'll come to you, my lad.

    Come down the back stairs when ye come to court me;
    Come down the back stairs when ye come to court me:
    Come down the back stairs, and let naebody see;
    And come as ye were na' coming to me.

First-line title in SC

  1, 2, 4 lad] jo *Thomson's alteration in MS*   3 gae mad] say no *Thomson's alteration in MS*   4 Thy . . . ye] *first MS repeats l. 1*   9, 14 *Abbreviations of ll. 1–4 repeated in MS*

At kirk, or at market whene'er ye meet me,   10
Gang by me as tho' that ye car'd nae a flie;
But steal me a blink o' your bonie black e'e,
    Yet look as ye were na lookin at me—
    Yet look as ye were na lookin at me.—
      O whistle &c.

Ay vow and protest that ye care na for me,   15
And whyles ye may lightly my beauty a wee;
But court nae anither, tho' jokin ye be,
    For fear that she wyle your fancy frae me—
    For fear that she wyle your fancy frae me.—

421. Song—

Tune—Geordie's byre—

Andante

Song. *Text from the Huntington Library MS (HL), collated with the Dalhousie MS (Dal; letter to Thomson, August 1793) and SC, 1799 (66). HL has the subscription:* To Miss Phillis M^cmurdo—with the Bard's most respectful Compl^{nts}—*Four 8-line stanzas in SC, ll. 5–8 repeated after ll. 25–28 only*

I

Adown winding Nith I did wander,
  To mark the sweet flowers as they spring;
Adown winding Nith I did wander,
  Of Phillis to muse and to sing.—

Chorus

Awa wi' your Belles and your Beauties,   5
  They never wi' her can compare:
Wha-ever has met wi' my Phillis,
  Has met wi' the Queen o' the Fair.—

2

The Daisy amus'd my fond fancy,
  So artless, so simple, so wild: 10
Thou emblem, said I, o' my Phillis,
  *For she is simplicity's child.—
    Awa &c.—

3

The rose-bud's the blush o' my Charmer,
  Her sweet balmy lip when 'tis prest:
How fair and how pure is the lily,   15
  But fairer and purer her breast.—
    Awa &c.—

4

Yon knot of gay flowers in the arbour,
  They ne'er wi' my Phillis can vie:
Her breath is the breath o' the woodbine,
  Its dew-drop o' diamond, her eye.—   20
    Awa &c.—

* Here the *Poet* trusts that he shall also be found a *Prophet*; and that this charming feature will ever be a distinguishing trait in his Heroine.

---

10 So artless] *correcting* So simple *in Dal*   12 Note *in HL only. A cancelled stanza follows in Dal:*

> The primrose is o'er for the season,
>   But mark where the violet is blown;
> How modest it peeps from the covert,
>   So modesty sure is her own,

5

Her voice is the songs of the morning,
  That wake thro' the green-spreading grove;
When Phebus peeps over the mountains
  On music, and pleasure, and love.—
    Awa &c.

6

But Beauty, how frail and how fleeting,   25
  The bloom of a fine summer's day;
While Worth in the mind of my Phillis
  Will flourish without a decay.—
    Awa &c.—

422. Allan Water

Andante

21 songs] *correcting* voice *in Dal*   28 *Chorus repeated in full in Dal*

Allan Water. *Text from the Dalhousie MS (Dal; letter to Thomson, 19 August 1793),*

B^Y Allan-side I chanc'd to rove,
  While Phebus sank beyond Benledi*;
The winds were whispering thro' the grove,
  The yellow corn was waving ready:
I listen'd to a lover's sang,   5
  And thought on youthfu' pleasures mony;
And ay the wild-wood echoes rang—
  O dearly do I lo'e thee, Annie.—

O happy be the woodbine bower,
  Nae nightly bogle make it eerie;   10
Nor ever sorrow stain the hour,
  The place and time I met my Dearie!
Her head upon my throbbing breast,
  She, sinking, said, 'I'm thine for ever!'
While mony a kiss the seal imprest,   15
  The sacred vow, we ne'er should sever.—

The haunt o' Spring's the primrose-brae,
  The Simmer joys the flocks to follow;
How cheery, thro' her shortening day,
  Is Autumn in her weeds o' yellow: 20
But can they melt the glowing heart,
  Or chain the soul in speechless pleasure,
Or thro' each nerve the rapture dart,
  Like meeting H<small>ER</small>, our bosom's treasure.

* A mountain west of Strathallan 3009 feet high.

---

collated with the Lochryan MS (Loch; letter to Mrs. Dunlop, 25 August 1793) and SC,
1799 (79). Title in Loch Song; first-line title in SC
  1 -side] stream alternative in Dal: stream SC   2 note mountain] high
mountain Dal: high mountain Loch   3009 feet high] om. Loch   6, 15 mony]
many SC   8 O . . . Annie] O my love, Annie's very bonie alternative in Dal
22 chain] sieze alternative in Dal

423. Song

Tune, Cauld kail

COME, let me take thee to my breast,
   And pledge we ne'er shall sunder;
And I shall spurn, as vilest dust,
   The warld's wealth and grandeur:
And do I hear my Jeanie own,   5
   That equal transports move her?
I ask for dearest life alone
   That I may live to love her.

Thus in my arms, wi' a' thy charms,
   I clasp my countless treasure;   10
I seek nae mair o' Heaven to share,
   Than sic a moment's pleasure:
And by thy een, sae bonie blue,
   I swear I'm thine for ever!
And on thy lips I seal my vow,   15
   And break it shall I never!

Song. *Text from the Dalhousie MS (letter to Thomson, 28 August 1793), collated with
SC, 1799 (93). Thomson's note on tune in the MS: or for the pretty Irish air Alley
Croker the measure being the same. Set to Alley Croker in SC, with repetitions by
Thomson to suit*
  8 *Additional lines in SC:*

      To love, to love, that I may live to love her,
        I ask for dearest life alone,
        That I may live to love her.

9 Thus] *correcting* When *in MS*   11 I] I'll *Thomson's alternative in MS*
16 *Additional lines in SC:*

      Never, never, break it shall I never!
        And on thy lips I seal my vow,
        And break it shall I never!

424. Dainty Davie

Now rosy May comes in wi' flowers,
   To deck her gay, green spreading bowers;
And now comes in my happy hours,
   To wander wi' my Davie.—

Chorus

   Meet me on the warlock knowe,   5
   Dainty Davie, Dainty Davie;
   There I'll spend the day wi' you,
   My ain dear dainty Davie.—

The crystal waters round us fa',
   The merry birds are lovers a',   10
The scented breezes round us blaw,
   Awandering wi' my Davie.—
   Meet me &c.

As purple morning starts the hare,
   To steal upon her early fare,
Then through the dews I will repair,   15
   To meet my faithfu' Davie.—
   Meet me &c.

When day, expiring in the west,
   The curtain draws o' Nature's rest,
I'll flee to his arms I lo'e the best,
   And that's my ain dear Davie.—   20

Chorus

   Meet me on the warlock knowe,
   Bonie Davie, dainty Davie;
   There I'll spend the day wi' you,
   My ain dear dainty Davie.—

*Dainty Davie. Text from the Dalhousie MS (letter to Thomson, 28 August 1793),
collated with SC, 1799 (69). Set in SC in two stanzas (ll. 1–4 and 9–12, 13–16 and
17–20), each with chorus*
   13 As] *correcting* When *in MS: Thomson suggests* When *in margin of MS:* When
SC   19 his] 's *SC*   21 on] at *alternative in MS*   22 Bonie] Dainty *SC*

425. Robert Bruce's March to Bannockburn—

To its ain tune—

Scots, wha hae wi' WALLACE bled,
Scots, wham BRUCE has aften led,
Welcome to your gory bed,—
Or to victorie.—

Now's the day, and now's the hour;   5
See the front o' battle lour;
See approach proud EDWARD's power,
Chains and Slaverie.—

Robert Bruce's March to Bannockburn. *Text from the Dalhousie MS (letter to Thomson, c. 30 August 1793), collated with SC, 1803 (133); set to the air Hey tutti taiti. H–H. (iii. 478) record these variants in an 'early draft', not traced:*

6–8   See approach proud Edward's power,
    Sharply maun we bide the stour,
    Either they or we.

17–20   Do you hear your children cry:—
    'Were we born in chains to lie?'
    No! Come Death or Liberty!
    Yes, *they shall be free.*

Thomson's note in SC: The Poet *originally* intended this noble strain for the Air [*Hey tutti taiti*]; but, on a suggestion from the Editor of this Work, who then thought 'Lewie Gordon' a fitter tune for the words, they were united together. . . . The Editor, however, having since examined the Air 'Hey tutti taiti' with more particular attention, frankly owns that he has changed his opinion, and that he thinks it much better adapted for giving energy to the Poetry. . . . He therefore sent it to HAYDN, who has entered into the spirit of it with a felicity peculiar to himself . . .

Burns's revision for Lewie Gordon *(Dalhousie MS; letter to Thomson, 3 September 1793) has the following alterations:* 4 Or to glorious victorie   8 Edward! Chains and Slaverie!   12 Traitor! Coward! turn and flie!   16 Caledonian! on wi' me!   20 But they shall be—shall be free!   24 Forward! Let us Do, or Die!!! *Other MSS have* they shall, they shall *in l. 20*

The revised text appears also in the following: MSS Lochryan *(letter to Mrs. Dunlop, 20 December 1793),* Rosenbach *(To Mrs G. Burns, from her brother The Author),* Harvard *(letter to the Earl of Buchan, 12 January 1794),* Edinburgh *(at Lady Stair's House; given to Dr. Hughes of Hereford by Burns on 8 August 1795 at Dumfries),* Alloway *(A undated; B, 5 December 1793), and Dumfries; the* Morning Chronicle, *8 May 1794, SC, 1799 (74), and SMM, 1803 (577). Title in the Rosenbach MS* Bannockburn—Bruce to his Troops—Tune, Lewis Gordon; *variants of this in other MSS. The Edinburgh MS has a long note for Dr. Hughes on the battle of Bannockburn and the murder of Comyn at Dumfries. Note in Alloway A:* N.B. the thought in the last Stanza is borrowed from a Couplet in the modernised copy of the History of Wallace—a Couplet worthy of Homer—

    A false Usurper sinks in every foe,
    And Liberty returns with every blow.

Wha will be a traitor-knave?
Wha can fill a coward's grave?   10
Wha sae base as be a Slave?
—Let him turn and flie:—

Wha for SCOTLAND's king and law,
Freedom's sword will strongly draw,
FREE-MAN stand, or FREE-MAN fa',   15
Let him follow me.—

By Oppression's woes and pains!
By your Sons in servile chains!
We will drain our dearest veins,
But they *shall* be free!   20

Lay the proud Usurpers low!
Tyrants fall in every foe!
LIBERTY's in every blow!
Let us Do—OR DIE!!!

426. To Maria—

Epigram—On Lord Buchan's assertion, that 'Women ought always
to be flattered grossly, or not spoken to at all'——

'PRAISE Woman still!' his Lordship says,
   'Deserved, or not, no matter,'
But thee, Maria, while I praise,
   There Flattery cannot flatter.—

Maria, all my thought and dream,   5
   Inspires my vocal shell:
The more I praise my lovely Theme
   The more the truth I tell.—

To Maria. *Text from the Alloway MS (addressed on verso to* Mrs W. Riddell
Woodleypark *and signed* RB). *H–H. (ii. 253) use a MS (not traced) with the heading*
On my Lord Buchan's vociferating in an argument that 'Women must always be
flattered . . .' *and these variants:*
   1 says] roars *MS*   3 Maria . . . praise] whom all my soul adores *MS*

427. Down the burn Davie

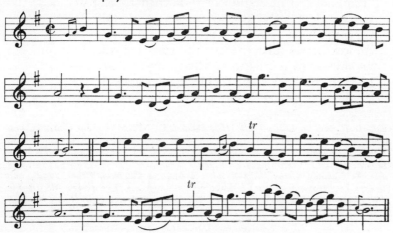

As down the burn they took their way,
And thro' the flowery dale;
His cheek to hers he aft did lay,
And love was ay the tale.—

With 'Mary, when shall we return,   5
Sic pleasure to renew;'
Quoth Mary, Love, I like the burn,
And ay shall follow you.—

428. [Passion's Cry]

'I cannot but remember such things were,
'And were most dear to me'—

In vain would Prudence, with decorous sneer,
Point out a cens'ring world, and bid me fear:
Above that world on wings of love I rise:
I know its worst and can that worst despise.—

Down the burn Davie. *Text from the Dalhousie MS (letter to Thomson, September 1793). See Commentary*

Passion's Cry. *Text from Ferguson's transcript of the Barrett MS (B; ?1793), collated*

1 decorous] her decent *alternative (not autograph) in B, with the note:* Her decent is found in a sketch of these lines among his papers & is better than decorous wh. is not rythm *(Ferguson)*

'Wronged, injured, shunned, unpitied, unredrest;   5
'The mocked quotation of the scorner's jest'—
Let Prudence' direst bodements on me fall,
Clarinda, rich reward! o'erpays them all.—
As low-borne mists before the sun remove,
So shines, so reigns unrivalled mighty LOVE.—   10
In vain the laws their feeble force oppose;
Chained at his feet, they groan Love's vanquished foes;

*with the Huntington Library MS (HL; headed To M^{rs} M^c— alias Clarinda, and
signed Sylvander), B.M. MS Egerton 1656, f. 15 (Eg; title, A Fragment), MSS
Cunningham (Cun; letter to Alexander Cunningham, 24 January 1789), Lochryan
(Loch A, entitled A Fragment; Loch B, letter to Mrs. Dunlop, 5 February 1789), Don
(title, Fragments), Lenox (ll. 1–8 only, in letter to Clarinda, ?June 1794), and
Stewart, Letters Addressed to Clarinda, &c., 1802 (p. 44). The 42-line MS listed in
E. C. Bigmore's reprint of the 1861 sale catalogue has not been traced. Hately Waddell
(1867; Appendix) prints six lines which may have been part of a MS of Passion's Cry:*

> Mild Zephyrs waft thee to life's farthest shore,
> Nor think of me and my distresses more,—
> Falsehood accurst! No! still I beg a place,
> Still near thy heart some little, little trace;
> For that dear trace the world I would resign:
> O let me live, and die, and think it mine!

See Commentary

5–6 Wronged . . . jest] *The remnant of the first fragment in Cun and Don:*

> By all I lov'd neglected and forgot,
> No friendly face e'er lights my squalid cot:
> Shunn'd, hated, wrong'd, unpitied, unredrest:
> The mock'd quotation of the scorner's jest:
> Even the poor support of my wretched life,   5
> Snatch'd by the violence of legal strife.
> Oft grateful for my very daily bread
> To those my Fam'ly's once large bounty fed:
> A welcome inmate at their homely fare,
> My griefs, my woes, my sighs, my tears they share;   10
> (Their vulgar souls unlike the souls refin'd,
> The fashion'd marble of the polish'd mind!)

2 squalid] lonely *Don*   10 griefs] *correcting* prayers *in Don*

11–26 In vain . . . die!!!] *A revision of HL Eg Loch A–B and the second fragment
in Cun and Don. HL begins:*

> 'I burn, I burn, as when thro' ripened corn
> 'By driving winds the crackling flames are borne!'

> Now maddening, wild, I curse that fatal night;
> Now bless the hour that charm'd my guilty sight:
> In vain the Laws . . .

Only HL, Eg and Loch A have the epigraph. Line 1 reads Now raving *in Eg Cun
Loch A; line 2 reads* Then bless *in Eg Cun*   11 their] his *Eg*

In vain Religion meets my shrinking eye;
I dare not combat, but I turn and fly:
Conscience in vain upbraids th' unhallowed fire;   15
Love grasps his scorpions, stifled they expire:
Reason drops headlong from his sacred throne,
Thy dear idea reigns, and reigns alone;
Each thought intoxicated homage yields,
And riots wanton in forbidden fields.—   20

By all on High, adoring mortals know!
By all the conscious villain fears below!
By, what, Alas! much more my soul alarms,
My doubtful hopes once more to fill thy arms!
E'en shouldst thou, false, forswear each guilty tie,   25
Thine, and thine only, I must live and die!!!

429. The Primrose—

Tune, Todlin Hame—

Slowish

16 his] her *HL Eg Loch A–B Don*   17 his] *correcting* her *in Don*: her *HL
Loch A–B*   18 Thy] Your *HL Eg Cun Loch A–B Don Stewart*   23–26 By
. . . die!!!] *HL Loch A̅ Eg Stewart have*

      'By your dear Self! the last great oath I swear
      'Not life nor soul were ever half so dear!'

25 each] the *Cun Loch B Don*   26 must] shall *Cun*

The Primrose. *Text from the Dalhousie MS (letter to Thomson, September 1793):
an old English song . . . altered . . . a little.*

Dost ask me, why I send thee here,
This firstling of the infant year?
Dost ask me, what this primrose shews,
Bepearled thus with morning dews?—

    I must whisper to thy ears,   5
    The sweets of love are wash'd with tears.

This lovely native of the dale
Thou seest, how languid, pensive, pale:
Thou seest this bending stalk so weak,
That each way yielding doth not break?   10

    I must tell thee, these reveal,
    The doubts and fears that lovers feel.

430. Thou hast left me ever

Fee him father

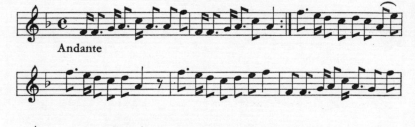

Andante

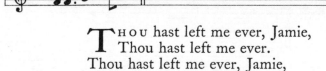

Thou hast left me ever, Jamie,
    Thou hast left me ever.
Thou hast left me ever, Jamie,
    Thou hast left me ever.

7–8 This . . . pale:] *correcting*
                Dost ask me of this floweret's hue,
                So yellow, green and sickly too?
in MS   9 Thou . . .bending] *correcting* Dost ask me of this *in MS*

Thou hast left me ever. *Text from the Dalhousie MS (letter to Thomson, September
1793), collated with SC, 1799 (90). Title from SC. Written for the air* Fee him,
father; *set to* The Lammy *in SC, with ll. 9 and 18 omitted to suit*
   1 *et passim* Jamie] Tam *SC*

Aften hast thou vow'd that Death, 5
  Only should us sever:
Now thou's left thy lass for ay—
  I maun see thee never, Jamie,
  I'll see thee never.—

Thou hast me forsaken, Jamie, 10
  Thou hast me forsaken:
Thou hast me forsaken, Jamie,
  Thou hast me forsaken.
Thou canst love anither jo,
  While my heart is breaking: 15
Soon my weary een I'll close—
  Never mair to waken, Jamie,
  Ne'er mair to waken.

431. Song—

Tune, Oran gaoil—

5 Aften] Often *SC*   7 thou's] thou'st *SC*   8 maun] must *SC*   14 anither
jo] another maid *SC*   16 een] eyes *SC*   17 mair] more *SC*

Song. *Text from the Dalhousie MS (letter to Thomson, September 1793), collated with the Watson MS (1134; letter to Clarinda, 27 December 1791) and SC, 1805 (154). Title in Watson* Song—To an old Scots tune—; *first-line title in SC*

B EHOLD the hour, the boat arrive;
    Thou goest, thou darling of my heart:
Severed from thee, can I survive,
    But Fate has willed—and we must part.
I'll often greet this surging swell,   5
    Yon distant Isle will often hail:
'E'en here, I took the last farewell;
    'There, latest marked her vanished sail.'

Along the solitary shore,
    While flitting sea-fowl round me cry,   10
Across the rolling, dashing roar
    I'll west-ward turn my wistful eye:
Happy, thou Indian grove, I'll say,
    Where now my Nancy's path may be!
While through thy sweets she loves to stray,   15
    O tell me, does she muse on me!

432. Fair Jenny—

Tune, The grey cock

2 Thou . . . heart:] My dearest Nancy, Oh, fareweel! *Watson*   3 from]
frae *Watson*   4–8 But . . . sail.] *Watson has*
                Frae thee wham I hae lov'd sae weel!
                Endless and deep shall be my grief,
                Nae ray o' comfort shall I see,
                But this most precious, dear belief!
                That thou wilt still remember me.

9 Along] Alang *Watson*   10 While] Where *Watson*   sea-fowl] sea-fowls *SC*
14 may] shall *Watson*   15 thy . . . loves to stray] your . . . holds her way *Watson*

Fair Jenny. *Text from the Dalhousie MS (Dal B; letter to Thomson, 15 September
1793), collated with MS Dal A (letter to Thomson, September 1793), and SC, 1801*

WHERE are the joys I have met in the morning,
    That danc'd to the lark's early song?
Where is the peace that awaited my wandring,
    At evening the wild-woods among?

No more a winding the course of yon river,   5
    And marking sweet flowerets so fair:
No more I trace the light footsteps of Pleasure,
    But Sorrow and sad-sighing Care.—

Is it that Summer's forsaken our vallies,
    And grim, surly Winter is near?   10
No, no! the bees humming round the gay roses
    Proclaim it the pride of the year.—

Fain would I hide, what I fear to discover,
    Yet long, long too well have I known:
All that has caused this wreck in my bosom,   15
    Is Jenny, fair Jenny alone.—

Time cannot aid me, my griefs are immortal,
    Not Hope dare a comfort bestow:
Come then, enamour'd and fond of my anguish,
    Enjoyment I'll seek in my woe.—   20

(*102*). *Title in Dal A* ~~Song~~ Fragment—tune, Saw ye my Father; *first-line title in SC;*
after The grey cock *in Dal B Thomson adds* or Saw ye my father. *Dewar collated a
draft, probably earlier than Dal A, in which* are (*l. 1*) *corrects* is, light (*l. 7*) *corrects*
gay, A' that has caused (*l. 15*) *corrects* She, the sweet cause o', fair (*l. 16*) *corrects*
sweet, *and ll. 17–20 are lacking*
   1 have] hae *Dal A*   2 song] sang *Dal A*   4 evening . . . among?] e'enin
amang. *Dal A*   5, 7 No more . . . of] Nae mair . . . o' *Dal A*   6 so] sae
Dal A   9 Summer] Simmer *Dal A*   12 of] o' *Dal A*   13 would] wad
Dal A   14 long, long . . . have] lang, lang . . . hae *Dal A*   15 All . . .
this] A' . . . the *Dal A*   20 *Dal A ends with* Cetera desunt.

433. On Captⁿ W—— R–dd–ck of C–rb—ton—

LIGHT lay the earth on Billy's breast,
  His chicken heart so tender:
But build a castle on his head,
  His scull will prop it under.—

434. Thine am I, my Chloris fair

THINE am I, my Chloris fair,
  Well thou may'st discover;
Every pulse along my veins
  Tells the ardent Lover.

To thy bosom lay my heart,   5
  There to throb and languish:
Tho' Despair had wrung its core,
  That would heal its anguish.

Take away these rosy lips,
  Rich with balmy treasure: 10
Turn away thine eyes of love,
  Lest I die with pleasure!

What is Life when wanting Love?
  Night without a morning:
Love's the cloudless summer sun,   15
  Nature gay adorning.

*On Captⁿ W—— R–dd–ck. Text from the Glenriddell MS (p. 160), collated with
the Adam MS (letter to Mrs W. Riddell, October 1793), letter to Patrick Millar,
?1 May 1794 (Ferguson's text), and the Huntington Library MS (letter to Creech, 30
May 1795). Title in Millar* Epigram—On a noted coxcomb—; *signed*—Clincher.—
4 prop] *alternative to* bear *in Adam*

Thine am I. *Text from the Dalhousie MS (Dal A; letter to Thomson, 29 October 1793),
corrected from Dalhousie MSS B and C (letters to Thomson, 19 October 1794 and 3
August 1795), the Adam MS (letter to Mrs. Riddell, October 1793), the Alloway (Al)
and Liverpool City Library (L) MSS, and SC, 1799 (59; not in later edns.). Title in Al*
Nancy—a Song—Tune, Leiger m: choss. *First-line title in SC; set in 8-line stanzas
to the air* Up in the morning early. *See Commentary*
  1 Chloris fair *Dal C*: faithful Fair *Adam Al Dal A–B SC, corrected to* lovely Kate *L*
2 Well . . . discover *Dal B L (correcting* Thine, my lovely Nancy) *SC*: Thine, my
lovely Nancy *Adam Al Dal A*   4 Tells the ardent Lover *Dal B L (correcting*
Ev'ry roving fancy) *SC*: Ev'ry roving fancy *Adam Al Dal A*   5 lay] take *L*

435. [Bonie Mary]

Tune, Minnie's ay glowerin o'er me—

Chorus

COME cowe me, minnie, come cowe me;
Come cowe me, minnie, come cowe me;
The hair o' my a— is grown into my c—t,
And they canna win to, to m—we me.

1

When Mary cam over the Border,   5
When Mary cam over the Border;
As eith 'twas approachin the C—t of a hurchin,
Her a— was in sic a disorder.—

2

But wanton Wattie cam west on't,
But wanton Wattie cam west on't,   10
He did it sae tickle, he left nae as meikle
'S a spider wad bigget a nest on't.—

Bonie Mary. *Text from the Bixby MS (letter to Cleghorn, 25 October ? 1793) collated
with MMC (pp. 121–2).*
    4 to,] too, *MS:* in for *MMC*   7 As eith] In troth *MMC*

3

And was nae Wattie a Clinker,
He m—w'd frae the Queen to the tinkler,
Then sat down, in grief, like the Macedon chief ₁₅
For want o' mae warlds to conquer.—

4

And O, what a jewel was Mary!
And O, what a jewel was Mary!
Her face it was fine, and her bosom divine,
And her c—nt it was theekit wi' glory.—   ₂₀
Come cowe &c.—

436. Act Sederunt of the Session—A Scots Ballad—

Tune—O'er the muir amang the heather—

I N Edinburgh town they 've made a law,
  In Edinburgh at the Court o' Session,
That standing pr—cks are fauteors a',
  And guilty of a high transgression.—

13 Clinker] blinker *MMC*

Act Sederunt of the Session. *Text from the Bixby MS (letter to Cleghorn, 25 October ? 1793), collated with MMC (p. 94)*
  1–2 Edinburgh] Embrugh *MMC*

Chorus

Act Sederunt o' the Session,   5
Decreet o' the Court o' Session,
That standing pr—cks are fauteors a',
And guilty of a high transgression.

2

And they 've provided dungeons deep,
Ilk lass has ane in her possession;   10
Untill the wretches wail and weep,
They there shall lie for their transgression.—

Chorus

Act Sederunt o' the Session,
Decreet o' the Court o' Session,
The rogues in pouring tears shall weep,   15
By act Sederunt o' the Session.—

437. To Capt.ⁿ G——, on being asked why
I was not to be of the party with him and his
brother K—nm—re at Syme's—

D os t ask, dear Captain, why from Syme
    I have no invitation,
When well he knows he has with him
    My first friends in the nation?

Is it because I love to toast,   5
    And round the bottle hurl?
No! there conjecture wild is lost,
    For *Syme* by God's no churl!—

Is 't lest with bawdy jests I bore,
    As oft the matter of fact is?   10
No! *Syme* the theory can't abhor—
    Who loves so well the practice.—

11 wretches] fau'tors *MMC*

To Capt.ⁿ G——. *Text from the Alloway MS*
  9 Is 't . . . bore] *correcting* Is 't because that a bawdy jest I love *in MS*
11 can't abhor] *correcting* must approve *in MS*

Is it a fear I should avow
Some heresy seditious?
No! *Syme* (but this is entre nous)   15
Is quite an old Tiresias.—

In vain Conjecture thus would flit
Thro' mental clime and season:
In short, dear Captain, Syme's a Wit—
Who asks of Wits a reason?—   20

Yet must I still the sôrt deplore
That to my griefs adds one more,
In balking me the social hour
With you and noble Kenmure.—

438. Impromptu, on Mrs. W. Riddell's Birthday, 4th Novr. 1793

O LD Winter, with his frosty beard,
  Thus once to Jove his prayer prefered.
What have I done of all the year,
To bear this hated doom severe?
My chearless suns no pleasure know;   5
Night's horrid car drags, dreary, slow:
My dismal months no joys are crowning,
But spleeny English, hanging, drowning.

Now, Jove, for once be mighty civil;
To counter balance all this evil;   10
Give me, and I've no more to say,
Give me MARIA's natal day!
That brilliant gift will so enrich me,
Spring, Summer, Autumn, cannot match me.

'Tis done!!! says Jove: so ends my story,   15
And Winter once rejoiced in glory.

Impromptu. *Text from the Adam MS, sent to Mrs. Riddell, collated with Currie (iv. 379)*

439. Occasional Address, Spoken by Miss Fontenelle, on her Benefit-Night, Decr. 4th. 1793.—Written by Mr Burns—

STILL anxious to secure your partial favor,
And not less anxious sure, this night than ever,
A Prologue, Epilogue, or some such matter,
'Twould vamp my Bill, thought I, if nothing better;
So, sought a Poet, roosted near the skies,   5
Told him, I came to feast my curious eyes;
Said, nothing like his works was ever printed,
And last, my Prologue-business, slily hinted.

   Ma'am, let me tell you, quoth my Man of RHYMES,
I know your bent—these are no laughing times;   10
Can you, but Miss, I own I have my fears,
Dissolve in pause—and sentimental tears—
With laden sighs, and solemn-rounded sentence,
Rouse from his sluggish slumbers, fell Repentance;
Paint Vengeance, as he takes his horrid stand,   15
Waving on high the desolating brand,
Calling the storms to bear him o'er a guilty La nd!

   I could no more—askance the creature eyeing,
D'ye think, said I, this face was made for crying?
I'll laugh, that's pos—nay more, the world shall know it; 20
And so, your servant, gloomy Master Poet.

Occasional Address. *Text from the Kilmarnock MS, collated with the Alloway MS
(Al; bound with a letter from Miss Fontenelle), the Lochryan MS (Loch; letter to Mrs.
Dunlop, 24 December 1793), and Currie (ii. 450–1). Wrongly dated 1795 in Currie*
   4 'Twould] Would *Al*   thought] said *Loch Currie*   5 roosted . . . skies]
alternative to in his skyey dome *in Al*   6 I . . . eyes] *alternative to* ~~that to
admire him~~ in admiration I was come *in Al*   8 *Deletion follows in Al:*

         'O Ma'am!' replied the silly, strutting creature,
         Screwing each self-important, aukward feature,
         'Flatt'ry I hate, as I admire your taste
         'At once so just, correct, profound and chaste.'—

9 Ma'am] *alternative to* But *in Al*

Firm as my creed, Sirs, 'tis my fix'd belief,
That Misery's another word for Grief:
I also think—so may I be a Bride!
That so much laughter, so much life enjoy'd.   25

Thou man of crazy care, and ceaseless sigh,
Still under bleak Misfortune's blasting eye;
Doom'd to that sorest task of man alive—
To make three guineas do the work of five;
Laugh in Misfortune's face—the beldam witch!   30
Say, you'll be merry—tho' you can't be rich.

Thou other man of care, the wretch in love,
Who long with jiltish arts and airs hast strove;
Who, as the boughs all temptingly project,
Measur'st, in desp'rate thought—a rope—thy neck—   35
Or, where the beetling cliffs o'erhang the deep
Peerest, to meditate the healing leap:
[For shame! for shame! I tell thee, thou art no man:
This for a giddy, vain, capricious woman?
A creature, though I say 't, you know, that should not;   40
Ridiculous with her idiot, 'Would and Would not.']
Wouldst thou be cur'd, thou silly, moping elf?
Laugh at her follies; laugh e'en at thyself:
Learn to despise those frowns, now so terrific;
And love a kinder—that's your grand specific!   45

To sum up all—be merry! I advise;
And as we're merry, may we still be wise.

22 Firm . . . Sirs] *alternative to* Believe me, Gentles *in Al*   24 may . . .
Bride] come my soul to bliss *Al*   25 life enjoy'd] happiness *Al*   26–30
Thou . . . Laugh in] *written on facing page in Al to replace:*

        Thou Man of Care, whose task is, to contrive
        To make three guineas do the work of five . . .

26 and ceaseless sigh] *correcting* that only pines *in Al*   31 merry] *correcting*
happy *in Al*   36 cliffs o'erhang] cliff o'erhangs *Loch Currie*   38–41 For . . .
not.'] *om. Loch Currie. In Al ll. 42–45 are written on facing page to replace ll. 38–41
and a first version of l. 44:* Laugh at her airs—these frowns no more terrific
39 giddy] *correcting* silly *in Al*   45 a kinder] *correcting* another *in Al*

440. On seeing Miss Fontenelle in a Favourite Character

SWEET naïveté of feature,
 Simple, wild, enchanting elf,
Not to thee, but thanks to nature,
 Thou art acting but thyself.

Wert thou awkward, stiff, affected,   5
 Spurning nature, torturing art;
Loves and graces all rejected,
 Then indeed thou'd'st act a part.

441. English song

To the tune—My joe Janet—

HUSBAND, husband, cease your strife,
 Nor longer idly rave, Sir:
Tho' I am your wedded wife,
 Yet I am not your slave, Sir.

'One of two must still obey,   5
 'Nancy, Nancy;
'Is it Man or Woman, say,
 'My Spouse Nancy.'

On seeing Miss Fontenelle. *Text from Cunningham, 1834 (iii. 257)*

English song. *Text from the Dalhousie MS (Dal; letter to Thomson, December 1793), collated with B.M. MS Eg. 1656, f. 25 (Eg), the Alloway MS (Al), and SC, 1799 (62). Title from Al. First-line title in SC; set in 8-line stanzas. Lines 1–8 lacking in Eg. In Al the stanzas, marked* He *and* She, *are numbered in pairs*

If 'tis still the lordly word,
   Service and obedience;   10
I'll desert my Sov'reign lord,
   And so, good b'ye, Allegiance!

'Sad will I be, so bereft,
   'Nancy, Nancy;
'Yet I'll try to make a shift,   15
   'My Spouse Nancy.'—

My poor heart then break it must,
   My last hour I am near it:
When you lay me in the dust,
   Think how you will bear it.—   20

'I will hope and trust in Heaven,
   'Nancy, Nancy;
'Strength to bear it will be given,
   'My Spouse Nancy.'—

Well, Sir, from the silent dead,   25
   Still I'll try to daunt you;
Ever round your midnight bed
   Horrid sprites shall haunt you.—

'I'll wed another, like my Dear,
   'Nancy, Nancy;
'Then all hell will fly for fear,   30
   'My Spouse, Nancy.'—

9–12 If . . . Allegiance!] *Eg and Al have*

       If the word is still, Obey!
          Always, love & fear you!
       I will take myself away,
          And never more come near you.—

15 Yet] Still *Eg*   18 I am] I'm *Eg Al*   20 Think how] Think, think
how *Thomson's alteration in Dal, SC*   25 Sir] even *Eg*: then *Al*   26 Still]
Sir, *Eg Al*   I'll] I will *Thomson's alteration in Dal, SC*

XI

POEMS
1794

DUMFRIES

442. To Miss Graham of Fintray—

Here, where the Scotish Muse immortal lives,
    In sacred strains and tuneful numbers join'd,
Accept the gift; though humble he who gives,
    Rich is the tribute of the grateful mind.

So may no ruffian feeling in thy breast   5
    Discordant jar thy bosom-chords among;
But Peace attune thy gentle soul to rest,
    Or love ecstatic wake his seraph song.

Or Pity's notes, in luxury of tears,
    As modest want the tale of woe reveals;   10
While conscious Virtue all the strain endears,
    And heaven-born Piety her sanction seals.

443. Monody on Maria—

How cold is that bosom which folly once fired,
    How pale is that cheek where the rouge lately glistened;
How silent that tongue which the echoes oft tired,
    How dull is that ear which to flattery so listened.—

If sorrow and anguish *their* exit await,   5
    From friendship and dearest affection removed;
How doubly severer, Maria, thy fate,
    Thou diedst unwept, as thou livedst unloved.—

To Miss Graham of Fintray. *Text from the Dalhousie MS (letter to Thomson, July 1794), collated with the Fintry MS (inscribed in a copy of SC and dated* Dumfries 31st Jany 1794) *and the Huntington Library MS (HL; laid in a copy of* Orpheus Caledonius, *1733, i). Title from Fintry*
    1 Here, *Fintry IIL:* Here *Dalhousie*   2 sacred . . . tuneful] tuneful . . . sacred *Fintry, corrected to* strains divine and sacred *in HL*   10 tale of woe] *alternative in HL to* secret tale. *The deletion of* secret tale *looks later and may not be autograph*
Monody on Maria. *Text from the Watson MS (1135; letter to Clarinda, 25 June? 1794), collated with the Lochryan MS (Loch; letter to Mrs. Dunlop, ? 13 March 1794). Title from Loch; title in Watson* Monody; *in Currie (iv. 370–1)* Monody, on a lady famed for her Caprice. *Currie follows Watson, substituting* Eliza *for* Maria *at ll. 7 and 12*
    1 bosom] breast now *Loch*   2 cheek] face *Loch*   3 silent] mute is *Loch*
5–8 If . . . unloved.] *not in Loch*

Loves, Graces, and Virtues, I call not on you;
   So shy, grave and distant, ye shed not a tear: 10
But come, all ye offspring of folly so true,
   And flowers let us cull for Maria's cold bier.—

We'll search through the garden for each silly flower,
   We'll range through the forest for each idle weed;
But chiefly the nettle, so typical, shower,   15
   For none e'er approached her but rued the rash deed.—

We'll sculpture the marble, we'll measure the lay;
   Here Vanity* strums on her idiot lyre;
Here keen Indignation shall dart on his prey,
   Which spurning Contempt shall redeem from his ire.— 20

THE EPITAPH—
Here lies, now a prey to insulting Neglect,
   What once was a butterfly gay in life's beam:
Want only of wisdom denied her respect,
   Want only of goodness denied her esteem.—

444. Wilt thou be my Dearie—
Tune, The Sutor's dochter—

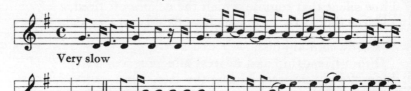

Very slow

* N.B. the lady affected to be a Poetess.

17–20 We'll . . . ire.] *not in Loch*
Wilt thou be my Dearie. *Text from the Hastie MS, f. 145 (Ha), collated with the*

W ILT thou be my Dearie;
   When sorrow wrings thy gentle heart,
O wilt thou let me chear thee:
By the treasure of my soul,
   That's the love I bear thee!   5
I swear and vow, that only thou
   Shalt ever be my Dearie—
Only thou, I swear and vow,
   Shalt ever be my Dearie.—

Lassie, say thou lo'es me;   10
Or if thou wilt na be my ain,
   Say na thou'lt refuse me:
If it winna, canna be,
   Thou for thine may chuse me,
Let me, Lassie, quickly die,   15
   Trusting that thou lo'es me—
Lassie, let me quickly die,
   Trusting that thou lo'es me.—

445. Sonnet, on the Death of Robert Riddel, Esq. *of Glen Riddel, April* 1794

N o more, ye warblers of the wood, no more,
   Nor pour your descant, grating, on my soul:
Thou young-eyed spring, gay in thy verdant stole,
More welcome were to me grim winter's wildest roar.

Alloway MSS, the Adam MSS (Aa, Ab), the Morning Chronicle, *10 May 1794, SMM, 1796 (470; signed B), and SC, 1799 (77).*

A MS collated by Dewar, and presented To the sweet, lovely Girl, who is the theme of the foregoing Song . . . as a mark of brotherly affection and unalterable regard, *has* O wilt (*l. 3*), And that's (*l. 5*), *and* Jeanie (*ll. 10, 15, 17*)

   3 O] *added in Ha in another hand*   5 That's] *correcting* And that's *in Ha:* And that's *Aa*   7, 9 Shalt] Shall *SMM SC*   10 Lassie] Jeany *Aa*   15, 17 Lassie] Jeany *Aa:* Jeanie *Ab*

Sonnet. *Text from Currie, 1801 (iv. 368–9), collated with the* Dumfries Journal, *22 April 1794, the* Morning Chronicle, *5 May 1794, the* Gentleman's Magazine, *May 1794, and Currie, 1800 (iv. 370, Currie 1)*
   2 soul] ear *Currie 1*   3 gay . . . stole,] thy charms I cannot bear; *Currie 1*

How can ye charm, ye flow'rs, with all your dyes?   5
   Ye blow upon the sod that wraps my friend:
How can I to the tuneful strain attend?
That strain flows round th' untimely tomb where Riddel
   lies.

Yes, pour, ye warblers, pour the notes of woe,
   And soothe *the Virtues* weeping on this bier: 10
The *Man of Worth,* and has not left his peer,
Is in his 'narrow house' for ever darkly low.

Thee, Spring, again with joy shall others greet,
Me, mem'ry of my loss will only meet.

446. On Robert Riddel

To Riddel, much-lamented man,
   This ivied cot was dear;
Reader, dost value matchless worth?
   This ivied cot revere.

447. Banks of Cree

Here is the glen, and here the bower,
   All underneath the birchen shade;
The village-bell has told the hour,
   O what can stay my lovely maid.

'Tis not Maria's whispering call;   5
   'Tis but the balmy breathing gale,
Mixt with some warbler's dying fall
   The dewy star of eve to hail.

   5 charm] please *Currie 1*   6 sod] soil *periodicals*   8 flows] pours *Currie 1*
8 *Currie 1 ends*   11 and has] who hath *periodicals*

On Robert Riddel. *Text from Cunningham, 1834 (iii. 308; copied from a window at Friars Carse)*

Banks of Cree. *Text from the Dalhousie MS (letter to Thomson, ? May 1794), collated with SC, 1798 (27). Set in 8-line stanzas in SC, to the air* The Flowers of Edinburgh, *with first-line title*

It is Maria's voice I hear;
   So calls the woodlark in the grove   10
His little, faithful Mate to chear,
   At once 'tis music—and 'tis love.

And art thou come! and art thou true!
   O welcome dear to love and me!
And let us all our vows renew   15
   Along the flowery banks of Cree.

448. Pinned to M^{rs} R——'s carriage—

IF you rattle along like your Mistress's tongue,
   Your speed will outrival the dart:
But, a fly for your load, you'll break down on the road,
   If your stuff be as rotten 's her heart.—

449. In answer to one who affirmed of a well-known Character here, D^r B——, that there was Falsehood in his very looks—

THAT there is Falsehood in his looks,
   I must and will deny;
They say, their Master is a Knave—
   —And sure they do not lie.—

Pinned to M^{rs} R—'s carriage. *Text from the Huntington Library MS (letter to Creech,
30 May 1795), collated with the Glenriddell MS (p. 161), the Watson MS (1135),
and Ferguson's text of letter to Patrick Millar, May 1794 (Millar). Title in Glenriddell* . . . W–lt–r R–dd–ll's . . . ; *in Watson,* . . . coach; *in Millar,* Extempore,
Pinned to a Lady's coach—. *Signed*—Nith.—*in Millar*

In answer. *Text from the Lochryan MS (letter to Mrs Dunlop, ? March 1794), collated
with the Glenriddell MS (Glen; p.160) and the Huntington Library MS (HL; letter
to Creech, 30 May 1795). Title in Glen* On hearing it said that there was falsehood in
D^r B–b–ngton's very looks—; *in HL* On hearing it asserted . . . in the Rev^d D^r
B——'s very looks—

450. Extempore [on The *Loyal Natives'* Verses]

[Ye sons of sedition give ear to my song,
Let Syme, Burns, and Maxwell pervade every
      throng,
With Craken the attorney, and Mundell the
      quack,
Send Willie the monger to hell with a smack.]

Y E true 'Loyal Natives', attend to my song,
    In uproar and riot rejoice the night long;
From *envy* and *hatred* your corps is exempt;
But where is your shield from the *darts of contempt?*

451. Ode [For General Washington's Birthday]

N o Spartan tube, no Attic shell,
    No lyre Eolian I awake;
'Tis Liberty's bold note I swell,
    Thy harp, Columbia, let me take.
See gathering thousands, while I sing,   5
A broken chain, exulting, bring,
    And dash it in a tyrant's face!
And dare him to his very beard,
And tell him, he no more is feared,
No more the Despot of Columbia's race.   10
    A tyrant's proudest insults braved,
They shout, a People freed! They hail an Empire saved.

Where is Man's godlike form?
Where is that brow erect and bold,
That eye that can, unmoved, behold   15
The wildest rage, the loudest storm,
That e'er created fury dared to raise!
Avaunt! thou caitiff, servile, base,
That tremblest at a Despot's nod,
Yet, crouching under th' iron rod,   20

Extempore. *Text of* The Loyal Natives' Verses *and Burns's reply from Cromek,*
Reliques, *1808 (p. 168)*

Ode. *Text from the Adam MS (Dewar's transcript), collated with the Alloway MS*
(Al; draft of ll. 44–62 in letter to Mrs. Dunlop, 25 June 1794)
    8 dare] *correcting* brave *in Adam*

Canst laud the arm that struck th' insulting blow!
    Art thou of man's imperial line?
    Dost boast that countenance divine?
    Each sculking feature answers, No!
    But come, ye sons of Liberty,   25
    Columbia's offspring, brave as free,
In danger's hour still flaming in the van:
Ye know, and dare maintain, The Royalty of Man.

    Alfred, on thy starry throne,
    Surrounded by the tuneful choir,   30
The Bards that erst have struck the patriot lyre,
And roused the freeborn Briton's soul of fire,
    No more thy England own.—
Dare injured nations form the great design,
    To make detested tyrants bleed?   35
Thy England execrates the glorious deed!
    Beneath her hostile banners waving,
    Every pang of honor braving,
England in thunders calls—'The Tyrant's cause is mine!'
That hour accurst, how did the fiends rejoice,   40
And hell thro' all her confines raise th' exulting voice,
    That hour which saw the generous English name
Linkt with such damned deeds of everlasting shame!

    Thee, Caledonia, thy wild heaths among,
    Famed for the martial deed, the heaven-taught song,   45
    To thee, I turn with swimming eyes.—
    Where is that soul of Freedom fled?
    Immingled with the mighty Dead!
Beneath that hallowed turf where WALLACE lies!
Hear it not, Wallace, in thy bed of death!   50
    Ye babbling winds in silence sweep;
    Disturb not ye the hero's sleep,
    Nor give the coward secret breath.—
Is this the ancient Caledonian form,
Firm as her rock, resistless as her storm?   55

45 Famed . . . heaven-taught] Thee, famed for martial deed and sacred *Al*
54–55 Is . . . storm ?] *Al has*
                Is this the Power in freedom's war
                That wont to bid the battle rage ?

Shew me that eye which shot immortal hate,
  Blasting the Despot's proudest bearing:
Shew me that arm which, nerved with thundering fate,
  Braved Usurpation's boldest daring!
  Dark-quenched as yonder sinking star,   60
  No more that glance lightens afar;
That palsied arm no more whirls on the waste of war.

452. On W. R——, Esq.

So vile was poor Wat, such a miscreant slave,
That the worms even damn'd him when laid in his grave.
'In his scull there is famine!' a starv'd reptile cries;
'And his heart it is poison!' another replies.

453. A red red Rose

Major Graham

56 Shew me] Behold *Al*   57 Blasting] Crushing *Al*   58 Shew me] *not in Al*
which] *correcting* once *in Adam*   60–62 Dark-quench'd . . . war.] *Al has*

> One quenched in darkness like the sinking star,
> And one the palsied arm of tottering, powerless Age.

On W. R——, Esq. *Text from the Lochryan MS (letter to Mrs Dunlop, September
1794), collated with Stewart, 1802 (p. 304). Title in Stewart* Epitaph on Walter
S——.

  1 So . . . poor] Sic a reptile was *Stewart*   such] sic *Stewart*   3 scull there is]
flesh there's a *Stewart*   4 And . . . it is] An' . . . is rank *Stewart*

A red red Rose. *Text from the Hastie MS, f. 114 (Ha), collated with the Cunningham
MS (letter to Cunningham, Autumn 1794; Cun), a MS owned by Mr. Frank B.*

O MY Luve's like a red, red rose,
    That's newly sprung in June;
O my Luve's like the melodie
    That's sweetly play'd in tune.—

As fair art thou, my bonie lass,   5
    So deep in luve am I;
And I will love thee still, my Dear,
    Till a' the seas gang dry.—

Till a' the seas gang dry, my Dear,
    And the rocks melt wi' the sun: 10
I will love thee still, my Dear,
    While the sands o' life shall run.—

And fare thee weel, my only Luve!
    And fare thee weel, a while!
And I will come again, my Luve,   15
    Tho' it were ten thousand mile!—

Bemis, Boston, SMM, 1796 (402, 403; signed R), and SC, 1799 (89). See Commentary.
Title from SMM; title in Cun and Bemis Song; *first-line title in SC. Text in SC* From
a MS. in the editor's possession, *not ascribed to Burns. Cancellation in Ha* Tune,
Ceud soraidh nam do'n Ailleagan *followed by* Tune, Major [   ]. *Air in SC*
Wishaw's Favourite
    1 a] the *Cun Bemis SC*   3 O] *added in Ha; om. Cun SC*   6 in luve] in
love, in love *SC*   7 will] *corrected to* can *in Bemis:* can *Cun SC*   8 *SC*
repeats ll. 5–8   10 the rocks] th' rocks *Bemis*   12 the sands] th' sands
Bemis   13–16 *om. SMM* (402)   13 only] dearest *Bemis*   14 And] O
Cun Bemis SC   a while] a little while *SC*   16 it were] 'twere *Cun Bemis SC*
16 *SC repeats ll. 13–16*

454. On the seas and far away—

Tune, O'er the hills &c.

I

How can my poor heart be glad,
When absent from my Sailor lad;
How can I the thought forego,
He's on the seas to meet the foe:
Let me wander, let me rove,   5
Still my heart is with my Love;
Nightly dreams and thoughts by day
Are with him that's far away.

Chorus

On the seas and far away,
On stormy seas and far away,   10
Nightly dreams and thoughts by day
Are ay with him that's far away.

2

[When in summer noon I faint,
As weary flocks around me pant,
Haply in this scorching sun   15
My Sailor's thundering at his gun:

On the seas and far away. *Text from the Dalhousie MS (letter to Thomson, 30 August
1794), collated with SC, 1805 (161). First-line title in SC*
    13–24 deleted (? by Thomson) in MS; om. SC

Bullets spare my only joy!
Bullets spare my darling boy!
Fate do with me what you may,
Spare but him that's far away.   20

Chorus

On the seas and far away,
On stormy seas and far away,
Fate do with me what you may,
Spare but him that's far away.]

3

At the starless midnight hour   25
When Winter rules with boundless power;
As the storms the forest tear,
And thunders rend the howling air:
Listening to the doubling roar,
Surging on the rocky shore,   30
All I can—I weep and pray
For his weal that's far away.

Chorus

On the seas and far away,
On stormy seas and far away,
All I can—I weep and pray   35
For his weal that's far away.

4

Peace thy olive wand extend,
And bid wild War his ravage end,
Man with brother Man to meet,
And as a brother kindly greet: 40
Then may Heaven with prosperous gales
Fill my Sailor's welcome sails,
To my arms their charge convey,
My dear lad that's far away.

21–24, 33–36 *abbreviated in MS*

Chorus
On the seas and far away,   45
On stormy seas and far away,
To my arms their charge convey,
My dear lad that's far away.

455. To Dr Maxwell, on Miss Jessy Staig's recovery

MAXWELL, if merit here you crave,
That merit I deny:
You save fair Jessy from the grave!
An ANGEL could not die.

456. Ca' the yowes to the knowes [B]

Chorus—
CA' the yowes to the knowes,
Ca' them whare the heather grows,
Ca' them whare the burnie rowes,
My bonie Dearie.

1
Hark, the mavis' evening sang   5
Sounding Clouden's woods amang;
Then a faulding let us gang,
My bonie Dearie.
Ca' the &c.

2
We'll gae down by Clouden side,
Through the hazels spreading wide   10
O'er the waves, that sweetly glide
To the moon sae clearly.
Ca' the &c.

45-48 On . . . away.] Chorus as usual *MS*

To Dr Maxwell. *Text from the Dalhousie MS (letter to Thomson, September 1794), collated with the Lochryan MS (letter to Mrs. Dunlop, September 1794)*

Ca' the yowes to the knowes. *Text from the Dalhousie MS (letter to Thomson, September 1794)*

3

Yonder Clouden's silent towers,
Where at moonshine midnight hours
O'er the dewy bending flowers 15
   Fairies dance sae cheary.
  Ca' the &c.

4

Ghaist nor bogle shalt thou fear;
Thou'rt to Love and Heaven sae dear,
Nocht of Ill may come thee near,
   My bonie Dearie. 20
  Ca' the &c.

5

Fair and lovely as thou art,
Thou hast stown my very heart;
I can die—but canna part,
   My bonie Dearie.
  Ca' the &c.

457. She says she lo'es me best of a'—

She says she lo'es me best of a'. *Text from the Hastie MS, f. 134 (Ha), collated with*

S AE flaxen were her ringlets,
   Her eyebrows of a darker hue,
Bewitchingly o'erarching
   Twa laughing een o' bonie blue.—
Her smiling, sae wyling,   5
   Wad make a wretch forget his woe;
What pleasure, what treasure,
   Unto these rosy lips to grow:
Such was my Chloris' bonie face,
   When first her bonie face I saw;   10
And ay my Chloris' dearest charm,
   She says, she lo'es me best of a'.—

Like harmony her motion;
   Her pretty ancle is a spy,
Betraying fair proportion,   15
   Wad make a saint forget the sky.—
Sae warming, sae charming,
   Her fauteless form and gracefu' air;
Ilk feature—auld Nature
   Declar'd that she could do nae mair: 20
Hers are the willing chains o' love,
   By conquering Beauty's sovereign law;
And ay my Chloris' dearest charm,
   She says, she lo'es me best of a'.—

Let others love the city,   25
   And gaudy shew at sunny noon;
Gie me the lonely valley,
   The dewy eve, and rising moon
Fair beaming, and streaming
   Her silver light the boughs amang;   30
While falling, recalling,
   The amorous thrush concludes his sang;

the Alloway MS (Al; ll. 25–36 only), the Dalhousie MS (Dal; letter to Thomson, September 1794), SMM, 1796 (447; signed B), and SC, 1805 (190). Ha marked Cronoch *in Burns's hand on verso. First-line title in SC*
  4 bonie] lovely *Dal*   6 Wad] Would *Dal SC*   10 her *SMM*: that *Ha Dal*
11 ay *SMM Dal SC*: still *Ha*   16 Wad] Would *Dal SC*   23 ay] still *Dal*
25 city] ally *Al*   28 dewy] scented *Al*   32 his] her *Al*

There, dearest Chloris, wilt thou rove
By wimpling burn and leafy shaw,
And hear my vows o' truth and love,   35
And say, thou lo'es me best of a'.—

458. Saw ye my Phely (quasi dicat, Phillis)

Tune, When she cam ben she bobbit—

O saw ye my dearie, my Phely?
  O saw ye my dearie, my Phely?
She's down i' the grove, she's wi' a new Love,
  She winna come hame to her Willy.—

What says she, my dearest, my Phely?   5
What says she, my dearest, my Phely?
She lets thee to wit that she has thee forgot,
  And for ever disowns thee her Willy.—

O had I ne'er seen thee, my Phely!
O had I ne'er seen thee, my Phely!   10
As light as the air, and fause as thou's fair,
  Thou 's broken the heart o' thy Willy.—

33 wilt thou] let us *Al*   34 and] or *Al*

Saw ye my Phely. *Text from the Dalhousie MS (Dal A; letter to Thomson, 19 October
1794), collated with MS Dal B (letter to Thomson, 19 November 1794) and Currie*
(iv. 174). *Title in Dal B Song—. See Commentary*
  1, 2 dearie] Dear *Thomson's alteration in Dal A, Dal B Currie*   1, 2 *et*
passim Phely] Mary *Dal B*   4 *et passim* Willy] Harry *Dal B*   5, 6 dearest]
Dear *Dal B*   7 that] *om. Dal B*

459. How lang and dreary is the night

A Galick Air

Slow

How lang and dreary is the night,
    When I am frae my Dearie;
I restless lie frae e'en to morn,
    Though I were ne'er sae weary.—

Chorus

For Oh, her lanely nights are lang;   5
And Oh, her dreams are eerie;
And Oh, her widow'd heart is sair,
That's absent frae her Dearie.—

When I think on the lightsome days
    I spent wi' thee, my Dearie;   10
And now what seas between us roar,
    How can I be but eerie.—
    For Oh, &c.

How lang and dreary. Text from the Dalhousie MS (letter to Thomson, 19 October 1794), collated with SMM, 1788 (175), and SC, 1798 (31). Title from SC. MS heading Tune, Cauld kail in Aberdeen. *Set in SMM to* A Galick Air, *with the third and fourth lines of each stanza repeated. SMM lacks ll. 5–8*
1 lang] long *SMM*   3 restless] sleepless *SMM*   5, 6 Oh] *correcting* Och
in MS   lanely nights are lang] *correcting* nights are $\frac{lanely}{wintry}$ lang *in MS*
8 absent] *alternative* distant *in MS*   9 lightsome] happy *SMM*   10 thee]
you *SMM*   11 seas . . . roar] lands . . . lie *SMM*

How slow ye move, ye heavy hours;
　The joyless day, how dreary:
It was na sae ye glinted by,   15
　When I was wi' my Dearie.—
　　For Oh, &c.

460. Song—

Tune, Duncan Gray—

LET not Woman e'er complain
　　Of inconstancy in love;
Let not Woman e'er complain,
　Fickle Man is apt to rove:
Look abroad through Nature's range,   5
Nature's mighty law is CHANGE;
Ladies would it not be strange
　Man should then a monster prove.—

Mark the winds, and mark the skies;
　Oceans ebb, and oceans flow: 10
Sun and moon but set to rise;
　Round and round the seasons go:
Why then ask of silly Man,
To oppose great Nature's plan?
We'll be constant while we can—   15
　You can be no more, you know.

14 The . . . dreary:] As ye were wae and weary! *SMM*

Song. *Text from the Dalhousie MS (letter to Thomson, 19 October 1794), collated with SC, 1798 (48)*

461. The auld man's winter thought—

Very slow

But lately seen in gladsome green
    The woods rejoiced the day,
Thro' gentle showers the laughing flowers
    In double pride were gay:
But now our joys are fled—   5
    On winter blasts awa!
Yet maiden May, in rich array,
    Again shall bring them a'.—

But my white pow—nae kindly thowe
    Shall melt the snaws of Age;   10
My trunk of eild, but buss or beild,
    Sinks in Time's wintry rage.—
Oh, Age has weary days!
    And nights o' sleepless pain!
Thou golden time o' Youthfu' prime,   15
    Why comes thou not again!

The auld man's winter thought. *Text from the Hastie MS, f. 155, collated with the Dalhousie MS (Dal; letter to Thomson, 19 October 1794), SMM, 1796 (486; signed B), and SC, 1801 (139). Title from Dal. Title in SMM* The winter of life; *first-line title in SC, set to the air* The death of the Linnet

5 But now our joys] Tho' now all Nature's sweets *SC, with footnote on MS reading* being too short for the air   13 weary] weary, weary *SC*   16 comes] com'st *Dal SC*

462. The Lovers morning salute to his Mistress—

Tune, Deil tak the wars

S LEEP'ST thou, or wauk'st thou, fairest creature;
    Rosy morn now lifts his eye,
Numbering ilka bud which Nature
    Waters wi' the tears o' joy.
    Now, to the streaming fountain,   5
    Or up the heathy mountain,

The Lovers morning salute. *Text from the Dalhousie MS (Dal B; letter to Thomson, November 1794), collated with MS Dal A (letter to Thomson, 19 October 1794) and SC, 1805 (157). Title from Dal A; first-line title in SC*
  3 ilka] every SC   5–9 Now . . . pours;] *Dal A has*
               Now through the leafy woods,
               And by the reeking floods,
      Wild Nature's tenants, freely, gladly, stray;
               The lintwhite in his bower
               Chants, o'er the breathing flower:

The hart, hind, and roe, freely, wanton stray;
  In twining hazel bowers,
  His lay the linnet pours;
  The lavrock, to the sky   10
  Ascends, wi' sangs o' joy:
While the sun and thou arise to bless the day.

Phebus, gilding the brow of morning,
  Banishes ilk darksome shade,
Nature gladdening and adorning;   15
  Such, to me, my lovely maid.
  When frae my Chloris parted,
  Sad, chearless, broken-hearted,
Then night's gloomy shades o'ercast my sky:
  But when she charms my sight,   20
  In pride of Beauty's light;
  When through my very heart,
  Her beaming glories dart;
'Tis then—'tis then I wake to life and joy!

463. On seeing Mrs Kemble in Yarico—

K EMBLE, thou cur'st my unbelief
  Of Moses and his rod:
At Yarico's sweet notes of grief
  The rock with *tears* had flow'd.—

7 wanton] ~~wildly~~-wanton *Dal B, restored in SC*   13 of] o' *Dal A*: of the *SC*
17 Chloris] Jeanie *SC*   17–21 When . . . light] *Dal A has*
           When absent frae my Fair,
           The murky shades o' Care
       With starless gloom o'ercast my sullen sky;
           But, when in beauty's light,
           She meets my ravish'd sight;
19 shades o'ercast] shades, ~~cloudy, dark,~~ o'ercast *Dal B, restored in SC*   24 'Tis . . .
life] 'Tis then I wake to life, to light *Dal A*

On seeing Mrs Kemble in Yarico. *Text from the Huntington Library MS (letter to Creech, 30 May 1795), collated with the Lochryan MS (letter to Mrs. Dunlop, 29 October 1794), a transcript of Mrs. Kemble's copy (sold by Dobell, 1936), and Stewart, 1801 (p. 62). Mrs. Kemble's copy, headed To Mrs Kemble on seeing her in Yarico— Extempore—and signed R.B., is endorsed by the antiquary Thomas Davidson of Newcastle-upon-Tyne: Given to me by Mrs. Stephen Kemble to whom it was* addressed and presented by the Celebrated Writer Rob. Burns.
    4 with] in *Kemble MS*

464. To the Honble Mr R. M——, of P–nm–re, on his high Phaeton

Tʜᴏᴜ fool, in thy Phaeton towering,
  Art proud when that Phaeton's
    prais'd?
'Tis the pride of a Thief's exhibition
When higher his pillory's rais'd.

465. Song, altered from an old English one—

Iᴛ was the charming month of May,
  When all the flowers were fresh and gay,
One morning, by the break of day,
    The youthful, charming Chloe;
From peaceful slumber she arose,   5
Girt on her mantle and her hose,
And o'er the flowery mead she goes,
    The youthful, charming Chloe.

Chorus

    Lovely was she by the dawn,
      Youthful Chloe, charming Chloe,   10
    Tripping o'er the pearly lawn,
      The youthful, charming Chloe.

The feather'd people, you might see,
Perch'd all around on every tree,
In notes of sweetest melody   15
    They hail the charming Chloe;
Till, painting gay the eastern skies,
The glorious sun began to rise,
Out-rivall'd by the radiant eyes
    Of youthful, charming Chloe.   20
    Lovely was she &c.

To the Honble Mr R. M——. *Text from the Lochryan MS (letter to Mrs. Dunlop, 29 October 1794)*

Song. *Text from the Dalhousie MS (letter to Thomson, November 1794), collated with SC, 1799 (69; alternative words)*

466. Lassie wi' the lintwhite locks—

Tune, Rothiemurche's rant

Chorus

LASSIE wi' the lintwhite locks,
Bonie lassie, artless lassie,
Wilt thou wi' me tent the flocks,
An wilt thou be my Dearie O.—

Now Nature cleeds the flowery lea,   5
And a' is young and sweet like thee,
O wilt thou share its joys wi' me,
And say thou'lt be my Dearie O.—
Lassie &c.—

The primrose bank, the wimpling burn,
The cuckoo on the milkwhite thorn,   10
The wanton lambs at rosy morn
Shall glad thy heart, my Dearie O.
Lassie &c.—

Lassie wi' the lintwhite locks. *Text from the Esty MS (Dewar's transcript), collated with the Dalhousie MSS (Dal A, letter to Thomson, September 1794; Dal B, letter to Thomson, November 1794), the Huntington Library MS (HL; letter to Findlater?, September 1794), the Kilmarnock MS (Kil), and SC, 1801 (121). MSS Dal A and HL have ll. 1–12 only; ll. 9–12 omitted in Dal B. The Esty MS has a marginal note on the tune, and may have been sent to Johnson. See Commentary*

4 An wilt] *correcting* Wilt *in Esty:* Wilt *Dal A–B HL Kil SC*   11 rosy]
early *Dal A HL Kil*   12 glad thy heart] welcome thee *Dal A HL Kil*

And when the welcome simmer shower
Has chear'd ilk drooping little flower,
We'll to the breathing woodbine bower   15
At sultry noon, my Dearie O.
　　Lassie, &c.—

As Cynthia lights, wi' silver ray,
The weary shearer's hameward way,
Through yellow waving fields we'll stray,
And talk o' love, my Dearie O.   20
　　Lassie &c.—

And should the howling wintry blast
Disturb my lassie's midnight rest,
I'll fauld thee to my faithfu' breast,
And comfort thee, my Dearie O.
　　Lassie &c.—

467. [To Chloris]

AH, Chloris, since it may not be,
　　That thou of love wilt hear;
If from the lover thou maun flee,
　　Yet let the *friend* be dear.

Altho' I love my Chloris, mair   5
　　Than ever tongue could tell;
My passion I will ne'er declare—
　　I'll say, I wish thee well.

Tho' a' my daily care thou art,
　　And a' my nightly dream,   10
I'll hide the struggle in my heart,
　　And say it is esteem.

14 ilk] each *Kil*   17 As] When *Dal B Kil SC*   21 should] when *Dal B
Kil SC*   22 Disturb] Disturbs *Dal B Kil SC*   23 I'll fauld thee] Enclasped
to *Dal B SC*: Enfaulded to *Kil*   24 And] I'll *Dal B Kil SC*

To Chloris. *Text from Scott Douglas (iii. 209–10). Set to the air* Major Graham.
First published in the Aldine edition, 1839 (iii. 179)

468. Song—

Tune, The Sow's tail

He

O PHILLY, happy be that day
   When roving through the gather'd hay,
My youthfu' heart was stown away,
   And by thy charms, my Philly.—

She

O Willy, ay I bless the grove   5
   Where first I own'd my maiden love,
Whilst thou did pledge the Powers above
   To be my ain dear Willy.—

He

As Songsters of the early year
   Are ilka day mair sweet to hear,   10
So ilka day to me mair dear
   And charming is my Philly.—

She

As on the brier the budding rose
   Still richer breathes and fairer blows,
So in my tender bosom grows   15
   The love I bear my Willy.—

Song. *Text from the Dalhousie MS (Dal B; letter to Thomson, 19 November 1794),
collated with MS Dal A (letter to Thomson, September 1794; ll. 25–40 only) and SC,
1805 (160). First-line title in SC. Set in SC with ll. 37–40 as a duet chorus in which*
lass *and* Phely *are alternatives to* lad *and* Willy
  1 *et passim* Philly] Phely *SC*

He

The milder sun and bluer sky
That crown my harvest cares wi' joy,
Were ne'er sae welcome to my eye
    As is a sight o' Philly.—   20

She

The little swallow's wanton wing,
Tho' wafting o'er the flowery Spring,
Did ne'er to me sic tydings bring,
    As meeting o' my Willy.—

He

The bee that thro the sunny hour   25
Sips nectar in the opening flower,
Compar'd wi' my delight is poor,
    Upon the lips o' Philly.—

She

The woodbine in the dewy weet
When evening shades in silence meet,   30
Is nocht sae fragrant or sae sweet
    As is a kiss o' Willy.—

He

Let Fortune's wheel at random run;
And Fools may tyne, and Knaves may win;
My thoughts are a' bound up on ane,   35
    And that's my ain dear Philly.—

She

What's a' the joys that gowd can gie?
I care na wealth a single flie;
The lad I love's the lad for me,
    And that's my ain dear Willy.—   40

26 opening] breathing *Dal A*   28, 36 Philly] Jeanie *Dal A*   31 or] and
Dal A   32, 40 Willy] Geordie *Dal A*   35 on] in *Dal A SC*   37 gowd]
correcting wealth *in Dal A*   39 love] lo'e *Dal A*

469. Can you leave me thus, my Katy

Tune, Roy's Wife

Chorus

CANST thou leave me thus, my Katy,
Canst thou leave me thus, my Katy;
Well thou know'st my aching heart,
And canst thou leave me thus for pity.—

Is this thy plighted, fond regard,   5
Thus cruelly to part, my Katy:
Is this thy faithful swain's reward—
An aching broken heart, my Katy.—
Canst thou &c.

Farewel! and ne'er such sorrows tear
That fickle heart of thine, my Katy!   10
Thou mayest find those will love thee dear—
But not a love like mine, my Katy.—
Canst thou &c.

Can you leave me thus, my Katy. *Text from the Dalhousie MS (letter to Thomson,
19 November 1794), collated with the Alloway MSS (Al A, Al B), the Adam MS
(letter to Mrs. Riddell, ? March 1795), and SC, 1799 (70). Title in Al B* Song—An
English one, to the tune of Roy's wife; *in Adam* English Song—Tune, Roy's
Wife.—For Pleyel; *first-line title in SC. Al A has* Betty *for* Katy *in ll. 1, 2, 6, 8; but*
Katie *in ll. 10 and 12. See Commentary*
   1, 2, 4 Canst thou] Can you *Al A (correction in Dal)*   3 thou know'st]
you know *Al A (correction in Dal)*   aching] faithful *Al B*   12 a love like] such
love as *Al A*

470. Scotish Song—

Tune, My lodging is on the cold ground

Slowly

B<small>EHOLD</small>, my Love, how green the groves,
  The primrose banks how fair;
The balmy gales awake the flowers,
  And wave thy flaxen hair:
The lavrock shuns the palace gay,   5
  And o'er the cottage sings;
For Nature smiles as sweet, I ween,
  To shepherds as to kings.—

Let minstrels sweep the skillfu' string,
  In lordly, lighted ha';   10
The shepherd stops his simple reed,
  Blythe, in the birken shaw:

Scotish Song. Text from the Huntington Library MS (HLa; letter to Lady Mary Douglas, 2 May 1795), collated with the Dalhousie MS (Dal; letter to Thomson, November 1794), MSS Esty (letter to Mrs. Dunlop, 20 December 1794), Adam (letter to Mrs. Riddell, ? March 1795), HLb (sent with letter to Creech, 30 May 1795), and SC, 1818 (201). First-line title in SC

  1 Behold, my love] My Chloris, mark *Dal (replacing a heavily deleted start), Esty Adam HLb*   8 To] For *Adam*   9 Let] The *HLb*   sweep] *correcting* rouse *correcting* touch *in Dal*   12 birken *Dal (correcting* birchen) *HLb*: birchen *HLa*

The princely revel may survey
   Our rustic dance wi' scorn,
But are their hearts as light as ours   15
   Beneath the milkwhite thorn.——

The shepherd, in the flowery glen,
   In shepherd's phrase will woo;
The courtier tells a finer tale,
   But is his heart as true: 20
These wild-wood flowers I've pu'd, to deck
   That spotless breast o' thine;
The courtier's gems may witness love—
   But 'tis na love like mine.——

471. Song—

Lumps o' puddins

CONTENTED wi' little, and cantie wi' mair,
   Whene'er I forgather wi' Sorrow and Care,
I gie them a skelp, as they're creeping alang,
Wi' a cog o' gude swats and an auld Scotish sang.

Song. *Text from the Dalhousie MS (Dal; letter to Thomson, 19 November 1794),*
collated with the Alloway MSS (Al A, Al B) and SC, 1799 (65). First-line title in SC;
set in 8-line stanzas. Al A is a draft (lacking ll. 9–12) with an excise list on the verso;
Al B is a copy apparently made for a friend, headed A Scots lilt, new off the airns, *to*
the tune of, Lumps o' puddins—. *H–H. (iii. 465) record a holograph draft lacking*
ll. 9–12, with the original readings and corrections of Al A in ll. 7–8 and 15, and a
deleted version of l. 16: Approach, you are welcome, you lea'e me, good-bye.
   4 swats] ale *SC*

I whyles claw the elbow o' troublesome thought;   5
But Man is a soger, and Life is a faught:
My mirth and gude humour are coin in my pouch,
And my FREEDOM's my Lairdship nae monarch dare touch.

A towmond o' trouble, should that be my fa',
A night o' gude fellowship sowthers it a';   10
When at the blythe end of our journey at last,
Wha the deil ever thinks o' the road he has past.

Blind Chance, let her snapper and stoyte on her way;
Be 't to me, be 't frae me, e'en let the jade gae:
Come Ease, or come Travail; come Pleasure, or Pain;   15
My warst word is—'Welcome and welcome again!'

472. My Nanie's awa—

Tune, There'll never be peace—

Now in her green mantle blythe Nature arrays,
  And listens the lambkins that bleat o'er the braes,
While birds warble welcomes in ilka green shaw;
But to me it's delightless—my Nanie's awa.—

The snawdrap and primrose our woodlands adorn,   5
And violets bathe in the weet o' the morn;
They pain my sad bosom, sae sweetly they blaw,
They mind me o' Nanie—and Nanie's awa.—

6 soger] soldier *SC*   7–8 My . . . touch.] *correcting*
        For wealth, I am mirry—how can I be poor?
        And my Freedom's my birthright not kings shall injure.
in Al A, with merry good humour *in l.* 7   7 are] is *Al A*   15 Pleasure, or
Pain] *correcting* canker, or joy *in Al A*   16 word] *correcting* wish *in Al B*

My Nanie's awa. *Text from the Dalhousie MS (letter to Thomson, 9 December 1794),
collated with SC, 1799 (99). First-line title in SC; set to the air Coolun. A second MS,
in U.S.A. (photostat supplied by Dr. J. W. Egerer), has* springs *in l. 9 and shows no
other variation from the Dalhousie MS. The Aldine editor records a MS (not traced)
with these variants:* 1 blythe] gay *MS*   3 While] And *MS*   5 snawdrap
and primrose] primrose and daisy *MS*   woodlands] glens may *MS*   7 pain
my sad] torture my *MS*   13 and grey] array *MS*

Thou lavrock that springs frae the dews of the lawn
The shepherd to warn o' the grey-breaking dawn,   10
And thou mellow mavis that hails the night-fa',
Give over for pity—my Nanie's awa.—

Come Autumn, sae pensive, in yellow and grey,
And soothe me wi' tydins o' Nature's decay:
The dark, dreary Winter, and wild-driving snaw,   15
Alane can delight me—now Nanie's awa.—

473-479. [Dumfries Epigrams]

It was observed to R. B. that R—— of C—— face would make
a good painting.

C——D faithful likeness, friend Painter, would'st seize?
Keep out Worth, Wit and Wisdom: Put in what
     you please.

474.

Extempore on Miss E. I——, a Lady of a figure indicating amazonian
strength.

SHOULD he escape the slaughter of thine Eyes,
Within thy strong Embrace he struggling dies.

475.

To a Club in Dfrs. who styled themselves the Dumfries Loyal
Natives and exhibited violent party work and intemperate Loyalty . . .
10th June 1794

PRAY, who are these *Natives* the Rabble so ven'rate?
They're our true ancient *Natives*, and they breed
     undegen'rate
The ignorant savage that weather'd the storm,
When the *man* and the Brute differed but in the form.

9 springs] starts *alternative in Dal; SC*

Dumfries Epigrams. *Text from transcript of the MSS of John Syme of Ryedale*
(Burns Chronicle, *1932, pp. 16–22*). *Syme's note on 474:* R. B. says the above was
made by a young Lady of Spirit. *Title of 475 based on two transcripts*

476.

On an old acquaintance who seemed to pass the Bard without notice

[i] Dost hang thy head, Billy, asham'd that thou
    knowest me?
'Tis paying in kind a just debt that thou owest me.

[ii] Dost blush, my dear Billy, asham'd of thyself,
    A Fool and a Cuckold together?
The fault is not thine, insignificant elf,
    Thou wast not consulted in either.

477.

Immediate extempore on being told by W L of the Customs Dublin that Com^y Goldie did not seem disposed to push the bottle.

Friend Commissar, since we're met and are happy,
    Pray why should we part without having more
    nappy!
Bring in t'other bottle, for faith I am dry—
Thy drink thou can't part with and neither can I.

478.

On Mr. Burke by an opponent and a friend to Mr. Hastings.

Oft I have wonder'd that on Irish ground
    No poisonous Reptile ever has been found:
Revealed the secret stands of great Nature's work:
She preserved her poison to create a Burke!

479.

At the election of Magistrates for Dumfries, 1794, John M'Murdo, Esqr., was chosen Provost and a Mr. Swan one of the Baillies; and at the Entertainment usually given on the occasion Burns, seeing the

477. 4 can't] can'st *transcript*

Provost's Supporters on the Bench, took his pencil and wrote the following.

B AILLIE Swan, Baillie Swan,
  Let you do what you can,
God ha' mercy on honest Dumfries:
  But e'er the year's done,
  Good Lord! Provost John
Will find that his *Swans* are but *Geese*.

480. On Chloris requesting me to give her a spray of a sloe-thorn in full blossom—

F ROM the white-blossom'd sloe, my dear
    Chloris requested
A sprig, her fair breast to adorn:
No, by Heavens! I replied, let me perish for
    ever,
  Ere I plant in that bosom a *thorn*!

On Chloris. *Text from the Alloway MS (signed R.B.), collated with the Huntington Library MS (HL; letter to Creech, 30 May 1795) and Stewart, 1802 (p. 304). Title in HL* On a lady requesting . . . a sprig of blossomed thorn—. *Title in Stewart* Spoke extempore on a young lady desiring him to pull her a sprig of sloe-thorn to adorn her breast. *Dewar collated a MS (not traced) with the title* On a lady's asking me for a spray from a sloe-bush in blossom: *and the readings of HL*
    1 Chloris] Chloe *Stewart*   3 No, by Heavens!] Nay, by heaven, *Stewart* I replied] I exclaim'd *HL*: said I *Stewart*   let me . . . for] may I . . . if *Stewart* 4 Ere I . . . that] I . . . your *Stewart*

XII

POEMS
1795–1796

DUMFRIES

481. Ode to Spring—

Tune, The tither morn—

Lively with expression

W<small>HEN</small> maukin bucks, at early f—s,
  In dewy glens are seen, Sir;
And birds, on boughs, take off their m—s,
  Amang the leaves sae green, Sir;
Latona's sun looks liquorish on   5
  Dame Nature's grand impètus,
Till his p—go rise, then westward flies
  To r—ger Madame Thetis.

Yon wandering rill that marks the hill,
  And glances o'er the brae, Sir,   10
Slides by a bower where many a flower
  Sheds fragrance on the day, Sir;
There Damon lay, with Sylvia gay,
  To love they thought no crime, Sir;
The wild-birds sang, the echoes rang,   15
  While Damon's a—se beat time, Sir.

Ode to Spring. *Text from the Dalhousie MS (letter to Thomson, January 1795),
collated with MMC (pp. 49–50). Tune in MMC* Push about the jorum. *A bowdlerized
version of ll. 9–16 was printed as a* Fragment *in the* Edinburgh Magazine, *January
1818*
  3 And] When *MMC*   7 p–go] pego *MMC*   14 no] nae *MMC*

First, wi' the thrush, his thrust and push
Had compass large and long, Sir;
The blackbird next, his tuneful text,
    Was bolder, clear and strong, Sir: 20
The linnet's lay came then in play,
And the lark that soar'd aboon, Sir;
Till Damon, fierce, mistim'd his a—,
And f—'d quite out o' tune, Sir.

482. Song—For a' that and a' that—

I s there, for honest Poverty
    That hings his head, and a' that;
The coward-slave, we pass him by,
    We dare be poor for a' that!
For a' that, and a' that,   5
    Our toils obscure, and a' that,
The rank is but the guinea's stamp,
    The Man's the gowd for a' that.—

What though on hamely fare we dine,
    Wear hoddin grey, and a' that.   10
Gie fools their silks, and knaves their wine,
    A Man's a Man for a' that.
For a' that, and a' that,
    Their tinsel show, and a' that;
The honest man, though e'er sae poor,   15
    Is king o' men for a' that.—

Song. *Text from the Dalhousie MS (Dal; letter to Thomson, January 1795), collated
with the Adam MS (endorsed Burns. 1794), the* Glasgow Magazine *(GM), August
1795, the* Oracle, *2 June 1796, and SC, 1805 (163). For other early printings, see
H-H., iii. 490–1. A MS in a copy of* Poems *1794, recorded in H-H. but not certainly
holograph, has the* Oracle *readings. Title in SC* The Honest Man the Best of Men; *set
to the air* Up and war them a' Willy
      1–8 Is . . . that.] *not in GM, Oracle*   1 Is there] Where's he *SC, with note
that* The Editor has taken the liberty to alter . . . for the sake of the Music, and
because there is an ellipsis in the line as it stands   for] *correcting* at *in Dal*: at *Adam*
3 The] A *Adam*   16 king] chief *GM*

Ye see yon birkie ca'd, a lord,
      Wha struts, and stares, and a' that,
Though hundreds worship at his word,
      He's but a coof for a' that.   20
      For a' that, and a' that,
      His ribband, star and a' that,
The man of independant mind,
      He looks and laughs at a' that.—

A prince can mak a belted knight,   25
      A marquis, duke, and a' that;
But an honest man's aboon his might,
      Gude faith he mauna fa' that!
      For a' that, and a' that,
      Their dignities, and a' that,   30
The pith o' Sense, and pride o' Worth,
      Are higher rank than a' that.—

Then let us pray that come it may,
      As come it will for a' that,
That Sense and Worth, o'er a' the earth   35
      Shall bear the gree, and a' that.
      For a' that, and a' that,
      Its comin yet for a' that,
That Man to Man the warld o'er,
      Shall brothers be for a' that.—   40

483. Sweet fa's the eve on Craigieburn

SWEET fa's the eve on Craigieburn,
      And blythe awakes the morrow,
But a' the pride o' Spring's return
      Can yield me nocht but sorrow.—

19 worship . . . word] beckon . . . nod *Oracle*   22 ribband, star] dignities
Oracle   23 The] A *GM*   24 He looks and laughs] Can look and laugh
GM: Can sing and laugh *Oracle*   25 A prince] The king *GM*   30 Their
dignities] His dignities *GM*: His garters, stars *Oracle*   32 higher rank] grander
far *GM*: better far *Oracle*   than] for *Adam*   33 that come it may] the time
may come *Oracle*   34 As] And *Oracle*   will] shall *GM*   35 That]
When *GM*   36 and] for *Oracle*   38 Its comin yet] An' come it will *Oracle*
39 That] The *Dal*: And *GM*   to] and *GM*   40 brothers] *correcting* equals
in Dal   for] and *GM*

Sweet fa's the eve. *Text from the Dalhousie MS (letter to Thomson, January 1795),*

I see the flowers and spreading trees,   5
   I hear the wild birds singing;
But what a weary wight can please,
   And Care his bosom wringing.—

Fain, fain would I my griefs impart,
   Yet dare na for your anger;   10
But secret love will break my heart,
   If I conceal it langer.
If thou refuse to pity me;
   If thou shalt love anither;
When yon green leaves fade frae the tree,   15
   Around my grave they'll wither.—

484. The Dumfries Volunteers

Tune, Push about the jorum

collated *with SC, 1798 (32). Set to the air* Craigieburn Wood *in SC, with Thomson's
note:* This Song was addressed to a Miss LORIMER, who lived at Craigieburn Wood,
near Moffat; the same lady who, (under the name of CHLORIS), is celebrated in
several other Songs by Burns.
   14 anither *Ed.:* another *MS*

The Dumfries Volunteers. *Text from the Philadelphia MS (headed* For the Edin^r
Courant—A Ballad by Mr Burns), *collated with the Alloway MS, the Lochryan MS
(sent to Mrs. Dunlop, autumn 1795), SMM, 1803 (546; unsigned), and SC, 1809 (47).*

Does haughty Gaul invasion threat,
    Then let the louns bewaure, Sir,
There's WOODEN WALLS upon our seas,
    And VOLUNTEERS on shore, Sir:
The *Nith* shall run to *Corsincon*,* 5
    And *Criffell*† sink in *Solway*,
E'er we permit a Foreign Foe
    On British ground to rally.

O, let us not, like snarling tykes,
    In wrangling be divided, 10
Till, slap! come in an *unco loun*,
    And wi' a rung decide it!
Be BRITAIN still to BRITAIN true,
    Amang oursels united;
For never but by British hands 15
    Must British wrongs be righted.

The *kettle* o' the Kirk and State,
    Perhaps a clout may fail in't;
But deil a foreign tinkler-loun
    Shall ever ca' a nail in't: 20
Our FATHERS' BLUDE the *kettle* bought,
    And wha wad dare to spoil it,
By Heavens, the sacreligious dog
    Shall fuel be to boil it!

The wretch that would a *Tyrant* own, 25
    And the wretch, his true-sworn brother,
Who'd set the *Mob* above the *Throne*,
    May they be damn'd together!

* A high hill at the source of the Nith.
† A high hill at the confluence of the Nith with Solway Frith.

Tune in the Alloway MS Callum Shiarghlas, *in SC* Rise up and bar the Door. *The piece was published in the* Edinburgh Courant, *4 May 1795, the* Dumfries Journal, *5 May, and the* Caledonian Mercury, *7 May 1795. In SMM the last two lines of each stanza are repeated as chorus. The notes on ll. 5–6 are in the Philadelphia MS only*
    5 run] *om. Al*   7 E'er we] We'll ne'er *SMM (repeat only)*   15 never] only *Loch*   16 Must] Maun *SMM Al Loch*   22 wha wad] who wou'd *SC*   23 Heavens] heav'n *SC*   26 true-sworn] true-born *SC*   27 Who'd] *correcting* Whoud *in Phil MS*: Who would *Al SMM*: Who'd *SC*

Who will not sing, GOD SAVE THE KING,
Shall hang as high 's the steeple;　30
But while we sing, GOD SAVE THE KING,
We'll ne'er forget THE PEOPLE!
Fal de ral &c.

485. Let me in this ae night—

Will ye lend me your loom Lass

Slowish

O LASSIE, art thou sleeping yet,
　Or art thou wakin, I would wit,
For Love has bound me, hand and foot,
　And I would fain be in, jo.

Let me in this ae night. *Text from the Dalhousie MS (Dal C; letter to Thomson,
6 February 1795), collated with MSS Dal A and B (letters to Thomson, 13 August 1793
and September 1794) and SC, 1805 (156). Title from Dal A. Title in Dal C Song;
first-line title in SC. Dal B has ll. 1–4 and 9–16 only, with chorus indicated*
　1, 2 art thou] are ye *Dal B*　　　2 would] wad *Dal A B*

Chorus
O let me in this ae night,   5
This ae, ae, ae night;
For pity's sake this ae night
O rise and let me in, jo.

Thou hear'st the winter wind and weet,
Nae star blinks thro' the driving sleet;   10
Take pity on my weary feet,
And shield me frae the rain, jo.—
O let me in &c.

The bitter blast that round me blaws
Unheeded howls, unheeded fa's;
The cauldness o' thy heart's the cause   15
Of a' my grief and pine, jo.—
O let me in &c.

HER ANSWER
O tell na me o' wind and rain,
Upbraid na me wi' cauld disdain,
Gae back the gate ye cam again,
I winna let ye in, jo.—   20

Chorus
I tell you now this ae night,
This ae, ae, ae night,
And ance for a' this ae night,
I winna let you in, jo.

7 For pity's sake] O let me in *Dal A*   8 O rise . . . in] I'll no come back
again *Dal A*   9 Thou . . . winter] O hear'st thou not the *Dal A*: O hear'st
thou na the *Dal B*   11 Take] Tak *Dal A, B*   13–16 The . . . pine, jo.]
Dal B ends. Dal A has a cancelled stanza:

> Thy kith and kin look down on me,
> A simple lad o' low degree;
> Sae I maun try frae love to flee,
>   Across the raging main, jo.

Autograph note: I do not know but this stanza may as well be omitted.
21–36 HER ANSWER] *Dal A has*

> Tho' never durst my tongue reveal,
> Lang, lang my heart to thee's been leal;
> O lassie dear, ae last farweel,
>   For pity's cause alane, jo.
>   O let me in &c.

The snellest blast, at mirkest hours,   25
That round the pathless wanderer pours,
Is nocht to what poor She endures,
    That's trusted faithless Man, jo.—
      I tell you now &c.

The sweetest flower that deck'd the mead,
Now trodden like the vilest weed—   30
Let simple maid the lesson read,
    The wierd may be her ain, jo.—
      I tell you now &c.

The bird that charm'd his summer day,
And now the cruel Fowler's prey,
Let that to witless woman say   35
    The gratefu' heart o' man jo.—
      I tell you now &c.

     O wyte na me untill thou prove
     The fatal force o' mighty Love;
     Then should on me thy fancy rove,
       Count my care by thy ain, jo.
       O let me in &c.

     O pity's ay to woman dear,
     She heav'd a sigh, she drapt a tear—
     "Twas love for me that brought him here,
       'Sae how can I complain, jo.'

          Chorus
     O come your ways, this ae night,
      This ae, ae, ae night;
     O come your ways this ae night,
      But ye maunna do't again, jo.

33–36 The . . . jo.] *Postscript correction—*By G— I have thought better!—*in Dal C
of:*
     The bird that charm'd his summer-day,
     Is now the cruel Fowler's prey;
     Let witless, trusting Woman say
       How aft her fate's the same, jo.

Cancelled version in SC. See Commentary

486. Fragment—Epistle from Esopus to Maria

FROM these drear solitudes and frowzy Cells,
    Where Infamy with sad repentance dwells;
Where Turnkeys make the jealous portal fast,
Then deal from iron hands the spare repast;
Where truant 'prentices, yet young in sin,   5
Blush at the curious stranger peeping in;
Where strumpets, relics of the drunken roar,
Resolve to drink—nay half, to whore—no more;
Where tiny thieves, not destined yet to swing,
Beat hemp for others riper for the string:—   10
From these dire scenes my wretched lines I date,
To tell Maria her Esöpus' fate.
    'Alas, I feel I am no actor here!'
'Tis *real* Hangmen *real* scourges bear.
Prepare, M****, for a horrid tale   15
Will turn thy very rouge to deadly pale;
Will make thy hair, tho erst from gypsey poll'd,
By Barber woven and by Barber sold,
Tho twisted smooth by *Harry*'s* nicest care,
Like Boary bristles to erect and stare.   20
The Hero of the mimic scene, no more
I start in Hamlet, in Othello roar;
Or haughty Chieftan, mid the din of arms,
In highland bonnet woo Malvina's charms;
While Sans Culotes stoop up the mountain high   25
And steal from me Maria's prying eye.

* her Servant.

Fragment. *Text from Syme's transcript (S), collated with Cunningham, 1834, iii. 230–3 (Cun). S is printed in the* Burns Chronicle, *1935, pp. 35–38. A copy (dated 1815; not holograph) has been recorded with these variants:* 1 these drear solitudes] dank and noisome vaults *MS*   3 Turnkeys . . . jealous portal] jealous turnkeys . . . portal *MS*   11 these . . . my] such . . . those *MS*   19 twisted smooth] crimp'd and crispt *MS*   31 her face] thee court *MS*   63 thy . . . Vagrants] on us thy vengeance *MS*   64 save] but *MS*   66 a] one *MS*   69 Or] And *MS. Cunningham's transcript is in a copy of the* Merry Muses *(?1825). See Commentary*

Title in Cun Epistle . . . Maria: *in S* Fragment—part description of a Correction house. The whole letter is now extended as follows—addressed to Maria—
    1 these] those *Cun*   4 Then] And *Cun*   9 tiny] *corrects* vagrant *in S*
19 twisted smooth] *correcting* crimp'd & frizz'd *in S*   by] with *Cun: correcting* with *in S*   20 Boary] hoary *Cun*

Blest highland Bonnet! once my proudest dress!
Now, prouder still, Maria's temples press!
I see her wave thy tow'ring plumes afar,
And call each Coxcomb to the wordy war.   30
I see her face the first of Ireland's Sons,*
And even out-irish his Hibernian bronze.
The Crafty Colonel† leaves the tartan'd lines
For other wars, where He a hero shines:
The hopeful youth,‡ in Scottish Senate bred,   35
Who owns a B——y's heart $^{\text{but not}}_{\text{without}}$ the head,
Comes, 'mid a string of coxcombs, to display
That veni, vidi, vici is his way.
The shrinking Bard§ adown an alley sculks,
And dreads a meeting worse than Woolwich hulks—   40
Tho' there his heresies in Church and State
Might well award him Muir and Palmer's fate:
Still she, undaunted, reels and rattles on,
And dares the public like a noontide sun!

What scandal call'd Maria's janty stagger   45
The ricket reeling of a crooked swagger?
What slander nam'd her seeming want of art
The flimsey wrapper of a rotten heart—
Whose spite e'en worse than Burns's venom when
He dips in gall unmixed his eager pen,   50
And pours his vengeance in the burning line?
Who christen'd thus Maria's Lyre divine,
The idiot strum of vanity bemused,
And e'en th' abuse of poesy abused?
Who called her verse a parish workhouse, made   55
For motely, foundling fancies, stolen or strayed?

A Workhouse! ah, that sound awakes my woes,
And pillows on the thorn my racked repose!

---

* Captn. R.G.   † Col. McD—   ‡ B. M—d   § R.B.

27 dress] *correcting* boast *in S*   36 B——y's] Bushby's *Cun*   36 *Cun has*
without *only*   43 undaunted] *correcting* unheeded *in S*   45–56 *parenthesis*
in Cun   47–48 What . . . heart] *om. Cun and 1815 copy*   49 spite] spleen
Cun and 1815 copy

In durance vile here must I wake and weep,
And all my frowzy Couch in sorrow steep;   60
That straw where many a rogue has lain of yore,
And vermin'd Gypseys litter'd heretofore.
Why, L——dale, thus thy wrath on Vagrants pour?
Must Earth no Rascal save thyself endure?
Must thou alone in crimes immortal swell,   65
And make a vast Monopoly of Hell?
Thou knowest the Virtues cannot hate thee worse;
The Vices also, must *they* club their curse?
Or must no tiny sin to others fall,
Because thy guilt's supreme enough for all?   70
  Maria, send me too thy griefs and cares;
In all of thee, sure, thy Esopus shares.
As thou at all mankind the flag unfurls,
Who on my fair one Satire's vengeance hurls?
Who calls thee pert, affected, vain Coquette,   75
A wit in folly and a fool in wit?
Who says that Fool alone is not thy due,
And quotes thy treacheries to prove it true?
Our force united on thy foes we'll turn,
And dare the war with all of woman born: 80
For who can write and speak as thou and I—
My periods that decyphering defy,
And thy still matchless tongue that conquers all reply?

487. On Miss J. Scott, of Ayr

OH! had each SCOT of ancient times,
   Been, JEANY SCOTT, as thou art,
The bravest heart on English ground,
   Had yielded like a coward.

65 crimes] guilt *Cun and 1815 copy*   70 guilt 's *Cun*: guilt *S*   81-83 *Editor's
bracket*   83 *note in S* The foregoing is quite private

On Miss J. Scott, of Ayr. *Text from Stewart, 1801 (p. 59). Wallace published
a variant from a letter (Dumfries, 30 April 1815) in the papers of Alexander Laing
and Peter Buchan (Chambers-Wallace, iv. 193):*
      O had each Scot on English ground
      Been bonnie Scott, as thou art,
      The stoutest heart of English kind
      Had yielded like a coward.

488. Song—

Tune, We'll gang nae mair to yon town—

O WAT ye wha's in yon town,
   Ye see the e'enin Sun upon,
The dearest maid's in yon town,
   That e'enin Sun is shining on.

Now haply down yon gay green shaw   5
   She wanders by yon spreading tree;
How blest ye flow'rs that round her blaw,
   Ye catch the glances o' her e'e.
     O wat ye wha's, &c.

How blest ye birds that round her sing,
   And welcome in the blooming year,   10
And doubly welcome be the spring,
   The season to my Jeanie dear.
     O wat ye wha's, &c.

The sun blinks blyth on yon town,
   Amang the broomy braes sae green;
But my delight in yon town,   15
   And dearest pleasure, is my Jean.
     O wat ye wha's, &c.

Song. *Text from SMM, 1796 (458; signed B), collated with the Dalhousie MS (letter to Thomson, April 1795), the* Glasgow Magazine, *September 1795 (GM), and SC, 1799 (53). Title from Dal. First-line title in SC, which has* yonder town *throughout, set to the air* Fy gar rub her o'er wi' strae *which appears to the Editor a much better Air for singing. Dal, GM and SC set in three twelve-line stanzas, ll. 1–4 not repeated as a chorus. In the Dalhousie MSS (letter to Thomson, 7 February 1795) is a draft of the chorus and a stanza:*

> O sweet to me yon spreading tree,
>   Where Jeanie wanders aft her lane;
> The hawthorn flower that shades her bower,
>   Oh, when shall I behold again!

3 dearest maid's] fairest dame's *Dal:* fairest maid's *SC*   10 welcome] wanton *GM*   11 And] But *GM*   12 Jeanie] Lucy *Dal SC*   14 Amang . . . green] And on yon bonie braes of Ayr *Dal SC*   broomy] bloomy *GM*   15 delight *Dal GM SC*: delight's *SMM*   16 pleasure, is my Jean] joy, is Lucy fair *Dal SC*

Without my fair, not a' the charms
O' Paradise could yeild me joy;
But gie me Jeanie in my arms,
And welcome Lapland's dreary sky.   20
  O wat ye wha's, &c.

My cave wad be a lovers' bow'r,
Tho' raging winter rent the air;
And she a lovely little flower,
That I wad tent and shelter there.
  O wat ye wha's, &c.

O sweet is she in yon town,   25
The sinkin Sun's gane down upon:
A fairer than's in yon town,
His setting beam ne'er shone upon.
  O wat ye wha's, &c.

If angry fate is sworn my foe,
And suffering I am doom'd to bear;   30
I careless quit aught else below,
But, spare me, spare me Jeanie dear.
  O wat ye wha's, &c.

For while life's dearest blood is warm,
Ae thought frae her shall ne'er depart,
And she—as fairest is her form,   35
She has the truest kindest heart.
  O wat ye wha's, &c.

17 fair] Love *Dal SC*   19 Jeanie] Lucy *Dal SC*   23 a] the *GM*
26 The] Yon *Dal SC*   27 A fairer than's] The dearest maid's *GM*   28 ne'er]
e'er *GM*   29 is] be *GM*   31 I] I'd *GM*   32 me,] oh! *GM*   Jeanie]
Lucy *Dal SC*   33 For] And *SC*   is] runs *GM*   34 Ae thought] My
thoughts *GM*   35 And ... fairest] For as most lovely *GM*

489. Song—(On Chloris being ill)

Tune, Ay wakin O—

Chorus—

LONG, long the night,
    Heavy comes the morrow,
While my soul's delight
Is on her bed of sorrow.—

1

Can I cease to care,   5
    Can I cease to languish,
While my darling Fair
Is on the couch of anguish.—
Long, &c.—

2

Ev'ry hope is fled;
    Ev'ry fear is terror;   10
Slumber even I dread,
    Ev'ry dream is horror.
Long, &c.

3

Hear me, Powers Divine!
    Oh, in pity, hear me!
Take aught else of mine,   15
But my Chloris spare me!
Long, &c.

Song. *Text from the Dalhousie MS (letter to Thomson, April 1795), collated with the
Adam MS (letter to Mrs. Riddell, ? March 1795) and SC, 1801 (111). Heading in
Adam* English verses for the air Ay wakin O—See the Scots Musical Museum. (On
Chloris being ill.) *Title in SC* Ay Waking, O! *In SC Thomson interpolates a first
stanza based on 287, ll. 5–12; sets the Dalhousie MS text in three 9-line stanzas, each
opening with the chorus; and adds a line to each for the sake of the Music. Lines 8 and
12 are followed by* O this love, this love!; *line 16 by* Spare, O spare my Love!
    16 Chloris] DARLING *Adam*

490. Elegy on Mʳ William Cruikshank A. M.

Now honest William's gaen to Heaven,
    I wat na gin 't can mend him:
The fauts he had in Latin lay,
    For nane in English kend them.——

491–494. [The Heron Ballads, 1795]

[Tune, For a' that, and a' that]

Wham will we send to London town,
    To Parliament, and a' that,
Wha maist in a' the country round,
    For worth and sense may fa' that.——
      For a' that, and a' that,   5
      Thro' Galloway and a' that,
      Whilk is the Laird, or belted Knight,
      That best deserves to fa' that?

2

Wha sees Kirouchtree's open yett,
    And wha is 't never saw that,   10
Or wha e'er wi' Kirouchtree met,
    That has a doubt of a' that?
      For a' that and a' that,
        Here's Heron yet for a' that;
      The independant Patriot,   15
      The Honest Man, and a' that.

3

Tho' wit and worth, in either sex,
    Saint Mary's Isle can shaw that;
Wi' Lords and Dukes let Selkirk mix,
    For weel does Selkirk fa' that.   20

Elegy on Mʳ William Cruikshank. *Text from the Watson MSS, 1118*

The Heron Ballads. I. *Text from the Alloway MS, collated with the 1795 broadside (95) and Cunningham, 1834 (iii. 261–3; Cun). See Commentary*
  1 Wham will we] Whom will you *Cun*   3 Wha maist] Or wha *95 Cun*   4 For . . . may] The best deserves to *95 Cun*   7 Whilk] Whare *95 Cun*   11 Or wha e'er] Whaever *95 Cun*   met] meets *Cun*   12 That] And *95 Cun*   17 Tho'] *correcting* For *in MS*   19 Lords and Dukes] dukes an' lords *Cun*   20 For] And *95 Cun*

For a' that and a' that,
    Here's Heron yet for a' that;
An independant Commoner
    Maun bear the gree and a' that.

4

To paughty Lordlings shall we jouk,   25
    And it against the law, that:
For even a Lord may be a gowk,
    Tho' sprung frae kings and a' that.
    For a' that and a' that,
        Here's Heron yet for a' that;   30
    A lord may be a lousy loun,
        Wi' ribband, star and a' that.—

5

Yon beardless boy comes o'er the hills,
    Wi 's uncle's gowd, and a' that:
But we'll hae ane frae 'mang oursels   35
    A man we ken and a' that.—
    For a' that and a' that,
        Here's Heron yet for a' that;
    We are na to the market come
        Like nowt and naigs and a' that.—   40

6

If we are to be knaves and fools,
    And bought and sauld and a' that,
A truant callan frae the schools
    It's ne'er be said did a' that.
    For a' that, and a' that,   45
        Here's Heron yet for a' that;
    And Master Dicky, thou shalt get
        A gird and stick to ca' that.—

---

24 Maun . . . and] Shall be the Man for 95 *Cun*   25 To . . . we] But why
should we to Nobles 95 *Cun*   26 it] its *Cun*   27 For] And 95   even]
correcting why *in MS*: why, *Cun*   28 Tho' . . . kings] Wi' ribban, star 95
Cun   33 Yon] A 95 *Cun*   34 gowd] purse 95 *Cun*   39 the market
come] *correcting* be bought *in MS*: be bought and sauld 95 *Cun*   41–48 If
we . . . ca' that.] *not in* 95 *Cun*

[7]

[Then let us drink the *Stewartry*,
  Kirochtree's Laird, and a' that,   50
Our Representative to be,
For weel he's worthy a' that.
  For a' that, and a' that,
    Here's Heron yet for a' that;
  A House o' Commons such as he,   55
    They wad be blest that saw that.]

492. The Election: A New Song

Tune—Fy, let us a' to the Bridal

F Y, let us a' to K[IRKCUDBRIGHT],
    For there will be bickerin there;
For M——'s *light horse* are to muster,
And O, how the heroes will swear!

49–56 Then let us . . . saw that. *not in MS. Text from 95*

The Heron Ballads. II. The Election. *Text from the 1795 broadside (95) collated with the Cowie MS (early fragment; sequence ll. 25–28, 17–20, 21–24, 45–48 and a quatrain later rejected, 37–40, 29–32), the Huntington Library MS (HL; ll. 1–28 only), and Cunningham, 1834, iii. 264–7 (Cun). Title in HL A Ballad—*

And there will be *M*—— commander,   5
And *G*—— the battle to win;
Like brothers they'll stand by each other,
Sae knit in alliance and kin.

And there will be black-nebbit *Johnie*,
The tongue o' the trump to them a';   10
An he get na H–ll for his haddin,
The Deil gets nae justice ava.
And there will be *K*————'s birkie,
A boy no sae black at the bane;
But as to his fine *Nabob* fortune,   15
We'll e'en let the subject alane.

And there will be *W*————'s new *Sh*————*ff*,
Dame Justice fu' brawlie has sped;
She's gotten the heart of a *B*————,
But Lord! what's become o' the head?   20
And there will be *C*————, Esquire,
Sae mighty in *C*————'s eyes;
A wight that will weather d–mn–tion,
The Devil the prey will despise.

And there will be ————*ses* doughty,   25
New-christening towns far and near;
Abjuring their democrat doings
By kissin the a—— of a *Peer*.
And there will be *K*————, sae gen'rous,
Whase honour is proof to the storm;   30
To save them from stark reprobation,
He lent them his name to the *Firm*.

6 the battle to win] that keenly will start *HL*   7–8 Like . . . kin.] *HL has*
Why shameless her lane is the lassie,
E'en let her kind kin tak a part.
9 -nebbit] -lippit *Cun*   13 *K*————'s birkie] bubblie-jock WILLY *HL*   14 boy
no] B————y *HL*   15–16 But . . . alane.] *HL has*
Whate'er they may say o' his failins,
Sure gamin and reavin are nane.
20 head ?] *Cun:* head. *95 HL*   29 *K*————, sae gen'rous] *correcting* generous
Kenmore *in Cowie*   31 stark reprobation] *correcting* bankrupt damnation *in*
Cowie   32 lent them . . . to] threw in . . . in *Cowie*

But we winna mention *R*——*stle*,
    The *body*, e'en let him escape:
He'd venture the gallows for siller,   35
    An 'twere na the cost o' the rape.
And where is our King's *L*—— *L*——*t*,
    Sae fam'd for his *gratefu'* return?
The billie is gettin his questions,
    To say in *S*—*nt St*–*ph*–*n's* the morn.   40

And there will be Lads o' the g–sp–l,
    M——, wha's as *gude* as he's *true*:
And there will be *B*——*'s Apostle*,
    Wha's mair o' the *black* than the *blue*:
And there will be Folk frae *Saint MARY*'s,   45
    A *house* o' great merit and note;
The deil ane but honours them highly,
    Tho' deil ane will gie them his vote.

And there will be wealthy young *RICHARD*—
    Dame Fortune should hing by the neck   50
For prodigal thriftless bestowing—
    His merit had won him respect.
And there will be rich brother *Nabobs*,
    Tho' *Nabobs*, yet men of the first:
And there will be *C*–*ll*–*ston's* whiskers,   55
    And *Quintin*, o' lads not the warst.

And there will be *Stamp-office Johnie*,
    Tak tent how ye purchase a dram:
And there will be gay *C*–*ss*–*ncary*,
    And there will be gleg *Colonel Tam*.   60

39 billie] birkie *Cowie*   45–48 And there . . . his vote.] *Cowie has*

    And there will the isle o' Saint Mary's
    Exult in the worth of her Youth:
    Alas, for the Isle o' Saint Mary's,
    In trusting to reason and truth!

    But where is the Doggerbank hero
    That made Hogan Mogan to sculk?
    Poor *Keith*'s gane to h–ll to be fuel,
    The auld rotten wreck of a Hulk.

50 neck] neck; *Cun*   51 prodigal thriftless bestowing—] prodigal, thriftless,
bestowing, *Cun*

And there will be trusty KIROCHTREE,
   Whase honour was ever his law;
If the VIRTUES were packt in a parcel
   His WORTH might be sample for a'.

And can we forget the auld MAJOR,   65
   Wha'll ne'er be forgot in the *Greys*;
Our flatt'ry we'll keep for some other,
   HIM, only it's justice to praise.
And there will be maiden *K–lk–rran*,
   And also *B–rsk–m–n*'s gude Knight;   70
And there will be roaring *B–rtwhistle*,
   Yet, luckily roars in the right.

And there, frae the *N–ddisd–le* border,
   Will mingle the *M–xw–lls* in droves;
Teugh *Jockie*, staunch *Geordie*, and *Walie*,   75
   That greens for the fishes and loaves.
And there will be *L–g–n M––d–w–l*,
   Sculdudry—and he will be there;
And also the *Wild Scot o' Galloway*,
   Sogering, gunpowder *Bl––r*.   80

Then hey the *chaste Int'rest* o' *B––––*,
   And hey for the blessins 'twill bring;
It may send *B––––* to the *C––––ns*,
   In *S–d–m* 'twould make him a King.
And hey for the sanctified *M––––*,   85
   Our land wha wi' *Ch–p–ls* has stor'd:
He founder'd his horse amang harlots,
   But gied the auld naig to the L–rd!

68 it 's] 'tis *Cun*   72 Yet,] Wha, *Cun*   73 *N–ddisd–le*] Niddisdale's *Cun*
78 *Sculdudry*—and] Sculdudd'ry an' *Cun*

493. Johnie B——'s lament—

Tune, The babes o' the wood

'TWAS in the seventeen hunder year
   O' Christ and ninety-five,
That year I was the waest man
   Of any man alive.—

On March, the three and twentieth morn,   5
   The sun raise clear and bright,
But Oh, I was a waefu' man
   Ere toofa' o' the night.—

Earl G——y lang did rule this land
   With *equal* right and fame;   10
Fast knit in *chaste* and haly bands
   Wi' B——n's noble name.—

Earl G——y's man o' men was I,
   And chief o' B——n's host:
So twa blind beggars on a string   15
   The faithfu' tyke will trust.—

The Heron Ballads. III. Johnie B—'s Lament. *Text from the Huntington Library MS,
collated with Cunningham, 1834 (iii. 268; Cun, quotation of ll. 1–16 only), and Hogg
and Motherwell, 1834 (i. 312–14; HM). Sequence in HM: lines 1–12, a variant of
17–20, 21–28, an additional stanza, 29–36, 41–56, 37–40. See Commentary*
  3 waest] saddest *Cun*   5 On . . . morn] In . . . day *Cun HM*   11–12 Fast . . .
name.] *Cun HM have*
              And thereto was his kinsman join'd
              The Murray's noble name!
13–20 Earl . . . gane.] *Cun HM have*
              Yerl Galloway lang did rule the land,
              Made me the judge o' strife;
              But now Yerl Galloway's sceptre 's broke,
              And eke my hangman's knife.
Cun ends with note: The succeeding verses . . . are too personal for insertion

But now Earl G———y's sceptre's broke,
And B———n's wi' the slain;
And I my ancient craft may try,
Sen honestie is gane.———   20

'Twas on the bonie banks o' Dee,
Beside K———t towers,
The St———t and the M———y there
Did muster a' their powers.———

The M———y on his auld grey yad,   25
Wi' *winged spurs*, did ride;
That auld grey yad, a' Nidsdale rade,
He lifted by Nid-side.———

And there was B———ie, I ween,
I' th' front rank he wad shine;   30
But B———ie had better been
Drinking Madeira wine.———

And frae Gl–nk–ns cam to our aid
A Chief o' doughty deed:
In case that WORTH should wanted be,   35
O' K———re we had need.———

And by our banner march'd M———d,
And B———le was na slack,
Whase haly Priest-hoods nane could stain,
For wha can dye the BLACK.———   40

21 bonie banks o'] banks o' bonie *HM*   22 K———t] Kirkcudbright's *HM*
23, 25 St———t . . . M———y] Stewart . . . Murray *HM*   25 on his] on the *HM*
27 a'] yea, *HM*   28 He lifted by] Astray upon *HM*   28 *Additional stanza*
in HM:

          An there had been the Yerl himsel',
          O there had been nae play;
          But Garlies was to London gane,
          And sae the kye might stray.

29, 31 B———ie] Balmaghie *HM*   33 And frae Gl–nk–ns] Frae the Glenken
HM   36 K———re] Kenmure *HM*   37 banner] banners *HM*   M———d]
Muirhead *HM*   38 B———le] Buittle *HM*   39 Priest-hoods] priesthood
HM   could] can *HM*

And there, sae grave, Squire C——ss
Look'd on till a' was done:
So, in the tower o' C——ss
A houlet sits at noon.—

And there led I the B——y clan;   45
My *gamesome* billie WILL,
And my son M——nd, *wise* as *brave*,
My footsteps followed still.—

The DOUGLAS and the HERON's name
We set nocht to their score: 50
The DOUGLAS and the HERON's name
Had felt our might before.—

Yet D——SES o' weight had we,
The pair o' lusty lairds,
For building cot-houses sae fam'd,   55
And christening kail-yards.—

And there R–dc–stle drew the sword
That ne'er was stain'd wi' gore;
Save on a wanderer, lame and blind,
To drive him frae his door.—   60

And last cam creeping C–l——n,
Was mair in fear than wrath:
Ae KNAVE was constant in his mind,
To keep that KNAVE frae scathe.—

*   *   *   *   *   *

41, 43 C——ss] Cardoness *HM*   45 B——y clan] Bushbys a' *HM*
47 M——nd] Maitland *HM*   52 might] weight *HM*   53 Yet D——SES]
But Douglasses *HM*   54 The . . . lusty] A . . . trusty *HM*   57–64 And . . .
scathe.] *Not in HM*   57 there] *followed by cancelled* drew *in MS*

494. Buy Braw Troggin. An Excellent New Song

Tune—Buy broom Besoms

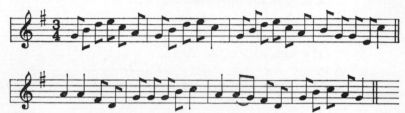

W^{HA} will buy my Troggin,
   Fine ELECTION WARE;
Broken trade o' *BR*——
   A' in high repair.

   Chorus
   Buy braw Troggin,   5
     Frae the Banks o' *Dee*l
   Wha want Troggin,
     Let them come to me.

Here's a noble Earl's
   Fame and high renown,   10
For an auld sang—
   It's thought the Gudes were stown.
   Buy braw Troggin, &c.

Here's the Worth o' *BR*——,
   In a *needle's e'e*:
Here's a reputation,   15
   Tint by *B*——.
   Buy braw Troggin, &c.

Here's an HONEST CONSCIENCE,
   Might a Prince adorn,
Frae the *Downs o' T*——,
   —So was never worn.   20
   Buy braw Troggin, &c.

The Heron Ballads. IV. Buy Braw Troggin. *Text from the 1795 broadside collated
with Cunningham, 1834 (iii. 269–71; Cun)*
   7–8, 55–56 want . . . them] wants . . . him *Cun*

Here's its Stuff and Lynin,
   C——*ss*'s Head;
Fine for a Soger,
   A' the wale o' lead.
     Buy braw Troggin, &c.

Here's a little Wadset,   25
   B——*ttle*'s scrap o' Truth;
Pawn'd in a gin-shop,
   Quenching haly drouth.
     Buy braw Troggin, &c.

Here's Armorial Bearings,
   Frae the Manse of ——;   30
The crest, an *auld crab-apple*,
   Rotten at the core.
     Buy braw Troggin, &c.

Here is Satan's Picture,
   Like a bizzard-gled,
Pouncing *poor* R——*tle*,   35
   Sprawlin as a tade.
     Buy braw Troggin, &c.

Here's the Font where *D*——
   Stane and mortar names;
Lately us'd at *C*——,
   Christening *M*——'s crimes.   40
     Buy braw Troggin, &c.

Here's the Worth and Wisdom
   C——*n* can boast;
By a *thievish Midge*
   They had been nearly lost.
     Buy braw Troggin, &c.

Here is *M*——'s Fragments   45
   O' the Ten Commands;
Gifted by BLACK JOCK
   —To get them off his hands.
     Buy braw Troggin, &c.

37–40 Here's . . . crimes.] *om. Cun*

Saw ye e'er sic Troggin?
If to buy ye're slack,   50
HORNIE's turning Chapman,
He'll buy a' the *Pack*!

Buy braw Troggin,
Frae the Banks o' *Dee*!
Wha want Troggin,   55
Let them come to me.

495. Address to the woodlark—

O STAY, sweet warbling woodlark stay,
  Nor quit for me the trembling spray,
A hapless lover courts thy lay,
Thy soothing fond complaining.—

Again, again that tender part,   5
That I may catch thy melting art;
For surely that wad touch her heart
Wha kills me wi' disdaining.—

Address to the woodlark. *Text from the Dalhousie MS (letter to Thomson, April 1795), collated with the Adam MS and SC, 1798 (26). Title in Adam* To a Woodlark; *first-line title in SC. See Commentary. Scott Douglas (iii. 275) records a holograph draft in pencil entitled* Song.—Composed on hearing a bird sing while musing on Chloris:

Sing on, sweet songster o' the brier,
Nae stealthy traitor-foot is near;
O soothe a hapless Lover's ear,
  And dear as life I'll prize thee.

Again, again that tender part,
That I may learn thy melting art,
For surely that would touch the heart,
  O' her that still denies me.

Oh was thy mistress, too, unkind,
And heard thee as the careless wind?
For nocht but Love and Sorrow join'd
  Sic notes of woe could wauken.
Thou tells, &c.

6 melting] tuneful *Adam*   7 wad] would *SC*

Say, was thy little mate unkind,
And heard thee as the careless wind?   10
Oh, nocht but love and sorrow join'd,
    Sic notes o' woe could wauken!

Thou tells o' never-ending care;
O' speechless grief, and dark despair:
For pity's sake, sweet bird, nae mair!   15
    Or my poor heart is broken!

496. Song—

11 nocht] nought *Adam SC*   13 tells o'] talks o' *Adam:* tell'st of *SC*
never-ending] grief, & endless *Adam*   14 O'] Of *SC*   grief] woe *Adam*

Song. *Text from the Dalhousie MS (letter to Thomson, April 1795), collated with the*
Adam MS (letter to Mrs. Riddell, ?March 1795), the Huntington Library MS (HL),
the Edinburgh Magazine, *May 1797, and SC, 1799 (95). Printed inaccurately in the*
London Star, *22 December 1796. First-line title in SC. Air in Adam and HL* Humors
of glen

T̶HEIR groves o' sweet myrtle let Foreign Lands reckon,
   Where bright-beaming summers exalt the perfume,
Far dearer to me yon lone glen o' green breckan
   Wi' th' burn stealing under the lang, yellow broom:
Far dearer to me are yon humble broom bowers,   5
   Where the blue-bell and gowan lurk, lowly, unseen;
For there, lightly tripping amang the wild flowers,
   A listening the linnet, oft wanders my JEAN.

Tho' rich is the breeze in their gay, sunny vallies,
   And cauld, CALEDONIA's blast on the wave;   10
Their sweet-scented woodlands that skirt the proud palace,
   What are they? The haunt o' the TYRANT and SLAVE.
The SLAVE's spicy forests, and gold-bubbling fountains,
   The brave CALEDONIAN views wi' disdain;
He wanders as free as the winds of his mountains,   15
   Save LOVE's willing fetters, the chains o' his JEAN.

497. Song—

Tune, Laddie lie near me

1 myrtle] myrtles *HL*   5 are] *om. Adam*   yon] these *HL*

Song. *Text from the Dalhousie MS (letter to Thomson, April 1795), collated with Currie (iv. 229–30)*

'Twas na her bonie blue e'e was my ruin;
     Fair tho' she be, that was ne'er my undoing:
'Twas the dear smile when naebody did mind us,
'Twas the bewitching, sweet, stown glance o'
     kindness.

Sair do I fear that to hope is denied me,   5
Sair do I fear that despair maun abide me;
But tho' fell Fortune should fate us to sever,
Queen shall she be in my bosom for ever.

Chloris I'm thine wi' a passion sincerest,
And thou hast plighted me love o' the dearest!   10
And thou'rt the angel that never can alter,
Sooner the sun in his motion would falter.

498. Altered from an old English song—

Tune, John Anderson my jo—

How cruel are the Parents
     Who riches only prize,
And to the wealthy booby
     Poor Woman sacrifice:
Meanwhile the hapless Daughter   5
     Has but a choice of strife;
To shun a tyrant Father's hate,
     Become a wretched Wife.—

The ravening hawk pursuing,
     The trembling dove thus flies,   10
To shun impelling ruin
     Awhile her pinions tries;
Till of escape despairing,
     No shelter or retreat,
She trusts the ruthless Falconer   15
     And drops beneath his feet.—

9 Chloris] Mary, *Currie*

Altered from an old English song. *Text from the Dalhousie MS (letter to Thomson,
? 3 May 1795), collated with SC, 1799 (51; alternative verses)*
     7 tyrant] *correcting* cruel *in MS*

499. Song

Tune, Deil tak the wars—

M̲A̲R̲K̲ yonder pomp of costly fashion,
  Round the wealthy, titled bride:
But when compar'd with real passion,
    Poor is all that princely pride.
     What are their showy treasures,   5
     What are their noisy pleasures,
The gay, gaudy glare of vanity and art:
     The polish'd jewel's blaze
     May draw the wond'ring gaze,
     And courtly grandeur bright   10
     The fancy may delight,
But never, never can come near the heart.—

But did you see my dearest Chloris,
  In simplicity's array;
Lovely as yonder sweet opening flower is,   15
    Shrinking from the gaze of day.
     O then, the heart alarming,
     And all resistless charming,
In Love's delightful fetters, she chains the willing
    soul!
     Ambition would disown   20
     The world's imperial crown,
     Even Av'rice would deny
     His worshipp'd deity,
And feel thro' every vein love's raptures roll.—

Song. *Text from the Dalhousie MS (letter to Thomson, ? 3 May 1795), collated with SC, 1805 (157; alternative verses)*

500. Address to the Tooth-Ache

(Written by the Author at a time when he was grievously tormented by that Disorder.)

MY curse on your envenom'd stang,
  That shoots my tortur'd gums alang,
An' thro' my lugs gies mony a bang
    Wi' gnawin vengeance;
Tearing my nerves wi' bitter twang,   5
    Like racking engines.

A' down my beard the slavers trickle,
I cast the wee stools owre the meikle,
While round the fire the hav'rels keckle,
    To see me loup;   10
I curse an' ban, an' wish a heckle
    Were i' their doup.

Whan fevers burn, or agues freeze us,
Rheumatics gnaw, or colics squeeze us,
Our neebors sympathize, to ease us,   15
    Wi' pitying moan;
But thou—the hell o' a' diseases,
    They mock our groan.

O' a' the num'rous human dools,
Ill har'sts, daft bargains, *cutty-stools*,   20
Or worthy friends laid i' the mools,
    Sad sight to see!
The tricks o' knaves, or fash o' fools,
    Thou bear'st the gree.

Address to the Tooth-Ache. *Text from Stewart, 1802 (pp. 316–17), collated with Currie, iv. 392–3 (following the printing in the* Scots Magazine, *October 1797). A MS recorded by H–H. (ii. 342–4; not traced) in a copy of* Poems 1786 *owned by Lady Blythswood has Currie's version of ll. 15 (with* does *for* may) *and 33,* In a' *at l. 19, and bears* at *ll. 24 and 29. Sub-title not in Currie*
    1 on your envenom'd] upon your venom'd *Currie*   3–5 bang . . . twang] twang . . . pang *Currie*   7–12, 13–18 *transposed in Currie*   7 A' down] Adown *Currie*   8 cast] throw *Currie*   9 While . . . hav'rels] As . . . giglets *Currie*   11 I curse . . . an'] While raving mad, I *Currie*   13 agues freeze us] ague freezes *Currie*   14 colics squeeze us] cholic squeezes *Currie*   15 neebors sympathize, to] neighbour's sympathy may *Currie*   17 thou—the] thee—thou *Currie*   18 They mock] Ay mocks *Currie. See Commentary*   21 laid] rak'd *Currie*

Whare'er that place be, priests ca' hell,   25
Whare a' the tones o' mis'ry yell,
An' plagues in ranked number tell
    In deadly raw,
Thou, *Tooth-ache*, surely bear'st the bell
    Aboon them a'!   30

O! thou grim mischief-makin chiel,
That gars the notes o' discord squeel,
Till human-kind aft dance a reel
    In gore a shoe thick,
Gie a' the faes o' Scotland's weal   35
    A Towmond's Tooth-Ache!

501. English Song—

Tune, Let me in this ae night—

FORLORN, my Love, no comfort near,
    Far, far from thee I wander here;
Far, far from thee, the fate severe
    At which I most repine, Love.—

        Chorus
    O wert thou, Love, but near me,   5
        But near, near, near me;
    How kindly thou wouldst chear me,
        And mingle sighs with mine, Love.—

Around me scowls a wintry sky,
Blasting each bud of hope and joy;   10
And shelter, shade, nor home have I,
    Save in these arms of thine, Love.
        O wert &c.—

26 Whare] Whence *Currie*   mis'ry *Currie*: mis'ry's *Stewart*   27–28 plagues
in ranked number . . . deadly] ranked plagues their numbers . . . dreadfu' *Currie*
30 Aboon] Amang *Currie*   33 human-kind aft] daft mankind aft *Currie*

English Song. *Text from the Dalhousie MS (Dal A; letter to Thomson, June 1795),
collated with Currie, iv. 246, and corrected from MS Dal B (ll. 13–16 only; letter to
Thomson, 3 August 1795). H–H. record a further MS with the earlier version of
ll. 13–14*
    10 Blasting] That blasts *Thomson's alteration in Dal A, Currie*   joy] *correct-
ing* sky *in Dal A*

Cold, alter'd friends with cruel art
Poisoning fell Misfortune's dart;—
Let me not break thy faithful heart,   15
And say that fate is mine, Love.—
O wert &c.—

But dreary tho' the moments fleet,
O let me think we yet shall meet!
That only ray of solace sweet
Can on thy Chloris shine, Love!   20
O wert &c.—

502. Scotch Song—

Now Spring has clad the grove in green,
   And strewed the lea wi' flowers:
The furrow'd waving corn is seen
   Rejoice in fostering showers.
While ilka thing in Nature join   5
   Their sorrows to forego,
O why thus all alone are mine
   The weary steps o' woe.—

The trout within yon wimpling burn
   That glides, a silver dart,   10
And safe beneath the shady thorn
   Defies the angler's art:
My life was ance that careless stream,
   That wanton trout was I;
But Love wi' unrelenting beam   15
   Has scorch'd my fountains dry.—

13-14 Cold . . . dart;—] Dal B. Dal A and Currie have
   Cold, alter'd friendship's cruel part,
   To poison Fortune's ruthless dart—

Scotch Song. *Text from the Dalhousie MS (Dal; letter to Alexander Cunningham, 3 August 1795), collated with the Cowie MS (letter to Mrs. Riddell, summer 1795) and SC, 1799 (91). First-line title in SC. The Cowie MS contains three 'detached Stanzas' only (ll. 9–32)*
   1 Spring has clad] *correcting* Nature cleeds *in Dal*   9 within yon] *correcting* that in yon *in Dal:* in yonder *Cowie*

The little floweret's peaceful lot
  In yonder cliff that grows,
Which save the linnet's flight, I wot,
  Nae ruder visit knows,   20
Was mine; till Love has o'er me past,
  And blighted a' my bloom,
And now beneath the withering blast
  My youth and joy consume.—

The waken'd lav'rock warbling springs   25
  And climbs the early sky,
Winnowing blythe her dewy wings
  In morning's rosy eye;
As little reckt I sorrow's power,
  Until the flowery snare   30
O' witching love, in luckless hour,
  Made me the thrall o' care.—

O had my fate been Greenland snows,
  Or Afric's burning zone,
Wi' man and nature leagu'd my foes,   35
  So Peggy ne'er I'd known!
The wretch whase doom is, hope nae mair,
  What tongue his woes can tell;
Within whase bosom save Despair
  Nae kinder spirits dwell.—   40

29 As *Cowie SC: Dal defective*   31 O' *Cowie*: Of *SC: Dal defective*
witching] *correcting* luckless *in Cowie*

503. Scotish Ballad—

Tune, the Lothian Lassie

Lively

Last May a braw wooer cam down the lang glen,
  And sair wi' his love he did deave me;
I said, there was naething I hated like men,
  The deuce gae wi'm, to believe me, believe me,
  The deuce gae wi'm, to believe me.   5

He spak o' the darts in my bonie black een,
  And vow'd for my love he was dying;
I said, he might die when he liked for JEAN—
  The Lord forgie me for lying, for lying,
  The Lord forgie me for lying!   10

A weel-stocked mailen, himsel for the laird,
  And marriage aff-hand, were his proffers:
I never loot on that I kend it, or car'd,
  But thought I might hae waur offers, waur offers,
  But thought I might hae waur offers.   15

Scotish Ballad. Text from the Dalhousie MS (Dal; letter to Thomson, 3 July 1795), collated with the Kilmarnock MS (Kil), SC, 1799 (52), Currie (iv. 248–50), and SMM 1803 (522). Title in Kil A Ballad; *first-line titles in SC and SMM. See Commentary*
  1 Last May] Ae day *SMM*   cam] came *Kil SMM*   3 I] But I *SMM*
4, 5 wi'm] wi' him *SC SMM*   6–10, 11–15 *transposed in SMM*   6 spak
spake *Kil SMM*   in] o' *SMM*   7 And vow'd] An' o *SMM*   8 liked]
liket *SMM*   9, 10 Lord] gude *SMM*   11 weel-stocked] weel stocket *SMM*
for] o't *SMM*   12 marriage] bridal *Kil SMM*   were his proffers] was the
proffer *SMM*   13 it, or] or I *SMM*   14, 15 hae waur offers] get a waur
offer *SMM*

But what wad ye think? in a fortnight or less,
   The deil tak his taste to gae near her!
He up the lang loan to my black cousin, Bess,
   Guess ye how, the jad! I could bear her, could
      bear her,
   Guess ye how, the jad! I could bear her.   20

But a' the niest week as I petted wi' care,
   I gaed to the tryste o' Dalgarnock;
And wha but my fine, fickle lover was there,
   I glowr'd as I'd seen a warlock, a warlock,
   I glowr'd as I'd seen a warlock.   25

But owre my left shouther I gae him a blink,
   Least neebors might say I was saucy:
My wooer he caper'd as he'd been in drink,
   And vow'd I was his dear lassie, dear lassie,
   And vow'd I was his dear lassie.   30

I spier'd for my cousin fu' couthy and sweet,
   Gin she had recover'd her hearin,
And how her new shoon fit her auld shachl't feet;
   But, heavens! how he fell a swearin, a swearin,
   But, heavens! how he fell a swearin.   35

He begged, for Gudesake! I wad be his wife,
   Or else I wad kill him wi' sorrow:
So e'en to preserve the poor body in life,
   I think I maun wed him tomorrow, tomorrow,
   I think I maun wed him tomorrow.—   40

16 wad] do *SMM*   17 The . . . her!] (The . . . her)] *SMM*   tak] 's in
SMM   18 He . . . my] He's down to the castle to *SMM*   lang loan]
Thomson's correction of gateslack *in Dal, SC. See Commentary*   19, 20 Guess
. . . bear] Think how the jade I cou'd endure *SMM*   21 But] An' *SMM*
week] ouk *SMM*   petted] fretted *Currie SMM*   22 Dalgarnock] Dulgarlock
SMM   23 fine . . . lover] bra' . . . wooer *SMM*   24, 25 I . . . I'd] Wha
. . . if he'd *SMM*   26 But] Out *SMM*   gae] gie'd *SMM*   27 Least
neebors might say] Lest neighbour shou'd think *SMM*   29, 30 I was his]
that I was a *SMM*   32 Gin she had] An' if she'd *SMM*   32–35 hearin
. . . swearin] hearing . . . swearing *SC*   33 her new] my auld *SMM with note:*
An old lover   fit] fitted *SMM*   auld] *om. SMM*   34, 35 But, heavens!]
Gude saf' us *SMM*   36 begged, . . . I wad] begg'd me . . . that I'd *SMM*
38 So e'en] An' just *SMM*   39, 40 maun] will *SMM*

504. Fragment

Tune, The Caledonian Hunt's delight—

WHY, why tell thy lover,
 Bliss he never must enjoy;
Why, why undecieve him,
 And give all his hopes the lie?

O why, while fancy, raptured, slumbers,   5
 Chloris, Chloris all the theme,
Why, why would'st thou cruel
 Wake thy lover from his dream.

505. Poetical Inscription, for an Altar to Independence At Kerrouchtry, the seat of Mr. Heron, written in Summer 1795

THOU, of an independent mind
 With soul resolv'd, with soul resigned;
Prepar'd pow'rs proudest frown to brave,
Who wilt not be, nor have a slave;
Virtue alone who dost revere,   5
Thy own reproach alone dost fear,
Approach this shrine, and worship here.

Fragment. *Text from the Dalhousie MS (letter to Thomson, 3 July 1795)*

Poetical Inscription. *Text from Currie, 1800 (iv. 369)*

506. [To Chloris]

Written on the blank leaf of a copy of the last edition of my Poems, presented to the lady whom in so many fictitious reveries of Passion but with the most ardent sentiments of *real* friendship, I have so often sung under the name of—CHLORIS—

'TIS Friendship's pledge, my young, fair
   FRIEND;
Nor thou the gift refuse,
Nor with unwilling ear attend
   The moralising Muse.

Since thou, in all thy youth and charms,   5
   Must bid the world adieu,
(A world 'gainst Peace in constant arms)
   To join the Friendly Few:

Since, thy gay morn of life o'ercast,
   Chill came the tempest's lour;   10
(And ne'er Misfortune's eastern blast
   Did nip a fairer flower:)

Since life's gay scenes must charm no more;
   Still much is left behind,
Still nobler wealth hast thou in store,   15
   THE COMFORTS OF THE MIND!

Thine is the self-approving glow,
   On conscious Honor's part;
And (dearest gift of Heaven below)
   Thine Friendship's truest heart.   20

To Chloris. *Text from the Dalhousie MS (Dal; with letter to Alexander Cunningham, 3 August 1795), collated with the Adam MS, the Cowie MS (defective: lacking ll. 13–18), and Currie (iv. 242–4). Lines 17–20 written in the margin in Dal. Title in Cowie* To Mᵣˢ—, *written on the blank leaf of my Poems*—
   5–8 Since . . . Few:] *following deleted lines in Adam:*
             Since thou, though all in youthful charms
             Bidd'st Public Life adieu,
             And shunn'st a world of woes and harms
             To bless the Friendly few.

   6 Must] Hast *Adam*   8 join] *correcting* bless *in Adam*   10 Chill came] *correcting* Succeeds *in Adam*   13 Since] Though *Adam*   scenes must charm] scenes delight *correcting* pleasures charm *in Adam*   15 nobler . . . in] rich art thou in nobler *Adam*

The joys refin'd of Sense and Taste,
With every Muse to rove:
And doubly were the Poet blest
These joys could he improve.—

507. Song—

Tune, This is no my ain house—

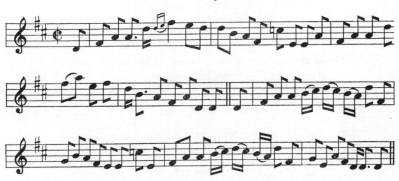

O THIS is no my ain lassie,
    Fair tho' the lassie be:
O weel ken I my ain lassie,
    Kind love is in her e'e.

I see a form, I see a face,   5
Ye weel may wi' the fairest place:
It wants, to me, the witching grace,
    The kind love that's in her e'e.

O this is no my ain lassie,
    Fair tho' the lassie be: 10
Weel ken I my ain lassie,
    Kind love is in her e'e.

24 could] *correcting* should *in Adam*

Song. *Text from the Dalhousie MS (Dal B; letter to Thomson, 3 August 1795), collated with the Dalhousie MS (Dal A; letter to Thomson, 3 July 1795), and SC, 1799 (56). Dal A has ll. 1–8, 13–16 only. First-line title in SC; the song set in 8-line stanzas each beginning with the chorus*
1 O] *added in Dal B*   1–3 lassie] BODY *Dal A*   3 O] *added in Dal B: om. after first stanza in SC*

She's bonie, blooming, straight and tall;
And lang has had my heart in thrall;
And ay it charms my very saul,   15
    The kind love that's in her e'e.
    O this is no &c.

A thief sae pawkie is my Jean
To steal a blink, by a' unseen;
But gleg as light are lovers' een,
    When kind love is in the e'e.   20
    O this is no &c.

It may escape the courtly sparks,
It may escape the learned clerks;
But weel the watching lover marks
    The kind love that's in her e'e.

508. Scotish Song—

I wish my love was in a mire

13 bonie, blooming] blooming, gracefu' *Dal A*   15 charms] chains *Dal A*
Scotish Song. *Text from the Dalhousie MS (letter to Alexander Cunningham, 3*

O BONIE was yon rosy brier,
    That blooms sae far frae haunt o' man;
And bonie she, and ah, how dear!
    It shaded frae the e'enin sun.—

Yon rosebuds in the morning dew   5
    How pure, amang the leaves sae green;
But purer was the lover's vow
    They witness'd in their shade yestreen.—

All in its rude and prickly bower
    That crimson rose how sweet and fair;   10
But love is far a sweeter flower
    Amid life's thorny path o' care.—

The pathless wild, and wimpling burn,
    Wi' Chloris in my arms, be mine;
And I the warld nor wish nor scorn,   15
    Its joys and griefs alike resign.—

509. Song

Tune, Morag—

Slow

August 1795), collated with the Adam MS (letter to Mrs. Riddell, August 1795) and
SC, 1801 (115). First-line title in SC; set to the air The Wee, Wee Man

Song. *Text from Edinburgh University MS Laing II. 210–12 (letter to Cleghorn,*

O WAT ye wha that lo'es me,
   And has my heart a keeping?
O sweet is she that lo'es me,
   As dews o' summer weeping,
   In tears the rosebuds steeping.——   5

Chorus——
O that's the lassie o' my heart,
   My lassie, ever dearer;
O that's the queen o' womankind,
   And ne'er a ane to peer her.——

If thou shalt meet a lassie   10
   In grace and beauty charming,
That e'en thy chosen lassie,
   Erewhile thy breast sae warming,
   Had ne'er sic powers alarming.——
     O that's &c.——

If thou hast heard her talking,   15
   And thy attention's plighted,
That ilka body talking
   But her, by thee is slighted;
   And thou art all delighted.——
     O that's &c.——

If thou hast met this Fair One,   20
   When frae her thou hast parted,
If every other Fair One,
   But her, thou hast deserted,
   And thou art broken hearted.——
O that's the lassie o' my heart,   25
   My lassie, ever dearer:
O that's the queen o' womankind,
   And ne'er a ane to peer her.——

January 1796), collated with the Alloway MS (Al) and SC, 1799 (67). First-line title
in SC. Al consists of ll. 1–5 and 10–14 only, with ll. 8–9 as chorus
    4 dews o' summer] correcting simmer e'enin in Al   5 tears] correcting dews
in Al   8 O] correcting And in Laing   23 But her] cancelled at end of l. 22
in Laing; inserted in l. 23

510. [To John Syme]

[A]. *On refusing to dine with him, after having been promised the first of company, and the first of Cookery, 17th December, 1795.*

No more of your guests, be they titled or not,
    And cook'ry the first in the nation:
Who is proof to thy personal converse and wit,
Is proof to all other temptation.

[B]. *With a present of a dozen of Porter.*

O HAD the malt thy strength of mind,
    Or hops the flavour of thy wit;
'Twere drink for first of human kind,
    A gift that e'en for S**e were fit.

Jerusalem Tavern, Dumfries.

511. On Mr Pit's hair-powder tax

PRAY Billy Pit explain thy rigs,
    This new poll-tax of thine!
'I mean to mark the GUINEA PIGS
    'From other common SWINE.'

512. [The Solemn League and Covenant]

THE Solemn League and Covenant
    Now brings a smile, now brings a tear.
But sacred Freedom, too, was theirs;
    If thou 'rt a slave, indulge thy sneer.

To John Syme. *Texts from Currie, 1801 (iv. 383)*

On Mr Pit's hair-powder tax. *Text from the Huntington Library MS*

The Solemn League and Covenant. *Text from the Dumfries MS (holograph footnote in Sinclair,* Statistical Account of Scotland). *Cunningham, 1834 (iii. 302), has*

> The Solemn League and Covenant
>   Cost Scotland blood—cost Scotland tears:
> But it sealed freedom's sacred cause—
>   If thou 'rt a slave, indulge thy sneers.

513. The Bob o' Dumblane

LASSIE, lend me your braw hemp-heckle,
   And I'll lend you my thripplin kame:
My heckle is broken, it canna be gotten,
   And we'll gae dance the Bob o' Dumblane.—

Twa gaed to the wood, to the wood, to the   5
   wood,
   Twa gaed to the wood, three cam hame:
An't be na weel bobbit, weel bobbit, weel
   bobbit,
An't be na weel bobbit, we'll bob it again.—

514. Poem

Addressed to Mr. Mitchell, Collector of Excise, Dumfries.

FRIEND o' the Poet, tried and leal,
   Wha, wanting thee, might beg, or steal:
Alake! Alake! the meikle Deil
      Wi' a' his witches
Are at it, skelpin! jig and reel,   5
      In my poor pouches.

The Bob o' Dumblane. *Text from the Watson MS (1136; letter to Johnson, autumn
1795)*

Poem. *Text from Dewar's transcript (MS not traced), collated with Currie, 1801 (iv.
386–7). Title from Currie, who dates the poem 1796*

Fu' fain I, modestly, would hint it,
That ONE POUND, ONE, I sairly want it;
If wi' the hizzie down ye sent it,
　　　　It would be kind;　　　　10
And while my heart wi' life-blood dunted,
　　　　I'd bear 't in mind.

So may the AULD YEAR gang out moaning,
To see the NEW come, laden, groaning,
With double plenty, o'er the loaning,　　　　15
　　　　To THEE and THINE;
DOMESTIC PEACE and COMFORT crowning
　　　　The hail DESIGN.

　　　　　　Hogmanai eve: 1795.
　　　　　　R. Burns.

Postscript.

Ye've heard this while how I've been licket,
And by fell Death 'maist nearly nicket;　　　　20
Grim loon! he gat me by the fecket,
　　　　And sair he sheuk;
But by good luck, I lap a wicket,
　　　　And turn'd a neuk.

But by that HEALTH, I've got a share o't!　　　　25
And by that LIFE, I'm promis'd mair o't!
My hale and weel I'll take a care o't
　　　　A tentier way:
So fareweel, FOLLY, hilt and hair o't,
　　　　For ance and ay!　　　　30

　　　　　　R. B.

---

7 Fu' . . . modestly,] I modestly fu' fain *Currie*　　8 POUND,] pound *Currie*
17 COMFORT] comforts *Currie*　　18 *date and signature om. Currie*
20 'maist] was *Currie*　　22 he] me *Currie*　　29 So fareweel, . . . hilt] Then
farewell . . . hide *Currie*

515. The Dean of Faculty—A new Ballad—

Tune, The dragon of Wantley

D<small>IRE</small> was the hate at old Harlaw
    That Scot to Scot did carry;
And dire the discord Langside saw,
    For beauteous, hapless Mary:
But Scot with Scot ne'er met so hot,   5
    Or were more in fury seen, Sir,
Than 'twixt H<small>AL</small> and B<small>OB</small> for the famous job—
    Who should be the F<small>ACULTY</small>'s D<small>EAN</small>, Sir.—

This H<small>AL</small> for genius, wit and lore
    Among the first was number'd;   10
But pious B<small>OB</small>, 'mid Learning's store,
    Commandment the tenth remember'd.
Yet simple B<small>OB</small> the victory got,
    And wan his heart's desire;
Which shews that Heaven can boil the pot   15
    Though the devil piss in the fire.—

The Dean of Faculty. *Text from B.M. MS Egerton 1656, f. 19, collated with Cromek,*
Reliques, *1808 (p. 416)*
    12 the] *om. Cromek*

Squire HAL besides had in this case
  Pretensions rather brassy,
For talents to deserve a place
  Are qualifications saucy;   20
So their Worships of the Faculty,
  Quite sick of Merit's rudeness,
Chose one who should owe it all, d'ye see,
  To their gratis grace and goodness.—

As once on Pisgah purg'd was the sight   25
  Of a son of Circumcision,
So may be, on this Pisgah height,
  Bob's purblind, mental vision:
Nay, BOBBY's mouth may be opened yet
  Till for eloquence you hail him,   30
And swear he has the angel met
  That met the ass of Balaam.—

In your heretic sins may ye live and die,
  Ye heretic Eight and thirty!
But accept, ye Sublime Majority,   35
  My congratulations hearty.—
With your Honors and a certain King
  In your servants this is striking—
The more incapacity they bring,
  The more they're to your liking.—   40

33–40 In . . . liking.] om. Cromek   37 With] correcting Twixt in MS

516. Hey for a lass wi' a tocher

Tune, Balinamona and ora

Awa wi' your witchcraft o' beauty's alarms,
The slender bit beauty you grasp in your arms:
O, gie me the lass that has acres o' charms,
O, gie me the lass wi' the weel-stockit farms.

Chorus
Then hey, for a lass wi' a tocher, then hey, for
a lass wi' a tocher,   5
Then hey, for a lass wi' a tocher; the nice
yellow guineas for me.

Your beauty's a flower, in the morning that blows,
And withers the faster the faster it grows;
But the rapturous charm o' the bonie green knowes,
Ilk Spring they're new deckit wi' bonie white yowes.   10
Then hey &c.

Hey for a lass wi' a tocher. *Text from the Dalhousie MS (letter to Thomson, February
1796), collated with SC, 1799 (100). First-line title in SC; chorus set in four lines. The
MS has a cancelled stanza after l. 6:*
      I grant ye, your Dearie is bonie and braw,
      She's genty, and strappin, and stately witha';
      But see yon strappin oaks at the head o' the shaw,
      Wi' the whack! of an ax how stately they'll fa'.
         Then hey &c.

And e'en when this Beauty your bosom has blest,
The brightest o' beauty may cloy, when possest;
But the sweet yellow darlings wi' Geordie imprest,
The langer ye hae them,—the mair they 're carest!
   Then hey &c.

517. Poem on Life

Addressed to Colonel De Peyster, Dumfries, 1796.

M Y honored colonel, deep I feel
   Your interest in the Poet's weal;
Ah! now sma' heart hae I to speel
         The steep Parnassus,
Surrounded thus by bolus pill,   5
         And potion glasses.

O what a canty warld were it,
Would pain and care, and sickness spare it;
And fortune favor worth and merit,
         As they deserve: 10
(And aye a rowth, roast beef and claret;
         Syne wha would starve?)

Dame life, tho' fiction out may trick her,
And in paste gems and frippery deck her;
Oh! flickering, feeble, and unsicker   15
         I've found her still,
Ay wavering like the willow wicker,
         'Tween good and ill.

Then that curst carmagnole, auld Satan,
Watches, like bawd'rons by a rattan,   20
Our sinfu' saul to get a claute on
         Wi' felon ire;
Syne, whip! his tail ye'll ne'er cast saut on,
         He's off like fire.

Poem on Life. *Text from Currie, 1801 (iv. 389–91)*

Ah! Nick, ah Nick it is na fair,   25
First shewing us the tempting ware,
Bright wines and bonnie lasses rare,
   To put us daft;
Syne weave, unseen, thy spider snare
    O' hell's damned waft.   30

Poor man the flie, aft bizzes bye,
And aft as chance he comes thee nigh,
Thy auld damned elbow yeuks wi' joy,
   And hellish pleasure;
Already in thy fancy's eye,   35
    Thy sicker treasure.

Soon heels o'er gowdie! in he gangs,
And like a sheep-head on a tangs,
Thy girning laugh enjoys his pangs
   And murdering wrestle,   40
As dangling in the wind he hangs
    A gibbet's tassel.

But lest you think I am uncivil,
To plague you with this draunting drivel,
Abjuring a' intentions evil,   45
   I quat my pen:
The Lord preserve us frae the devil!
    Amen! Amen!

518. Here's a health to ane I lo'e dear

Chorus

HERE's a health to ane I lo'e dear,
 Here's a health to ane I lo'e dear;
Thou art sweet as the smile when fond
 lovers meet,
And soft as their parting tear—Jessy.

Here's a health. *Text from the Dalhousie MS (Dal; letter to Thomson, May 1796),*
collated with the Watson MS (1140; letter to Alexander Cunningham, 12 July 1796)
and SC, 1799 (75). In Dal stanza 2 is followed by &c.—&c.—&c.—; and Thomson

1

Although thou maun never be mine,   5
Although even hope is denied;
'Tis sweeter for thee despairing,
Than aught in the warld beside—Jessy.
Here's a health &c.

2

I mourn thro' the gay, gaudy day,
As, hopeless, I muse on thy charms;   10
But welcome the dream o' sweet slumber,
For then I am lockt in thy arms—Jessy.
Here's a health &c.

519–522. [On Jessy Lewars]

[A]   TALK not to me of savages
         From Afric's burning sun,
No savage e'er can rend my heart
As, Jessy, thou hast done.

But Jessy's lovely hand in mine,   5
A mutual faith to plight,
Not even to view the heavenly choir
Would be so blest a sight.

noted on the MS: The Poet it is presumed never went farther with this Song. *An
additional stanza, found among Burns's MSS and printed in Currie (iv. 262) and
later editions of SC, looks like a draft only:*
        I guess by the dear angel smile,
        I guess by the love rolling e'e;
        But why urge the tender confession
        'Gainst fortune's fell cruel decree—
        Jessy!
11 dream] *correcting* hour *in Dal:* hour *Watson*

On Jessy Lewars. *Texts from Cunningham, 1834 (iii. 318–20). Titles in Cunningham:*
[A] Jessy Lewars; [B] The Toast; [C] On Miss Jessy Lewars; [D] The Recovery
of Jessy Lewars. *Title of* [A] *in H–H.* The Menagerie (*See Commentary*)

[A] 3 can *H–H.:* could *Cunningham*

520.

[B]

FILL me with the rosy wine,
    Call a toast—a toast divine;
Give the Poet's darling flame,
Lovely Jessy be the name;
Then thou mayest freely boast,   5
Thou hast given a peerless toast.

521.

[C]

SAY, sages, what's the charm on earth
    Can turn Death's dart aside?
It is not purity and worth,
    Else Jessy had not died.

522.

[D]

BUT rarely seen since Nature's birth,
    The natives of the sky;
Yet still one seraph's left on earth,
    For Jessy did not die.

523. To a Young Lady,
Miss Jessy L——, Dumfries;
With Books which the Bard presented her

THINE be the volumes, Jessy fair,
    And with them take the poet's prayer;
That fate may in her fairest page,
With every kindliest, best presage,
Of future bliss, enroll thy name: 5
With native worth, and spotless fame,
And wakeful caution still aware
Of ill—but chief, man's felon snare;

To a Young Lady. *Text from Currie, 1801 (iv. 381); signature and date from Henley and Henderson, who collated the original in the Rosebery collection*

All blameless joys on earth we find,
And all the treasures of the mind—　　　10
These be thy guardian and reward;
So prays thy faithful friend, *the bard.*
　　　　　　　　　　ROBERT BURNS.
June 26ᵗʰ 1796

524. [Oh wert thou in the cauld blast]

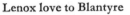

Lenox love to Blantyre

Slowish

O   H wert thou in the cauld blast,
　　　On yonder lea, on yonder lea;
My plaidie to the angry airt,
　　I'd shelter thee, I'd shelter thee:
Or did misfortune's bitter storms　　　5
　　Around thee blaw, around thee blaw,
Thy bield should be my bosom,
　　To share it a', to share it a'.

Or were I in the wildest waste,
　　Sae black and bare, sae black and bare,　　10
The desart were a paradise,
　　If thou wert there, if thou wert there.
Or were I monarch o' the globe,
　　Wi' thee to reign, wi' thee to reign;
The brightest jewel in my crown,　　　15
　　Wad be my queen, wad be my queen.

Oh wert thou in the cauld blast. *Text from Currie, 1801 (iv. 380)*

525. Song

Tune, Rothiemurchie

Chorus

FAIREST maid on Devon banks,
    Crystal Devon, winding Devon,
Wilt thou lay that frown aside,
And smile as thou wert wont to do.

1

Full well thou knowest I love thee dear,   5
Couldst thou to malice lend an ear!
O did not Love exclaim, 'Forbear,
'Nor use a faithful lover so.'—
    Fairest maid &c.

2

Then come, thou fairest of the fair,
Those wonted smiles O let me share;   10
And by thy beauteous self I swear,
No love but thine my heart shall know.—

526. To Mr S. McKenzie—

THE friend who wild from Wisdom's way
    The fumes of wine infuriate send,
(Not moony madness more astray)
Who but deplores that hapless friend?

Song. *Text from the Dalhousie MS (letter to Thomson, 12 July 1796), collated with SC, 1801 (121; alternative verses). First-line title in SC. Thomson's note on MS:* These I presume are the last verses which came from the great Bard's pen, as he died very soon after

To Mr S. McKenzie. *Text from the Huntington Library MS, collated with Currie (iv. 388). Title in Currie* Sent to a Gentleman whom he had offended.

The MS is signed RB *and dated* Monday noon. *The recipient's note runs:* Mr Robt Burns with a pretended excuse for having used my character ill—1796—Delivered to me by Mr Syme,—opposite the Inn possessed by Mrs. Riddick, in Bank Street.
    1 who] whom *Currie*   4 friend? *Currie*: friend. *MS*

Mine was th' insensate, frenzied part,   5
(Ah! why did I those scenes outlive,
Scenes so abhorrent to my heart!)
'Tis thine to pity and forgive.—

527. A Fragment—On Glenriddel's Fox breaking
his chain—

T HOU, Liberty, thou art my theme;
    Not such as idle Poets dream,
Who trick thee up a Heathen goddess
That a fantastic cap and rod has:
Such stale conceits are poor and silly;   5
I paint thee out, a Highland filly,
A sturdy, stubborn, handsome dapple,
As sleek 's a mouse, as round 's an apple,
That when thou pleasest can do wonders;
But when thy luckless rider blunders,   10
Or if thy fancy should demur there,
Wilt break thy neck ere thou go further.—

These things premis'd, I sing a fox,
Was caught among his native rocks,
And to a dirty kennel chain'd,   15
How he his liberty regain'd.—

Glenriddel, a Whig without a stain,
A Whig in principle and grain,
Couldst thou enslave a free-born creature,
A native denizen of Nature?   20
How couldst thou with a heart so good,
(A better ne'er was sluic'd with blood)
Nail a poor devil to a tree,
That ne'er did harm to thine or thee?

6 did] should *Currie*

A Fragment. *Text from the Glenriddell MS (pp. 146–9)*
    3 up] *correcting* out *in MS*   19 Couldst] *correcting catchword* How *in MS*

The staunchest Whig Glenriddel was,   25
Quite frantic in his Country's cause;
And oft was Reynard's prison passing,
And with his brother Whigs canvassing
The Rights of Men, the Powers of Women,
With all the dignity of Freemen.——   30

Sir Reynard daily heard debates
Of Princes' kings' and Nations' fates;
With many rueful, bloody stories
Of tyrants, Jacobites and tories:
From liberty how angels fell,   35
That now are galley-slaves in hell;
How Nimrod first the trade began
Of binding Slavery's chains on Man;
How fell Semiramis, G–d d–mn her!
Did first with sacreligious hammer,   40
(All ills till then were trivial matters)
For Man dethron'd forge hen-peck fetters;
How Xerxes, that abandon'd tory,
Thought cutting throats was reaping glory,
Untill the stubborn Whigs of Sparta   45
Taught him great Nature's Magna charta;
How mighty Rome her fiat hurl'd,
Resistless o'er a bowing world,
And kinder than they did desire,
Polish'd mankind with sword and fire: 50
With much too tedious to relate,
Of Ancient and of Modern date,
But ending still how Billy Pit,
(Unlucky boy!) with wicked wit,
Has gagg'd old Britain, drain'd her coffer,   55
As butchers bind and bleed a heifer.——

Thus wily Reynard by degrees,
In kennel listening at his ease,
Suck'd in a mighty stock of knowledge,
As much as some folks at a college.——   60
Knew Britain's rights and constitution,
Her aggrandizement, diminution,

How fortune wrought us good from evil;
Let no man then despise the devil,
As who should say, I ne'er can need him;   65
Since we to scoundrels owe our freedom.—

528. [To Captain Riddell]

Ellisland: Monday Even:

YOUR News and Review, Sir, I've read through and
  through, Sir,
With little admiring or blaming:
The Papers are barren of home-news or foreign,
No murders or rapes worth the naming.—

Our friends the Reviewers, those Chippers and Hewers,   5
Are judges of Mortar and Stone, Sir;
But of *meet*, or *unmeet*, in a *Fabrick* complete,
I'll boldly pronounce they are none, Sir.—

My Goose-quill too rude is to tell all your goodness
Bestowed on your servant, The Poet;   10
Would to God I had one like a beam of the Sun,
And then all the World should know it!
                              ROBT. BURNS

529. [Reply to Robert Riddell]

[Dear Bard
          To ride this day is vain
For it will be a steeping rain
    So come and sit with me
Wee'l twa or three leaves fill up with scraps
And whiles fill up the time with Cracks
    And spend the day with glee.
                              R. R.]

To Captain Riddell. *Text from the Liverpool City Library MS, collated with Cromek,* Reliques, *1808 (p. 401). Subtitle in Cromek* (Extempore Lines on returning a News-paper).
    6 and] *correcting* or *in MS*   12 World should] World, Sir, should *Cromek:* Sir *inserted in MS in another hand*

Reply to Robert Riddell. *Text of invitation and reply from Scott Douglas's facsimile of the original MS (ii. 198–9). Burns's lines are on the verso*

Ellisland

DEAR Sir, at ony time or tide
    I'd rather sit wi' you than ride,
Tho' 'twere wi' royal Geordie:
And trowth your kindness soon and late
Aft gars me to mysel look blate—   5
THE LORD IN HEAVEN REWARD YE!
                R. BURNS.

530. [Grim Grizzle]

GRIM Grizzel was a mighty Dame
    Weel kend on Cluden-side:
Grim Grizzel was a mighty Dame
    O' meikle fame and pride.

When gentles met in gentle bowers   5
    And nobles in the ha',
Grim Grizzel was a mighty Dame,
    The loudest o' them a'.

Where lawless Riot rag'd the night
    And Beauty durst na gang,   10
Grim Grizzel was a mighty Dame
    Wham nae man e'er wad wrang.

Nor had Grim Grizzel skill alane
    What bower and ha' require;
But she had skill, and meikle skill,   15
    In barn and eke in byre.

Ae day Grim Grizzel walkèd forth,
    As she was wont to do,
Alang the banks o' Cluden fair,
    Her cattle for to view.   20

The cattle sh— o'er hill and dale
    As cattle will incline,
And sair it grieved Grim Grizzel's heart
    Sae muckle muck to tine.

Grim Grizzle. *Text from H–H., ii. 459–61. See Commentary*

And she has ca'd on John o' Clods,   25
    Of her herdsmen the chief,
And she has ca'd on John o' Clods,
    And tell'd him a' her grief:—

'Now wae betide thee, John o' Clods!
    I gie thee meal and fee,   30
And yet sae meikle muck ye tine
    Might a' be gear to me!

'Ye claut my byre, ye sweep my byre,
    The like was never seen;
The very chamber I lie in   35
    Was never half sae clean.

'Ye ca' my kye adown the loan
    And there they a' discharge:
My Tammy's hat, wig, head and a'
    Was never half sae large!   40

'But mind my words now, John o' Clods,
    And tent me what I say:
My kye shall sh— ere they gae out,
    That shall they ilka day.

'And mind my words now, John o' Clods,   45
    And tent now wha ye serve;
Or back ye 'se to the Colonel gang,
    Either to steal or starve.'

Then John o' Clods he lookèd up
    And syne he lookèd down;   50
He lookèd east, he lookèd west,
    He lookèd roun' and roun'.

His bonnet and his rowantree club
    Frae either hand did fa';
Wi' lifted een and open mouth   55
    He naething said at a'.

At length he found his trembling tongue,
    Within his mouth was fauld:—
'Ae silly word frae me, madam,
    Gin I daur be sae bauld.   60

'Your kye will at nae bidding sh—,
    Let me do what I can;
Your kye will at nae bidding sh—
    Of onie earthly man.

'Tho' ye are great Lady Glaur-hole,   65
    For a' your power and art
Tho' ye are great Lady Glaur-hole,
    They winna let a fart.'

'Now wae betide thee, John o' Clods!
    An ill death may ye die!   70
My kye shall at my bidding sh—,
    And that ye soon shall see.'

Then she's ta'en Hawkie by the tail,
    And wrung wi' might and main,
Till Hawkie rowted through the woods   75
    Wi' agonising pain.

'Sh—, sh—, ye bitch,' Grim Grizzel roar'd,
    Till hill and valley rang;
'And sh—, ye bitch,' the echoes roar'd
    Lincluden wa's amang.   80

531. Burns grace at Kirkudbright

SOME have meat and cannot eat,
    Some can not eat that want it:
But we have meat and we can eat,
    Sae let the Lord be thankit.

Burns grace. *Text from the Grierson Papers* (Robert Burns: His Associates and Contemporaries, *ed. R. T. Fitzhugh, 1943, p. 49*)

532. [Graces——at the Globe Tavern]

Before Dinner

O LORD, when hunger pinches sore,
  Do thou stand us in stead,
And send us from thy bounteous store
  A tup- or wether-head!

               Amen.

After Dinner.

[A]

O LORD, since we have feasted thus,
  Which we so little merit,
Let Meg now take away the flesh,
  And Jock bring in the spirit!

               Amen.

[B]

L—D, we [thee] thank an' thee adore
  For temp'ral gifts we little merit;
At present we will ask no more,
  Let *William Hislop give the spirit.*

[Lines *Written on windows of the Globe Tavern, Dumfries*]

533. [A]

THE greybeard, old wisdom, may boast of his treasures,
  Give me with gay folly to live;
I grant him his calm-blooded, time-settled pleasures,
  But folly has raptures to give.

Graces. *Text of* Before Dinner *and* After Dinner [A] *from* Chambers, *1851 (iv. 50).*
Text of After Dinner [B] *from* Stewart, *1802 (p. 304; title* A Grace). *A variant of*
[A] *was published in the* Literary Magnet, *N.S., i (1826), 12:*

    O Lord, we do Thee humbly thank
      For that we little merit:
    Now Jean may take the flesh away,
      And Will bring in the spirit.

Lines. *Text of A, C and D from* Stewart, *1802 (p. 302; from the originals then at the*
Globe Tavern). *Text of B from the* Glenriddell MS, *p. 20, collated with the* Alloway
MS *and* Stewart. *Title in* Alloway On the great Recruiting in the year 17— during
the American war.—Tune, Gillicrankie—. *Lines 9–16 not in* Stewart

534. [B] Song—

I MURDER hate by field or flood,
   Tho' glory's name may screen us;
In wars at home I'll spend my blood,
   Life-giving wars of Venus:
The deities that I adore   5
   Are social Peace and Plenty;
I'm better pleased *to make one more,*
   Than be the death of twenty.—

I would not die like Socrates,
   For all the fuss of Plato;   10
Nor would I with Leonidas,
   Nor yet would I with Cato:
The Zealots of the Church, or State,
   Shall ne'er my mortal foes be,
But let me have bold *ZIMRI's fate,   15
   Within the arms of COSBI!—

535. [C]

MY bottle is a holy pool,
   That heals the wounds o' care an' dool;
And pleasure is a wanton trout,
An ye drink it, ye'll find him out.

536. [D]

IN politics if thou would'st mix,
   And mean thy fortunes be;
Bear this in mind, be deaf and blind,
   Let great folks hear and see.

* Vide. Numbers Chap. 25th Verse 8th—15th.—

537. Lines *Written on a window, at the King's Arms Tavern, Dumfries*

YE men of wit and wealth, why all this sneering
    'Gainst poor Excisemen? give the cause a hearing:
What are your landlords' rent-rolls? taxing ledgers:
    What premiers, what? even Monarchs' mighty gaigers:
Nay, what are priests? those seeming godly wisemen: 5
What are they, pray? but spiritual Excisemen.

538. [You're welcome, Willie Stewart]

[Chorus]   YOU'RE welcome, Willie Stewart,
            You're welcome, Willie Stewart;
        There's ne'er a flower that blooms in May
        That's half sae welcome 's thou art.

Come, bumpers high, express your joy,   5
    The bowl we maun renew it;
The tappit-hen gae bring her ben,
    To welcome Willie Stewart.

May foes be strang, and friends be slack,
    Ilk action may he rue it;   10
May woman on him turn her back,
    That wrangs thee, Willie Stewart.

539. [At Brownhill Inn]

AT Brownhill we always get dainty good cheer
    And plenty of bacon each day in the year;
We've a' thing that's nice, and mostly in season—
But why always *Bacon?*—come, tell me a reason.

Lines. *Text from Stewart, 1802 (p. 303)*
    3 landlords'] landlords *Stewart*   4 Monarchs'] Monarchs *Stewart*
6 they,] they *Stewart*

You're welcome, Willie Stewart. *Text from Lockhart, 1830 (p. 220)*

At Brownhill Inn. *Text from Chambers–Wallace, 1896 (iv. 60)*

540. On W—— Gr–h–m Esq: of M–sskn–w

'STOP thief!' dame Nature called to Death,
As Willie drew his latest breath:
How shall I make a fool again—
My choicest model thou hast ta'en.—

541. [Epitaph on Mr. Burton]

HERE, cursing swearing Burton lies,
A buck, a beau, or *Dem my eyes!*
Who in his life did little good,
And his last words were, *Dem my blood!*

542. Epitaph on D—— C——

HERE lies in earth a root of H–ll,
Set by the Deil's ain dibble;
This worthless body d——d himsel,
To save the L—d the trouble.

543. *Epitaph Extempore, On a person nicknamed the Marquis, who desired Burns to write one on him*

HERE lies a mock Marquis whose titles were shamm'd,
If ever he rise, it will be to be d——'d.

544. Epitaph on J–hn B–shby—

HERE lies J–hn B–shby, *honest man!*
Cheat him devil—if you can.—

On W— Gr–h–m. *Text from the Glenriddell MS (p. 161), collated with the Hunting-ton Library MS (letter to Creech, 30 May 1795)*

Epitaph on Mr. Burton. *Text from Scott Douglas (iii. 207)*

Epitaph on D—— C——. *Text from Stewart, 1802 (p. 252), collated with Cunning-ham, 1834 (iii. 317). Title in Cun* On a Suicide
  1 Here . . . root] Earth'd up here lies an imp *Cun*   2 Set . . . ain] Planted
by Satan's *Cun*   3 This . . . d——d] Poor silly wretch, he's damn'd *Cun*

Epitaph Extempore. *Text from Stewart, 1802 (p. 303)*

Epitaph. *Text from the Huntington Library MS (with letter to Creech, 30 May 1795), collated with the Glenriddell MS (p. 162) and Stewart, 1802 (p. 303). Title in Stewar*

545. On Captn L——lles—

WHEN L——lles thought fit from this world to depart,
Some friends warmly spoke of embalming his heart;
A bystander whispers—'Pray don't make so much o't,
'The subject is *poison*, no reptile will touch it.'—

546. [On John M'Murdo]

BLEST be M'Murdo to his latest day!
No envious cloud o'ercast his evening ray;
No wrinkle furrowed by the hand of care,
Nor ever sorrow add one silver hair!
O, may no son the father's honour stain,
Nor ever daughter give the mother pain!

547. [On Gabriel Richardson]

HERE brewer Gabriel's fire's extinct,
And empty all his barrels:
He's blest—if as he brew'd he drink—
In upright, honest morals.

548. On Commissary Goldie's Brains

LORD, to account who dares Thee call,
Or e'er dispute Thy pleasure?
Else, why within so thick a wall
Enclose so poor a treasure?

EPITAPH On J——n B——y, Writer, D——s. *Alexander Young's copy, got . . .
soon after it was made from my friend Mr. John Syme, had* Catch him devil *in l. 2*

On Captn L——lles. *Text from the Huntington Library MS (with letter to Creech, 30
May 1795), collated with the Glenriddell MS (p. 161)*
    3 o't] on't *Glenriddell*

On John M'Murdo. *Text from Cunningham, 1834 (iii. 114, note). See Commentary*

On Gabriel Richardson. *Text from Cunningham, 1834 (iii. 312). Henley and Henderson say that* honest (*l. 4*) *is erroneous, and read* virtuous

On Commissary Goldie's Brains. *Text from Chambers–Wallace, 1896 (iv. 311)*

549. The Hue and Cry of John Lewars—

A poor man ruined and undone by Robbery and Murder. Being an aweful WARNING to the young men of this age, how they look well to themselves in this dangerous, terrible WORLD.—

A THIEF, AND A MURDERER! stop her who can!
    Look well to your lives and your goods!
Good people, ye know not the hazard you run,
    'Tis the far-famed and much-noted WOODS.—

While I looked at her eye, for the devil is in it,   5
    In a trice she whipt off my poor heart:
Her brow, cheek and lip—in another sad minute,
    My peace felt her murderous dart.—

Her features, I'll tell you them over—but hold!
    She deals with your wizards and books;   10
And to peep in her face, if but once you're so bold,
    There's witchery kills in her looks.—

But softly—I have it—her haunts are well known,
    At midnight so slily I'll watch her;
And sleeping, undrest, in the dark, all alone—   15
    Good lord! the dear THIEF HOW I'LL CATCH HER!

550. [The Keekin' Glass]

H ow daur ye ca' me 'Howlet-face,'
    Ye blear-e'ed, wither'd spectre?
Ye only spied the keekin' glass,
    An' there ye saw your picture.

The Hue and Cry of John Lewars. *Text from the Alloway MS. Foot-notes in (?) Syme's hand:* John Lewars. Land Surveyor in Dumfries; Miss Woods, Governess at Miss M<sup>c</sup>Murdo's boarding school

The Keekin' Glass. *Text from Chambers–Wallace, 1896 (iv. 313; published by Chambers, 1851)*

551. [Inscription on a Goblet]

THERE's death in the cup—sae beware!
　Nay, more—there is danger in touching;
But wha can avoid the fell snare?
　The man and his wine's sae bewitching!

552. [On Andrew Turner]

IN Se'enteen Hunder 'n Forty-Nine
　The Deil gat stuff to mak a swine,
　　An' coost it in a corner;
But wilily he chang'd his plan,
An' shap'd it something like a man,
　An' ca'd it Andrew Turner.

553. [The Toadeater]

NO more of your titled acquaintances boast,
　　Nor of the gay groups you have seen;
A crab louse is but a crab louse at last,
　Tho' stack to the 　　　of a Queen.

Inscription on a Goblet. *Text from Cunningham, 1834 (iii. 305)*

On Andrew Turner. *Text from Chambers–Wallace, 1896 (iv. 316)*

The Toadeater. *Text from the Grierson Papers; editor's punctuation. Title from Cunningham. The earliest printed version is Lockhart's (1830):*

> Of lordly acquaintance you boast,
> 　And the dukes that you dined wi' yestreen,
> Yet an insect 's an insect at most,
> 　Tho' it crawl on the curl of a queen.

Cunningham (iii. 308) has:

> What of earls with whom you have supt,
> 　And of dukes that you dined with yestreen?
> Lord! a louse, Sir, is still but a louse,
> 　Though it crawl on the curls of a queen.

Chambers (1838) has Grierson's version of l. 1, And what nobles and gentles you've seen *in l. 2, and a variant of Lockhart's version in ll. 3–4. See Commentary*

XIII

LAST SONGS FOR *THE SCOTS MUSICAL MUSEUM*

554. The lovely lass o' Inverness—

Slow

THE luvely Lass o' Inverness,
  Nae joy nor pleasure can she see;
For e'en and morn she cries, Alas!
  And ay the saut tear blins her e'e:
Drumossie moor, Drumossie day,   5
  A waefu' day it was to me;
For there I lost my father dear,
  My father dear and brethren three!

Their winding-sheet the bludy clay,
  Their graves are growing green to see;   10
And by them lies the dearest lad
  That ever blest a woman's e'e!

The lovely lass o' Inverness. *Text from the Hastie MS, f. 113ʳ, collated with SMM,
1796 (401; signed B), and SC, 1818 (210). Air in SC* Fingal's Lament. *Note to l. 5 in
SC* Drumossie Muir, or Culloden Field, which proved so fatal to the Highland
Clans, fighting under Prince CHARL S STUART, against the English army comman-
ded by the Duke of CUMBERLAND

Now wae to thee, thou cruel lord,
A bludy man I trow thou be;
For mony a heart thou has made sair   15
That ne'er did wrang to thine or thee!

555. Song—

Tune, Cumnock Psalms—

Recitative

in time, very slow

Chorus

in time,

very slow

As I stood by yon roofless tower,
    Where the wa'-flower scents the dewy air,
Where the houlet mourns in her ivy bower,
    And tells the midnight moon her care:

Song. *Text from the Hastie MS, f. 115 (Ha), collated with the Alloway MS (Al), the Washington MS (W; Library of the Scottish Rite of Freemasonry; ll. 1–8 only), SMM, 1796 (405; signed B), and Currie (iv. 344–6). Title in SMM* A Lassie all alone. Recitative, *Written by Rob*^t *Burns; title in Currie* A Vision, *the text given from the poet's MS with his last corrections but without a chorus. The Alloway MS is a fragment (ll. 9–16, 17–20) on the verso of a holograph of* 469

    1 roofless] Abbey *W*   2 dewy] *correcting* gloamin *in W*

Chorus

A lassie all alone was making her moan,   5
　Lamenting our lads beyond the sea; [and a',
In the bluidy wars they fa', and our honor's gane
　And broken-hearted we maun die.—

The winds were laid, the air was still,
　The stars they shot alang the sky;   10
The tod was howling on the hill,
　And the distant-echoing glens reply.—
The lassie &c.

The burn, adown its hazelly path,
　Was rushing by the ruin'd wa',
Hasting to join the sweeping Nith   15
　Whase roarings seem'd to rise and fa'.—
The lassie &c.

The cauld, blae north was streaming forth
　Her lights, wi' hissing, eerie din;
Athort the lift they start and shift,
　Like Fortune's favors, tint as win.—   20
The lassie &c.

Now, looking over firth and fauld,
　Her horn the pale-fac'd Cynthia rear'd,
When, lo, in form of Minstrel auld,
　A stern and stalwart ghaist appear'd.—
The lassie &c.

5 all . . . moan] by her lane with a sigh and a grane *W*   6 Lamenting our]
Lamented the *W*   beyond] *correcting* that's far aw o'er *in W*   7 our honor's
gane and] thc wives are widows *W*   8 broken-hearted we maun] maidens we
may live and *W*   10 shot] shote *Al*   11 tod] fox *Currie*   12 *Chorus in*
Al Still the lassie &c.: A lassie, &c. *SMM*: A *corrected to* still *corrected to* The *in Ha*
13 burn] stream *Currie*   14 wa'] wa's *Currie*   15 Hasting . . . Nith] To
join yon river on the Strath *variant in Currie*   16 Whase . . . fa'] Whase distant roaring swells and fa's *Currie*   16 *Chorus indication in Ha:* A *corrected*
to The   17 blae] blue *Currie*   21–24 *quoted as a* variation *in Currie, whose*
text has two stanzas:

> By heedless chance I turn'd mine eyes,
> 　And, by the moon-beam, shook, to see
> A stern and stalwart ghaist arise,
> 　Attir'd as minstrels wont to be.

And frae his harp sic strains did flow,   25
    Might rous'd the slumbering Dead to hear;
But Oh, it was a tale of woe,
    As ever met a Briton's ear.—
The lassie &c.

He sang wi' joy his former day,
    He weeping wail'd his latter times: 30
But what he said it was nae play,
    I winna ventur't in my rhymes.—
The lassie &c.

556. The Wren's Nest

Slowish

T H E Robin cam to the wren's nest
    And keekit in and keekit in,
O weel's me on your auld pow,
    Wad ye be in, wad ye be in.
Ye'se ne'er get leave to lie without,   5
    And I within, and I within,
As lang's I hae an auld clout
    To row you in, to row you in.

*   *   *   *   *   *

Had I a statue been o' stane,
    His darin look had daunted me;
And on his bonnet grav'd was plain,
    The sacred posy—Liberty!

30 He *correcting* He, *in Ha*

The Wren's Nest. *Text from SMM, 1796 (406; unsigned)*

557. O an ye were dead Gudeman—

Chorus

O AN ye were dead gudeman,
A green turf on your head, gudeman,
I wad bestow my widowhood
Upon a rantin Highlandman.—

There's sax eggs in the pan, gudeman,   5
There's sax eggs in the pan, gudeman;
There's ane to you, and twa to me,
And three to our John Highlandman.—
O an ye &c.

A sheep-head's in the pot, gudeman,
A sheep-head's in the pot, gudeman;   10
The flesh to him the broo to me,
An the horns become your brow, gudeman.—

Chorus to the last verse—

Sing round about the fire wi' a rung she ran,
An rownd about the fire wi' a rung she ran:
Your horns shall tie you to the staw,   15
And I shall bang your hide, gudeman.—

O an ye were dead Gudeman. *Text from the Hastie MS, f. 112, collated with SMM,
1796 (409; unsigned). Title in SMM* O gin ye were dead Gudeman. *Lines 13–16
headed* Cho! *in SMM*

15–16 *follow cancellation in MS:*
Your horns may be a quarter lang,
I wat they're brawly sprung, gudeman.

558. Tam Lin

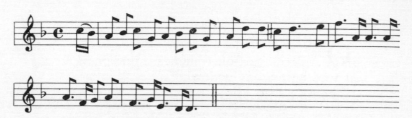

O I forbid you, maidens a'
     That wear gowd on your hair,
To come, or gae by Carterhaugh,
   For young Tom-lin is there.

There's nane that gaes by Carterhaugh   5
   But they leave him a wad;
Either their rings, or green mantles,
   Or else their maidenhead.

Janet has kilted her green kirtle,
   A little aboon her knee;   10
And she has broded her yellow hair
   A little aboon her bree;
And she's awa to Carterhaugh
   As fast as she can hie.

When she cam to Carterhaugh   15
   Tom-lin was at the well,
And there she fand his steed standing
   But away was himsel.

She had na pu'd a double rose,
   A rose but only tway,   20
Till up then started young Tom-lin,
   Says, Lady, thou's pu' nae mae.

Tam Lin. *Text from the Hastie MS, ff. 117–120ʳ, collated with SMM, 1796 (411; unsigned). Set in four-line stanzas throughout in SMM*
4, 16 Tom] *correcting* Tam *in MS:* Tam *SMM passim*

Why pu's thou the rose, Janet,
　And why breaks thou the wand?
Or why comes thou to Carterhaugh   25
　Withoutten my command?

Carterhaugh it is my ain,
　My daddie gave it me;
I'll come and gang by Carterhaugh
　And ask nae leave at thee.   30

Janet has kilted her green kirtle
　A little aboon her knee,
And she has snooded her yellow hair,
　A little aboon her bree,
And she is to her father's ha,   35
　As fast as she can hie.

Four and twenty ladies fair
　Were playing at the ba,
And out then cam the fair Janet,
　Ance the flower amang them a'.   40

Four and twenty ladies fair
　Were playing at the chess,
And out then cam the fair Janet,
　As green as onie glass.

Out then spak an auld grey knight,   45
　Lay o'er the castle-wa,
And says, Alas, fair Janet for thee
　But we'll be blamed a'.

Haud your tongue ye auld-fac'd knight,
　Some ill death may ye die,   50
Father my bairn on whom I will,
　I'll father nane on thee.

Out then spak her father dear,
　And he spak meek and mild,
And ever alas, sweet Janet, he says,   55
　I think thou gaes wi' child.

39 And] *added in MS*

If that I gae wi' child, father,
    Mysel maun bear the blame;
There's ne'er a laird about your ha,
    Shall get the bairn's name.   60

If my Love were an earthly knight,
    As he's an elfin grey;
I wad na gie my ain true-love
    For nae lord that ye hae.

The steed that my true-love rides on,   65
    Is lighter than the wind;
Wi' siller he is shod before,
    Wi' burning gowd behind.

Janet has kilted her green kirtle
    A little aboon her knee;   70
And she has snooded her yellow hair
    A little aboon her brie;
And she's awa to Carterhaugh
    As fast as she can hie.

When she cam to Carterhaugh,   75
    Tom-lin was at the well;
And there she fand his steed standing,
    But away was himsel.

She had na pu'd a double rose,
    A rose but only tway,   80
Till up then started young Tom-lin,
    Says, Lady thou pu's nae mae.

Why pu's thou the rose Janet,
    Amang the groves sae green,
And a' to kill the bonie babe   85
    That we gat us between.

O tell me, tell me, Tom-lin she says,
    For's sake that died on tree,
If e'er ye was in holy chapel,
    Or Christendom did see.   90

Roxbrugh he was my grandfather,
   Took me with him to bide,
And ance it fell upon a day
   That wae did me betide.

Ance it fell upon a day,   95
   A cauld day and a snell,
When we were frae the hunting come
   That frae my horse I fell.

The queen o' Fairies she caught me,
   In yon green hill to dwell,   100
And pleasant is the fairy-land;
   But, an eerie tale to tell!

Ay at the end of seven years
   We pay a tiend to hell;
I am sae fair and fu' o flesh   105
   I'm fear'd it be mysel.

But the night is Halloween, lady,
   The morn is Hallowday;
Then win me, win me, an ye will,
   For weel I wat ye may.   110

Just at the mirk and midnight hour
   The fairy folk will ride;
And they that wad their truelove win,
   At Milescross they maun bide.

But how shall I thee ken, Tom-lin,   115
   O how my truelove know,
Amang sae mony unco knights
   The like I never saw.

O first let pass the black, Lady,
   And syne let pass the brown;   120
But quickly run to the milk-white steed,
   Pu ye his rider down:

For I'll ride on the milk-white steed,
　　And ay nearest the town;
Because I was an earthly knight   125
　　They gie me that renown.

My right hand will be glov'd, lady,
　　My left hand will be bare;
Cockt up shall my bonnet be,
　　And kaim'd down shall my hair;   130
And thae's the tokens I gie thee,
　　Nae doubt I will be there.

They'll turn me in your arms, lady,
　　Into an ask and adder,
But hald me fast and fear me not,   135
　　I am your bairn's father.

They'll turn me to a bear sae grim,
　　And then a lion bold;
But hold me fast and fear me not,
　　As ye shall love your child.   140

Again they'll turn me in your arms
　　To a red het gaud of airn;
But hold me fast and fear me not,
　　I'll do to you nae harm.

And last they'll turn me, in your arms,   145
　　Into the burning lead;
Then throw me into well-water,
　　O throw me in wi' speed!

And then I'll be your ain truelove,
　　I'll turn a naked knight: 150
Then cover me wi' your green mantle,
　　And cover me out o sight.

Gloomy, gloomy was the night,
　　And eerie was the way,
As fair Jenny in her green mantle   155
　　To Milescross she did gae.

123 I'll . . . the] *correcting* I . . . a *in MS*

About the middle o' the night
  She heard the bridles ring;
This lady was as glad at that
  As any earthly thing.   160

First she let the black pass by,
  And syne she let the brown;
But quickly she ran to the milk-white steed,
  And pu'd the rider down.

Sae weel she minded what he did say   165
  And young Tom-lin did win;
Syne cover'd him wi' her green mantle
  As blythe's a bird in spring.

Out then spak the queen o' Fairies,
  Out of a bush o' broom;   170
Them that has gotten young Tom-lin,
  Has gotten a stately groom.

Out then spak the queen o' Fairies,
  And an angry queen was she;
Shame betide her ill-fard face,   175
  And an ill death may she die,
For she's ta'en awa the boniest knight
  In a' my companie.

But had I kend, Tom-lin, she says,
  What now this night I see,   180
I wad hae taen out thy twa grey een,
  And put in twa een o' tree.

165 did say] *correcting* had said *in MS*   167 Syne] *correcting* And *in MS*

559. Had I the wyte she bade me

Come kiss with me

Had I the wyte, had I the wyte,
    Had I the wyte, she bade me;
She watch'd me by the hie-gate-side,
    And up the loan she shaw'd me;
And when I wad na venture in,   5
    A coward loon she ca'd me:
Had Kirk and State been in the gate,
    I lighted when she bade me.—

Sae craftilie she took me ben,
    And bade me mak nae clatter;   10
'For our ramgunshoch, glum Goodman
    'Is o'er ayont the water:'
Whae'er shall say I wanted grace,
    When I did kiss and dawte her,
Let him be planted in my place,   15
    Syne, say, I was a fautor.—

Could I for shame, could I for shame,
    Could I for shame refus'd her;
And wad na Manhood been to blame,
    Had I unkindly us'd her: 20

Had I the wyte she bade me. *Text from the Hastie MS, f. 121, collated with SMM,
1796 (415; signed Z). A transcript of lines 13–16 (Cowie MS) is endorsed* On a pane
of glass at Brow

He claw'd her wi' the ripplin-kame,
　And blae and bluidy bruis'd her;
When sic a husband was frae hame,
　What wife but wad excus'd her?

I dighted ay her een sae blue,　　　　　　25
　And bann'd the cruel randy;
And weel I wat her willin mou
　Was e'en like succarcandie.
At glomin-shote it was, I wat,
　I lighted on the Monday;　　　　　　　30
But I cam thro' the Tiseday's dew
　To wanton Willie's brandy.—

560. Comin thro' the rye

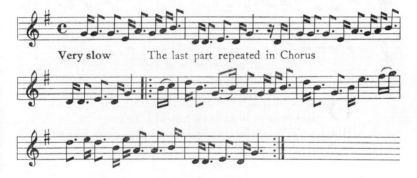

Very slow　　The last part repeated in Chorus

Comin thro' the rye, poor body,
　Comin thro' the rye,
She draigl't a' her petticoatie
　Comin thro' the rye.
　　Oh Jenny's a' weet, poor body,　　　5
　　Jenny's seldom dry;
　　She draigl't a' her petticoatie
　　Comin thro' the rye.

31 Tiseday's] *correcting* Tyseday's *in MS*

Comin thro' the rye. *Text from SMM, 1796 (417; signed B). Punctuation supplied in ll. 2, 6, 12*

Gin a body meet a body
Comin thro' the rye,   10
Gin a body kiss a body
Need a body cry.
    Cho.ᵉ Oh Jenny's a' weet, &c.

Gin a body meet a body
Comin thro' the glen;
Gin a body kiss a body   15
Need the warld ken!
    Cho.ᵉ Oh Jenny's a' weet, &c.

561. The rowin 't in her apron

Slow

O U R young lady's a huntin gane,
    Sheets nor blankets has she ta'en,
But she's born her auld son or she cam hame,
And she's row'd him in her apron.—

Her apron was o' the hollan fine,   5
Laid about wi' laces nine;
She thought it a pity her babie should tyne,
And she's row'd him in her apron.—

*The rowin 't in her apron. Text from the Hastie MS, f. 124, collated with the Watson
MS (1143) and SMM, 1796 (424; unsigned). Burns's note on Watson MS* The air of
the following verses is something like, For lake o' Gold, tho' *I suspect it to be a very
different tune. Opening stanza in Watson (followed by ll. 1–4):*

In Edinburgh braes there is a well,
An' it is as sweet as the sugar itsel,
An' our young lady has tasted sae weel
    Till it 's mounted up her apron.

1 a] to the *Watson*   2 has she ta'en] she's ta'en none *Watson*

Her apron was o' the hollan sma,
Laid about wi' laces a',   10
She thought it a pity her babe to let fa,
And she row'd him in her apron.—

   * * * * * *

Her father says within the ha,
Amang the knights and nobles a,
I think I hear a babie ca,   15
 In the chamber amang our young ladies.—

O father dear it is a bairn,
I hope it will do you nae harm,
For the daddie I lo'ed, and he'll lo'e me again,
 For the rowin't in my apron.—   20

O is he a gentleman, or is he a clown,
That has brought thy fair body down,
I would not for a' this town
 The rowin't in thy apron.—

Young Terreagles he's nae clown,   25
He is the toss of Edinborrow town,
And he'll buy me a braw new gown
 For the rowin't in my apron.—

   * * * * * *

Its I hae castles, I hae towers,
I hae barns, I hae bowers,   30
A' that is mine it shall be thine,
 For the rowin't in thy apron.—

12 *additional stanza in Watson:*
    To her chamber she did hie,
    Lest her mother should her spy;
    Till loud her sweet babie began for to cry,
     Weel row't up in her apron.

13 says] sat *Watson*   14 knights and nobles] lords an' ladies *Watson*
15 a babie] a young babie *Watson*   19–20 For . . . apron.] *Watson has*
    It smiles sae sweet as it lies in my arm,
     Weel row't up in my apron.

21 O] *not in Watson*   28 the] *not in Watson*   29–32 Its I . . . apron.]
Watson has

    I hae bow'rs an' castles fine,
    All that is mine it shall be thine;
    For the game it was guid an' we'll try it again,
     An' we'll row't once more i' your apron.

562. Charlie he's my darling

Lively

'T WAS on a monday morning,
    Right early in the year,
That Charlie cam to our town,
    The young Chevalier.—

Chorus
An' Charlie he's my darling, my darling, my darling,   5
Charlie he's my darling, the young Chevalier.—

As he was walking up the street,
    The city for to view,
O there he spied a bonie lass
    The window looking thro'.—   10
An Charlie &c.

Sae light's he jimped up the stair,
    And tirled at the pin;
And wha sae ready as hersel
    To let the laddie in.—
    An Charlie &c.

He set his Jenny on his knee,   15
    All in his Highland dress;
For brawlie weel he ken'd the way
    To please a bonie lass.—
    An Charlie &c.

Charlie he's my darling. *Text from the Hastie MS, f. 126, collated with SMM, 1796*
(*428; unsigned*)

Its up yon hethery mountain,
  And down yon scroggy glen,   20
We daur na gang a milking,
  For Charlie and his men.—
  An Charlie &c.

563. The Lass of Ecclefechan

Lively

G AT ye me, O gat ye me,
    O gat ye me wi' naethin,
Rock and reel and spinnin wheel
    A mickle quarter bason.
Bye attour, my Gutcher has   5
    A hich house and a laigh ane,
A' for bye, my bonnie sel,
    The toss of Ecclefechan.

O had your tongue now Luckie Laing,
    O had your tongue and jauner;   10
I held the gate till you I met,
    Syne I began to wander:
I tint my whistle and my sang,
    I tint my peace and pleasure;
But your green graff, now Luckie Laing,   15
    Wad airt me to my treasure.

The Lass of Ecclefechan. *Text from SMM, 1796 (430; unsigned), collated with the Hastie MS, f. 127. The MS has ll. 9–16 only, with a note* I believe I sent only the first stanza—

564. We'll hide the Couper behint the door—

Tune, Bab at the bowster—

Chorus

WE'LL hide the Couper behint the door,
   Behint the door, behint the door;
We'll hide the Couper behint the door,
   And cover him under a mawn O.—

The Couper o' Cuddy cam here awa,   5
   He ca'd the girrs out o'er us a';
And our gudewife has gotten a ca'
   That's anger'd the silly gudeman O.—
      We'll hide &c.

He sought them out, he sought them in,
   Wi', deil hae her! and, deil hae him!   10
But the body he was sae doited and blin',
   He wist na whare he was gaun O.—
      We'll hide &c.

We'll hide the Couper. *Text from the Hastie MS, f. 129ʳ, collated with SMM, 1796* (*431; unsigned*). *Title in SMM* The Couper o' Cuddy
   1, 2, 3 behint] *correcting* behind *in MS:* behind *SMM*

They couper'd at e'en, they couper'd at morn,
  Till our gudeman has gotten the scorn;
On ilka brow she's planted a horn,   15
  And swears that there they shall stan' O.—
  We'll hide &c.

565. Leezie Lindsay

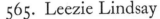
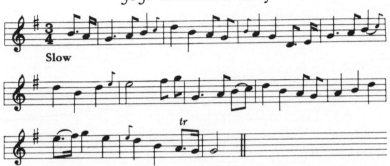

WILL ye go to the Highlands Leezie Lindsay,
    Will ye go to the Highlands wi' me;
Will ye go to the Highlands Leezie Lindsay,
  My pride and my darling to be.
        *   *   *   *   *   *

566. For the sake o' Somebody—

Leezie Lindsay. *Text from SMM, 1796 (434; unsigned)*

For the sake o' Somebody. *Text from the Hastie MS, f. 130, collated with SMM,
1796 (436; signed B)*

Mʏ heart is sair, I dare na tell,
   My heart is sair for Somebody;
I could wake a winter-night
   For the sake o' Somebody.—
      Oh-hon! for Somebody!   5
      Oh-hey! for Somebody!
I could range the warld round,
   For the sake o' Somebody.—

Ye Powers that smile on virtuous love,
   O, sweetly smile on Somebody!   10
Frae ilka danger keep him free,
   And send me safe my Somebody.—
      Ohon! for Somebody!
      Ohey! for Somebody!
I wad do—what wad I not—   15
   For the sake o' Somebody!

567. The cardin o't—

1 I *SMM*: & *MS*   3 I *SMM*: But I *MS*   4 the sake *SMM*: a sight *MS*
16 sake o'] sake o' Sake o' *MS*

The cardin o't. *Text from the Hastie MS, f. 131, collated with SMM, 1796 (437;
signed Z)*

I coft a stane o' haslock woo,
To mak a wab to Johnie o't;
For Johnie is my onlie jo,
I lo'e him best of onie yet.—

Chorus—

The cardin o't, the spinnin o't,   5
The warpin o't, the winnin o't;
When ilka ell cost me a groat,
The taylor staw the lynin o't.—

For though his locks be lyart grey,
And though his brow be beld aboon,   10
Yet I hae seen him on a day
The pride of a' the parishon.—
The cardin &c.

568. Sutors o' Selkirk—

Sutors o' Selkirk. *Text from the Hastie MS, f. 132, collated with SMM, 1796 (438 unsigned)*

ITS up wi' the Sutors o Selkirk,
  And down wi' the Earl o' Hume;
And here is to a' the braw laddies
  That wear the single sol'd shoon:
Its up wi' the Sutors o' Selkirk,   5
  For they are baith trusty and leal;
And up wi' the lads o' the Forest,
  And down wi' the Merse to the deil.—

＊   ＊   ＊   ＊   ＊   ＊

569. Tibbie Fowler

Slow

TIBBIE Fowler o' the glen,
  There's o'er mony wooin at her,
Tibbie Fowler o' the glen,
  There's o'er mony wooin at her.

Chorus

Wooin at her, pu'in at her,   5
  Courtin at her, canna get her:
Filthy elf, it's for her pelf,
  That a' the lads are wooin at her.

1, 5 Its] *added in MS*   3 laddies *SMM*: lads *MS*

Tibbie Fowler. *Text from SMM, 1796 (440; unsigned), where the stanzas are set as
long-lined couplets*

Ten cam east, and ten cam west,
  Ten came rowin o'er the water;   10
Twa came down the lang dyke side,
  There's twa and thirty wooin at her.
    Wooin at her, &c.

There's seven but, and seven ben,
  Seven in the pantry wi' her;
Twenty head about the door,   15
  There's ane and forty wooin at her.
    Wooin at her, &c.

She's got pendles in her lugs,
  Cockle-shells wad set her better;
High-heel'd shoon and siller tags,
  And a' the lads are wooin at her.   20
    Wooin at her, &c.

Be a lassie e'er sae black,
  An she hae the name o' siller,
Set her upo' Tintock-tap,
  The wind will blaw a man till her.
    Wooin at her, &c.

Be a lassie e'er sae fair,   25
  An she want the pennie siller;
A flie may fell her in the air,
  Before a man be even till her.
    Wooin at her, &c.

570. There's three true gude fellows

T HERE's three true gude fellows,
There's three true gude fellows,
There's three true gude fellows
Down ayont yon glen.

Its now the day is dawin,   5
But or night do fa' in,
Whase cock's best at crawin,
Willie thou sall ken.
There's three, &c.

571. The bonie lass made the bed to me—

There's three true gude fellows. *Text from SMM, 1796 (442; unsigned). Title in SMM* There's three gude fellow ayont yon glen. *SMM repeats chorus in full after l. 8*
6 do fa' in] to fain *SMM*

The bonie lass made the bed to me. *Text from the Hastie MS, f. 135, collated with SMM, 1796 (448; unsigned), Stewart, 1801 (pp. 63–65; S1) and 1802 (pp. 202–4; S2). Title in S1 and S2* The Lass that made the Bed to me. A Song: *set in eight-line stanzas*

WHEN Januar wind was blawing cauld,
 As to the north I took my way,
The mirksome night did me enfauld,
 I knew na whare to lodge till day.—

By my gude luck a maid I met,   5
 Just in the middle o' my care;
And kindly she did me invite
 To walk into a chamber fair.—

I bow'd fu' low unto this maid,
 And thank'd her for her courtesie;   10
I bow'd fu' low unto this maid,
 And bade her mak a bed for me.—

She made the bed baith large and wide,
 Wi' twa white hands she spread it down;
She put the cup to her rosy lips   15
 And drank, 'Young man now sleep ye sound.'—

She snatch'd the candle in her hand,
 And frae my chamber went wi' speed;
But I call'd her quickly back again
 To lay some mair below my head.—   20

A cod she laid below my head,
 And served me wi' due respect;
And to salute her wi' a kiss,
 I put my arms about her neck.—

Haud aff your hands young man, she says,   25
 And dinna sae uncivil be:
Gif ye hae ony luve for me,
 O wrang na my virginitie!—

---

1 Januar wind was] January winds were *S1 S2*   2 took] bent *S1 S2*
3 mirksome] darksome *S1 S2*   4 knew] kend *S1 S2*   5 maid] lass *S1 S2*
9 unto this] to this sam' *S1*   11 unto this] to this fair *S1*   14 Wi' twa]
Wi' her twa *S1*   15 lips] lip *S1*   20 below] beneath *S1*   21 below]
beneath *S1*   23 And] Syne *S1*   24 put] flang *S1*   25 she says] said
she *S1*

Her hair was like the links o' gowd,
   Her teeth were like the ivorie,   30
Her cheeks like lillies dipt in wine,
   The lass that made the bed to me.—

Her bosom was the driven snaw,
   Twa drifted heaps sae fair to see;
Her limbs the polish'd marble stane,   35
   The lass that made the bed to me.—

I kiss'd her o'er and o'er again,
   And ay she wist na what to say;
I laid her between me and the wa',
   The lassie thought na lang till day.—   40

Upon the morrow when we rase,
   I thank'd her for her courtesie:
But ay she blush'd, and ay she sigh'd,
   And said, Alas, ye've ruin'd me.—

I clasp'd her waist and kiss'd her syne,   45
   While the tear stood twinklin in her e'e;
I said, My lassie dinna cry,
   For ye ay shall mak the bed to me.—

She took her mither's holland sheets
   And made them a' in sarks to me: 50
Blythe and merry may she be,
   The lass that made the bed to me.—

The bonie lass made the bed to me,
   The braw lass made the bed to me;
I'll ne'er forget till the day that I die   55
   The lass that made the bed to me.—

33–36 follow 37–40 in S1   38 And ay] *correcting* The lassie *in MS*
39 between] 'tween *S1 S2*   43 blush'd . . . sigh'd,] sigh'd and cry'd, 'Alas! *S1*
44 And said, Alas,] 'Alas! young man, *S1 S2*   45 I . . . syne,] I look'd her
in her bonny face *S1*   47 My] Sweet *S1*   48 For] *om. S1*   53 bonie]
braw *S1*   54 braw] bonnie *S1*   55 forget] forsake *S1 S2* that] *om. S1*

572. Sae far awa—

O SAD and heavy should I part,
But for her sake sae far awa;
Unknowing what my way may thwart,
My native land sae far awa.—

Thou that of a' things Maker art, 5
That form'd this Fair sae far awa,
Gie body strength, then I'll ne'er start
At this my way sae far awa.—

How true is love to pure desert,
So love to her, sae far awa: 10
And nocht can heal my bosom's smart,
While Oh, she is sae far awa.—

Nane other love, nane other dart,
I feel, but her's sae far awa;
But fairer never touch'd a heart 15
Than her's, the Fair sae far awa.—

Sae far awa. *Text from the Hastie MS, f. 136, collated with SMM, 1796 (449; signed B)*
7 Gie] Gin *SMM*

573. The Reel o' Stumpie

Lively

W<small>AP</small> and rowe, wap and row,
   Wap and row the feetie o't,
I thought I was a maiden fair,
   Till I heard the greetie o't.

My daddie was a Fiddler fine,   5
   My minnie she made mantie O;
And I mysel a thumpin quine,
   And danc'd the reel o' Stumpie O.

574. I'll ay ca' in by yon town—

The Reel o' Stumpie. *Text from SMM, 1796 (457; unsigned)*
1 row,] row *SMM*

I'll ay ca' in by yon town. *Text from the Hastie MS, f. 137, collated with SMM,
1796 (458; unsigned)*

Chorus

I'LL ay ca' in by yon town,
   And by yon garden green, again;
I'll ay ca' in by yon town,
   And see my bonie Jean again.—

There's nane sall ken, there's nane sall guess,   5
   What brings me back the gate again,
But she, my fairest faithfu' lass,
   And stownlins we sall meet again.—
      I'll ay ca' &c.—

She'll wander by the aiken tree,
   When trystin time draws near again;   10
And when her lovely form I see,
   O haith, she's doubly dear again!
      I'll ay ca' &c.—

575. The rantin laddie—

Slow

A FTEN hae I play'd at the cards and the dice,
   For the love of a bonie rantin laddie;
But now I maun sit in my father's kitchen neuk,
   Below a bastart babie.—

The rantin laddie. *Text from the Hastie MS, f. 140, collated with SMM, 1796 (462; unsigned)*

For my father he will not me own,   5
    And my mother she neglects me,
And a' my friends hae lightlyed me,
    And their servants they do slight me.—

But had I a servant at my command,
    As aft-times I've had many,   10
That wad rin wi' a letter to bonie Glenswood,
    Wi' a letter to my rantin laddie.—

Oh, is he either a laird, or a lord,
    Or is he but a cadie,
That ye do him ca' sae aften by name,   15
    Your bonie, bonie rantin laddie.—

Indeed he is baith a laird and a lord,
    And he never was a cadie;
But he is the Earl o' bonie Aboyne,
    And he is my rantin laddie.—   20

O ye'se get a servant at your command,
    As aft-times ye've had many,
That sall rin wi' a letter to bonie Glenswood,
    A letter to your rantin laddie.—

When lord Aboyne did the letter get,   25
    O but he blinket bonie;
But or he had read three lines of it,
    I think his heart was sorry.—

O wha is he daur be sae bauld,
    Sae cruelly to use my lassie?   30

*   *   *   *   *

*   *   *   *

For her father he will not her know,
    And her mother she does slight her,
And a' her friends hae lightlied her,   35
    And their servants they neglect her.—

23 wi'] *correcting* to *in* MS

Go raise to me my five hundred men,
   Make haste and make them ready;
With a milkwhite steed under every ane,
   For to bring hame my lady.—   40

As they cam in thro Buchan shire,
   They were a company bonie,
With a gude claymore in every hand,
   And O, but they shin'd bonie.—

576. O May thy morn

The Rashes

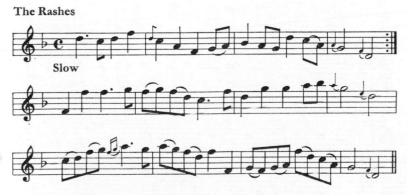

Slow

O MAY, thy morn was ne'er sae sweet,
   As the mirk night o' December;
For sparkling was the rosy wine,
   And private was the chamber:
And dear was she, I dare na name,   5
   But I will ay remember.—
And dear was she, I dare na name,
   But I will ay remember.—

And here's to them, that, like oursel,
   Can push about the jorum;   10
And here's to them that wish us weel,
   May a' that's gude watch o'er them:

O May thy morn. *Text from the Hastie MS, f. 141, collated with SMM, 1796 (464; signed B). Title from SMM*

And here's to them, we dare na tell,
    The dearest o' the quorum.—
And here's to them, we dare na tell,   15
    The dearest o' the quorum.—

577.   As I cam o'er the Cairney mount—

Slow

As I cam o'er the Cairney mount,
    And down amang the blooming heather,
Kindly stood the milkin-shiel
    To shelter frae the stormy weather.—

Chorus

O my bonie Highland lad,   5
    My winsome, weelfar'd Highland laddie;
Wha wad mind the wind and rain,
    Sae weel row'd in his tartan plaidie.—

＊   ＊   ＊   ＊   ＊

As I cam o'er the Cairney mount. *Text from the Hastie MS, f. 143, collated with SMM, 1796 (467; signed Z)*

Now Phebus blinkit on the bent,
And o'er the knowes the lambs were bleating: 10
But he wan my heart's consent,
To be his ain at the neist meeting.—
      O my bonie &c.—

578. Highland laddie—

Brisk

She

T H E bonniest lad that e'er I saw,
    Bonie laddie, highland laddie,
Wore a plaid and was fu' braw,
    Bonie Highland laddie.

On his head a bonnet blue,   5
    Bonie &c.
His royal heart was firm and true,
    Bonie &c.

He

Trumpets sound and cannons roar,
    Bonie lassie, Lawland lassie,   10
And a' the hills wi' echoes roar,
    Bonie Lawland lassie.

Highland laddie. *Text from the Hastie MS, f. 144ʳ, collated with SMM, 1796 (468; unsigned)*
    4, 24 Bonie Highland] *correcting* Bonie laddie Highland *in MS*   6 &c.]
SMM prints in full   12 Bonie Lawland] *correcting* Bonie lassie Lawland *in MS*

Glory, Honor, now invite
    Bonie &c.
For freedom and my King to fight   15
    Bonie &c.

        She

The sun a backward course shall take,
    Bonie laddie &c.
Ere ought thy manly courage shake;
    Bonie laddie &c.   20

Go, for yoursel procure renown,
    Bonie &c.
And for your lawful king his crown,
    Bonie Highland laddie.

579. Lovely Polly Stewart—

Tune, Ye're welcome Charlie Stewart

        Chorus
O LOVELY Polly Stewart!
    O charming Polly Stewart!
There's ne'er a flower that blooms in May
That's hauf sae sweet as thou art.—

Lovely Polly Stewart. *Text from the Hastie MS, f. 146, collated with SMM, 1796*
(471; unsigned)
    4 hauf sae sweet] half so fair *SMM*

The flower it blaws, it fades, it fa's,　　　5
And art can ne'er renew it;
But Worth and Truth eternal youth
Will gie to Polly Stewart.—
O lovely &c.

May he, whase arms shall fauld thy charms,
Possess a leal and true heart!　　　10
To him be given, to ken the Heaven
He grasps in Polly Stewart!
O lovely &c.

580. The Highland balou—

Slow

H EE-balou, my sweet, wee Donald,
Picture o' the great Clanronald;
Brawlie kens our wanton Chief
Wha got my wee Highland thief.—

Leeze me on thy bonie craigie,　　　5
And thou live, thou'll steal a naigie,
Travel the country thro' and thro',
And bring hame a Carlisle cow.—

Thro' the Lawlands, o'er the Border,
Weel, my babie, may thou furder:　　　10
Herry the louns o' the laigh Countrie,
Syne to the Highlands hame to me.—

*　　*　　*　　*　　*

The Highland balou. *Text from the Hastie MS, f. 147, collated with SMM, 1796*
(*472; unsigned*)
4 wee] young *SMM*

581. Bannocks o' bear-meal—

Chorus

Bannocks o' bear meal,
Bannocks o' barley,
Here's to the Highlandman's bannocks o' barley.—

Wha, in a brulzie, will first cry a parley?
Never the lads wi' the bannocks o' barley.—   5
Bannocks o' &c.

Wha, in his wae days, were loyal to Charlie?
Wha but the lads wi' the bannocks o' barley.—
Bannocks o' &c.

*   *   *   *   *

Bannocks o' bear-meal. *Text from the Hastie MS, f. 150, collated with SMM, 1796*
(*475; unsigned*). *In SMM the chorus precedes and follows the verse*
  9 Bannocks o' &c. *SMM: om. MS*

582. Wae is my heart

Very slow

W AE is my heart, and the tear's in my e'e;
Lang, lang joy's been a stranger to me:
Forsaken and friendless my burden I bear,
And the sweet voice o' pity ne'er sounds in my ear.

Love, thou hast pleasures, and deep hae I loved;   5
Love thou hast sorrows, and sair hae I proved:
But this bruised heart that now bleeds in my breast,
I can feel by its throbbings will soon be at rest.—

O, if I were, where happy I hae been;
Down by yon stream and yon bonie castle-green: 10
For there he is wandring, and musing on me,
Wha wad soon dry the tear frae his Phillis's e'e.—

Wae is my heart. *Text from the Hastie MS, f. 151, collated with SMM, 1796 (476; unsigned)*
    2 joy's] has Joy *Scott Douglas*   12 tear . . . e'e.] tear-drop that clings to my e'e. *Scott Douglas*

583A. Here's his health in water

A<small>LTHOUGH</small> my back be at the wa',
      And though he be the fautor,
Although my back be at the wa',
Yet here's his health in water.—

O wae gae by his wanton sides,   5
   Sae brawly's he could flatter;
Till for his sake I'm slighted sair,
   And dree the kintra clatter:
But though my back be at the wa',
   Yet here's his health in water.—   10

*   *   *   *

583B. Here's his health in water

Tune—The job o' journey-wark

A<small>LTHO</small>' my back be at the wa',
      An' tho' he be the fau'tor;
Altho' my back be at the wa',
I'll drink his health in water.

Here's his health in water. *Text from the Hastie MS, f. 128, collated with SMM, 1796 (480; signed Z)*

Here's his health in water. *Text from MMC (pp. 92–93). In his copy of MMC Scott Douglas writes the title of the tune over a reference to SMM*

O wae gae by his wanton sides,   5
  Sae brawly 's he cou'd flatter.
I for his sake am slighted sair,
  An' dree the kintra clatter;
But let them say whate'er they like,
  Yet, here's his health in water.   10

He follow'd me baith out and in,
  Thro' a' the nooks o' Killie;
He follow'd me baith out an' in,
  Wi' a stiff stanin' p–llie.
But when he gat atween my legs,   15
  We made an unco splatter;
An' haith, I trow, I soupled it,
  Tho' bauldly he did blatter;
But now my back is at the wa',
  Yet here's his health in water.   20

584. Gude Wallace

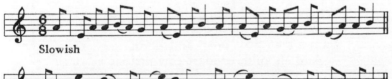

Slowish

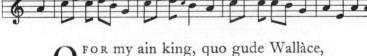

O FOR my ain king, quo gude Wallàce,
  The rightfu king o' fair Scotland;
Between me and my Sovereign Blude
I think I see some ill seed sawn.—

Wallàce out over yon river he lap,   5
  And he has lighted low down on yon plain,
And he was aware of a gay ladie,
  As she was at the well washing.—

7 am] I'm *MMC*   8 dree] drees *MMC*

Gude Wallace. *Text from the Hastie MS, f. 153, collated with SMM, 1796 (484; unsigned)*

What tydins, what tydins, fair lady, he says,
    What tydins hast thou to tell unto me;   10
What tydins, what tydins, fair lady, he says,
    What tydins hae ye in the South Countrie.——

Low down in yon wee Ostler house,
    There is fyfteen Englishmen,
And they are seekin for gude Wallàce,   15
    It's him to take and him to hang.——

There's nocht in my purse, quo gude Wallàce,
    There's nocht, not even a bare pennie;
But I will down to yon wee Ostler house
    Thir fyfteen Englishmen to see.——   20

And when he cam to yon wee Ostler house,
    He bad benedicite be there;

    *   *   *   *   *   *
      *   *   *   *   *

Where was ye born, auld crookit Carl,   25
    Where was ye born, in what countrie;
I am a true Scot born and bred,
    And an auld, crookit carl just sic as ye see.——

I wad gie fyfteen shilling to onie crookit carl,
    To onie crookit carl just sic as ye,   30
If ye will get me gude Wallàce,
    For he is the man I wad very fain see.——

He hit the proud Captain alang the chafft-blade,
    That never a bit o' meat he ate mair;
And he sticket the rest at the table where they sat, 35
    And he left them a' lyin sprawlin there.——

Get up, get up, gudewife, he says,
    And get to me some dinner in haste;
For it will soon be three lang days
    Sin I a bit o' meat did taste.——   40

The dinner was na weel readie,
    Nor was it on the table set,
Till other fyfteen Englishmen
    Were a' lighted about the yett.—

Come out, come out now, gude Wallàce,   45
    This is the day that thou maun die;
I lippen nae sae little to God, he says,
    Altho' I be but ill wordie.—

The gudewife had an auld gudeman,
    By gude Wallàce he stiffly stood,   50
Till ten o' the fyfteen Englishmen
    Before the door lay in their blude.—

The other five to the greenwood ran,
    And he hang'd these five upon a grain:
And on the morn wi' his merry men a'   55
    He sat at dine in Lochmaben town.—

585. The auld man's mare's dead—

Slowish

S H E was cut-luggit, painch-lippit,
    Steel-waimit, staincher-fittit,
Chanler-chaftit, lang-neckit,
    Yet the brute did die.—

The auld man's mare's dead. *Text from the Hastie MS, f. 154 (Ha), collated with the Adam MS and SMM, 1796 (485; unsigned)*

2 staincher-] stanchel- *Adam*   3 lang-neckit] and lang-neckit *Adam*: and
cancelled in Ha   4 Yet . . . die] *correcting* And yet the brute die *in Ha*: And
yet . . . die *Adam*

Chorus

The auld man's mare's dead,   5
The poor man's mare's dead,
The auld man's mare's dead
A mile aboon Dundee.——

Her lunzie-banes were knaggs and neuks,
She had the cleeks, the cauld, the crooks,   10
The jawpish and the wanton yeuks,
   And the howks aboon her e'e.——
   The auld &c.

My Master rade me to the town,
He ty'd me to a staincher round,
He took a chappin till himsel,   15
   But fient a drap gae me.

The auld man's mare's dead,
The poor man's mare's dead,
The peats and tours and a' to lead
And yet the bitch did die.   20

586. The Taylor—

13 My] *correcting* (?) When *in Ha*   rade] *correcting* took *in Ha:* ca't *Adam*
14 staincher] stanchel *Adam*   15 He took] *correcting* And f . . . *in Ha*   till]
to *Adam*   16 *catchword* and *in Ha*   19 The] *om. Adam*   a'] *correcting*
a's *in Ha:* a's *Adam*   20 bitch] *corrected to* jad *in another hand in Ha:* jad
SMM   did] inser*ted in Ha*

The Taylor. *Text from the Hastie MS, f. 156, collated with SMM, 1796 (490; un-*
signed). In SMM the chorus precedes and follows the verse

T H E Taylor he cam here to sew,
And weel he kend the way to woo,
For ay he pree'd the lassie's mou
As he gaed but and ben O.

Chorus
For weel he kend the way O   5
The way O, the way O,
For weel he kend the way O
The lassie's heart to win O.—

The Taylor rase and sheuk his duds,
The flaes they flew awa in cluds,   10
And them that stay'd gat fearfu' thuds,
The Taylor prov'd a man O.—

Chorus
For now it was the gloamin,
The gloamin, the gloamin,
For now it was the gloamin   15
When a' to rest are gaun O.—

*   *   *   *   *

587. There grows a bonie brier-bush &c.

Slowish

There grows a bonie brier-bush. *Text from the Hastie MS, f. 158, collated with SMM, 1796 (492; signed Z). Title from SMM*

THERE grows a bonie brier-bush in our kail-yard,
  There grows a bonie brier-bush in our kail-yard;
And below the bonie brier-bush there's a lassie and a lad,
And they're busy, busy courtin in our kail-yard.—

We'll court nae mair below the buss in our kail-yard,   5
We'll court nae mair below the buss in our kail-yard;
We'll awa to Athole's green, and there we'll no be seen,
Whare the trees and the branches will be our safe-guard.—

Will ye go to the dancin in Carlyle's ha',
Will ye go to the dancin in Carlyle's ha';   10
Whare Sandy and Nancy I'm sure will ding them a'?
I winna gang to the dance in Carlyle-ha'.

What will I do for a lad, when Sandy gangs awa?
What will I do for a lad, when Sandy gangs awa?
I will awa to Edinburgh and win a pennie fee,   15
And see an onie bonie lad will fancy me.—

He's comin frae the North that's to fancy me,
He's comin frae the North that's to fancy me;
A feather in his bonnet and a ribbon at his knee,
He's a bonie, bonie laddie and yon be he.—   20

588. Here's to thy health my bonie lass

Tune, Loggan burn

3 bonie . . . lad *SMM*: brier-buss there's a lad and a lass *MS*   4 they're]
correcting there *in MS*   15 and] *correcting* to *in MS*   19 bonnet . . . rib-
bon] *correcting* hat . . . buckle *in MS*   20 laddie] *correcting* lad *in MS*
Here's to thy health my bonie lass. *Text from SMM, 1796 (495; signed B), collated*

H ERE's to thy health, my bonie lass,
   Gudenight and joy be wi' thee:
I'll come nae mair to thy bower-door,
   To tell thee that I loe thee.
O dinna think, my pretty pink,   5
   But I can live without thee:
I vow and swear, I dinna care,
   How lang ye look about ye.

Thou'rt ay sae free informing me
   Thou hast nae mind to marry: 10
I'll be as free informing thee,
   Nae time hae I to tarry.
I ken thy friends try ilka means
   Frae wedlock to delay thee;
Depending on some higher chance,   15
   But fortune may betray thee.

I ken thcy scorn my low estate,
   But that does never grieve me;
For I'm as free as any he,
   Sma' siller will relieve me.   20
I'll count my health my greatest wealth,
   Sae lang as I'll enjoy it:
I'll fear nae scant, I'll bode nae want,
   As lang's I get employment.

But far-off fowls hae feathers fair,   25
   And ay until ye try them:
Tho' they seem fair, still have a care,
   They may prove as bad as I am. [bright,
But at twal at night, when the moon shines
   My dear, I'll come and see thee;   30
For the man that loves his mistress weel,
   Nae travel makes him weary.

---

with the Hastie MS, f. 160. Set in four-line stanzas in the MS, the third and fourth
lines of each repeated as chorus. Lines 5–8 inserted in the margin in the MS, marked
verse 2d.
   9 me] *om. SMM*   10 marry: *MS:* marry. *SMM*   13 try] *correcting* use
in MS   25 far-off *MS:* far off *SMM*   29 twal *MS:* twel *SMM*
30 I'll *MS:* I'd *SMM*   31 weel, *MS:* weel *SMM*

589. It was a' for our rightfu' king

IT was a' for our rightfu' king
   We left fair Scotland's strand;
It was a' for our rightfu' king,
   We e'er saw Irish land, my dear,
   We e'er saw Irish land.—   5

Now a' is done that men can do,
   And a' is done in vain:
My Love and Native Land fareweel,
   For I maun cross the main, my dear,
   For I maun cross the main.   10

He turn'd him right and round about,
   Upon the Irish shore,
And gae his bridle-reins a shake,
   With, Adieu for evermore, my dear,
   And adieu for evermore.   15

The soger frae the wars returns,
   The sailor frae the main,
But I hae parted frae my Love,
   Never to meet again, my dear,
   Never to meet again.   20

It was a' for our rightfu' king. *Text from the Cowie MS (facsimile in Scott Douglas,*
iii. 192), collated with SMM, 1796 (497; unsigned)
   10, 15, 20 *Repeat abbreviated in MS and SMM*   15 And] With, *SMM*

When day is gane, and night is come,
    And a' folk bound to sleep;
I think on him that's far awa,
    The lee-lang night and weep, my dear,
    The lee-lang night and weep.—   25

590. The Highland widow's lament

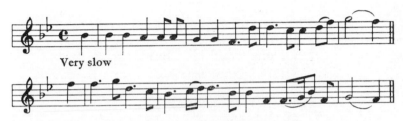

Very slow

OH, I am come to the low Countrie,
    Ochon, Ochon, Ochrie!
Without a penny in my purse
    To buy a meal to me.—

It was na sae in the Highland hills,   5
    Ochon, Ochon, Ochrie!
Nae woman in the Country wide
    Sae happy was as me.—

For then I had a score o' kye,
    Ochon, &c.—   10
Feeding on yon hill sae high,
    And giving milk to me.—

And there I had three score o' yowes,
    Ochon, &c.—
Skipping on yon bonie knowes,   15
    And casting woo to me.—

23 on him ...] *correcting* upon my abs *in MS*

The Highland widow's lament. *Text from the Hastie MS, f. 161, collated with SMM, 1796 (498; unsigned)*

I was the happiest of a' the Clan,
  Sair, sair may I repine;
For Donald was the brawest man,
  And Donald he was mine.—   20

Till Charlie Stewart cam at last,
  Sae far to set us free;
My Donald's arm was wanted then
  For Scotland and for me.—

Their waefu' fate what need I tell,   25
  Right to the wrang did yield;
My Donald and his Country fell
  Upon Culloden field.—

Ochon, O, Donald, Oh!
  Ochon, &c.—   30
Nae woman in the warld wide
  Sae wretched now as me.—

591. O steer her up and had her gaun

O steer her up and had her gaun. *Text from SMM, 1803 (504; unsigned)*

O STEER her up and had her gaun,
  Her mither's at the mill, jo;
An' gin she winna tak a man
  E'en let her tak her will, jo.
First shore her wi' a kindly kiss   5
  And ca' anither gill, jo;
An' gin she tak the thing amiss
  E'en let her flyte her fill, jo.

O steer her up and be na blate,
  An' gin she tak it ill, jo,   10
Then lea'e the lassie till her fate,
  And time nae langer spill, jo:
Ne'er break your heart for ae rebute,
  But think upon it still, jo,
That gin the lassie winna do't,   15
  Ye'll fin' anither will, jo.

592. Wee Willie Gray

A little lively

W EE Willie Gray, an' his leather wallet;
  Peel a willie wand, to be him boots and jacket.
The rose upon the breer will be him trouse an' doublet,
The rose upon the breer will be him trouse an' doublet.

13 ae] ay *SMM*

Wee Willie Gray. *Text from SMM, 1803 (514; unsigned;* Written for this Work by
R. Burns)

Wee Willie Gray, and his leather wallet;   5
Twice a lily-flower will be him sark and cravat;
Feathers of a flee wad feather up his bonnet,
Feathers of a flee wad feather up his bonnet.

593. Gudeen to you kimmer

Canty

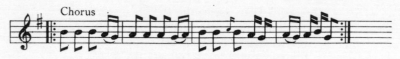

Chorus

Gudeen to you kimmer
        And how do ye do?
Hiccup, quo' kimmer,
        The better that I'm fou.

        Chorus
We're a' noddin, nid nid noddin,   5
        We're a' noddin at our house at hame,
We're a' noddin, nid nid noddin,
        We're a' noddin at our house at hame.

Kate sits i' the neuk,
        Suppin hen-broo;   10
Deil tak Kate
        An' she be na noddin too!
        We're a' noddin &c.

How's a' wi' you, kimmer,
        And how do ye fare?
A pint o' the best o't,   15
        And twa pints mair.
        We're a' noddin &c.

Gudeen to you kimmer. *Text from SMM, 1803 (523; signed B;* Corrected by Burns)

How's a' wi' you, kimmer,
And how do ye thrive;
How mony bairns hae ye?
    Quo' kimmer, I hae five.   20
    We're a' noddin &c.

Are they a' Johny's?
Eh! atweel no:
Twa o' them were gotten
When Johny was awa.
    We're a' noddin &c.

Cats like milk   25
    And dogs like broo;
Lads like lasses weel,
    And lasses lads too.
    We're a' noddin &c.

594. O ay my wife she dang me

A little lively

O ay my wife she dang me. *Text from SMM, 1803 (532; unsigned;* Written for this
Work by Robert Burns), *collated with the Rosenbach MS (R)*

A MS collated by H–H. (iii. 439) has My Wife she dang me *as ll. 1 and 2 and these*

Chorus

O AY my wife she dang me,
    An' aft my wife she bang'd me,
If ye gie a woman a' her will
    Gude faith she'll soon oergang ye.

On peace and rest my mind was bent,   5
    And fool I was I marry'd;
But never honest man's intent
    As cursedly miscarry'd.

Some sairie comfort still at last,
    When a' thir days are done, man,   10
My pains o' hell on earth is past,
    I'm sure o' bliss aboon, man.
    O ay my wife she &c.

595. Scroggam

Slowish

auld Cowl

T HERE was a wife wonn'd in Cockpen,
    Scroggam;
She brew'd gude ale for gentlemen,
    Sing auld Cowl, lay you down by me,
    Scroggam, my Dearie, ruffum.   5

The gudewife's dochter fell in a fever,
    Scroggam;
The priest o' the parish fell in anither,
    Sing auld Cowl, lay you down by me,
    Scroggam, my Dearie, ruffum.   10

variants: 3 If ye] And *MS*   6–8 marry'd . . . miscarry'd] marry . . . miscarry *MS*

   2 she bang'd] did bang *R*   3 If ye gie] An' gie ye *R*   11 is] are *R*

Scroggam. *Text from SMM, 1803 (539; signed B)*

They laid the twa i' the bed thegither,
         Scroggam;
That the heat o' the tane might cool the tither,
   Sing auld Cowl, lay you down by me,
   Scroggam, my Dearie, ruffum.   15

596. O gude ale comes &c.

Lively

O GUDE ale comes and gude ale goes,
  Gude ale gars me sell my hose,
Sell my hose and pawn my shoon,
Gude ale keeps my heart aboon.

O gude ale comes. *Text from the Paisley MS, collated with the Alloway MS (Al) and SMM, 1803 (542; unsigned; Corrected by R. Burns). Title from SMM. The Alloway MS has ll. 1–8, two additional stanzas, ll. 9–12, an additional stanza, and ll. 1–4 marked as chorus after each stanza*
    passim ale] yill *Al*   4, 8 Gude] *corrected to* For gude *in Al*

I had sax owsen in a pleugh,   5
They drew a' weel eneugh,
I sald them a', ane by ane,
Gude ale keeps my heart aboon.

Gude ale hauds me bare and busy,
Gars me moop wi' the servant hizzie,   10
Stand i' the stool when I hae done,
Gude ale keeps my heart aboon.

O gude ale comes and gude ale goes,
Gude ale gars me sell my hose;
Sell my hose and pawn my shoon,   15
Gude ale keeps my heart aboon.

5 had] *correcting* have *in Al*   6 They] *corrected to* And they *in Al*   a']
corrected to teugh & *in Al*   8 *Additional stanzas in Al:*

> I had forty shillin in a clout,
> Gude yill gart me pyke them out;
> That gear should moul I thought a sin,
> Gude yill keeps my heart aboon.—
>   Gude yill &c.
>
> The meikle pot upon my back,
> Unto the yill-house I did pack;
> It melted a' wi' the heat o' the moon,
> Gude yill keeps my heart aboon.—
>   Gude yill &c.

10 moop] jink *Al*   11 stool] kirk *Al*   12 *Additional stanza in Al.*

> I wish their fa' may be a gallows,
> Winna gie gude yill to gude fallows;
> And keep a soup till the afternoon,
> Gude yill keeps my heart aboon.—

597. My Lady's gown there's gairs upon 't

Chorus

Lively

Chorus

M Y Lady's gown there's gairs upon 't,
And gowden flowers sae rare upon 't;
But Jenny's jimps and jirkinet
My Lord thinks meikle mair upon 't.

My Lord a hunting he is gane,   5
But hounds or hawks wi' him are nane;
By Colin's cottage lies his game,
If Colin's Jenny be at hame.
    My Lady's gown &c.

My Lady's white, my Lady's red
And kith and kin o' Cassillis' blude,   10
But her tenpund lands o' tocher gude
Were a' the charms his Lordship lo'ed.
    My Lady's gown &c.

Out o'er yon moor, out o'er yon moss,
Whare gor-cocks thro' the heather pass,
There wons auld Colin's bonie lass,   15
A lily in a wilderness.
    My Lady's gown &c.

My Lady' gown there's gairs upon 't. *Text from SMM, 1803 (554; unsigned;* Written
for this Work by Robert Burns), *collated with the Rosenbach MS*
  10 Cassillis'] *correcting* noble *in MS*

Sae sweetly move her genty limbs,
Like music-notes o' Lovers hymns;
The diamond-dew in her een sae blue
Where laughing love sae wanton swims.   20
    My Lady's gown &c.

My Lady's dink, my Lady's drest,
The flower and fancy o' the west;
But the Lassie that a man loes best,
O that's the Lass to mak him blest.
    My Lady's gown &c.

598. Sweetest May

Kinloch of Kinloch

Slowish

SWEETEST May let love inspire thee;
Take a heart which he designs thee;
As thy constant slave regard it;
For its faith and truth reward it.

Proof o' shot to Birth or Money,   5
Not the wealthy, but the bonie;
Not high-born, but noble-minded,
In Love's silken band can bind it.

23 a MS: *om. SMM*

Sweetest May. *Text from SMM, 1803 (559; unsigned;* Written for this Work by Robert Burns)

5 99. Jockey's ta'en the parting kiss

A little lively

JOCKEY's ta'en the parting kiss,
  O'er the mountains he is gane;
And with him is a' my bliss,
  Nought but griefs with me remain.
Spare my love, ye winds that blaw,   5
  Plashy sleets and beating rain;
Spare my love, thou feath'ry snaw,
  Drifting o'er the frozen plain.

When the shades of evening creep
  O'er the day's fair, gladsome e'e,   10
Sound and safely may he sleep,
  Sweetly blythe his waukening be.
He will think on her he loves,
  Fondly he'll repeat her name;
For whare'er he distant roves   15
  Jockey's heart is still at hame.

Jockey's ta'en the parting kiss. *Text from SMM, 1803 (570; unsigned;* Written for this Work by Robert Burns)

600. O lay thy loof in mine lass

Chorus

O LAY thy loof in mine lass,
    In mine lass, in mine lass,
And swear on thy white hand lass,
    That thou wilt be my ain.

Song

A slave to love's unbounded sway,   5
    He aft has wrought me meikle wae;
But now, he is my deadly fae,
    Unless thou be my ain.
        O lay thy loof &c.

There's monie a lass has broke my rest,
    That for a blink I hae lo'ed best;   10
But thou art queen within my breast
    For ever to remain.
        O lay thy loof &c.

O lay thy loof in mine lass. *Text from SMM, 1803 (574; signed B). SMM repeats the chorus in full after l. 8*

601. Cauld is the e'enin blast

A little lively

C<small>AULD</small> is the e'enin blast
 O' Boreas o'er the pool,
And dawin it is dreary,
 When birks are bare at Yule.

O cauld blaws the e'enin blast   5
 When bitter bites the frost,
And in the mirk and dreary drift
 The hills and glens are lost.

Ne'er sae murky blew the night
 That drifted o'er the hill,   10
But bonie Peg a Ramsey
 Gat grist to her mill.

Cauld is the e'enin blast. *Text from SMM, 1803 (583; unsigned;* Written for this
Work by Robert Burns)

602. There was a bonie lass

Rather slow

THERE was a bonie lass,
   And a bonie, bonie lass,
And she lo'ed her bonie laddie dear;
   Till war's loud alarms
   Tore her laddie frae her arms,   5
Wi' monie a sigh and a tear.

Over sea, over shore,
   Where the cannons loudly roar;
He still was a stranger to fear:
   And nocht could him quail,   10
   Or his bosom assail,
But the bonie lass he lo'ed sae dear.

There was a bonie lass. *Text from SMM, 1803 (586; unsigned;* By R. Burns)

603. There 's news lasses news

A little lively

THERE'S news, lasses, news,
    Gude news I've to tell,
There's a boatfu' o' lads
    Come to our town to sell.

Chorus   The wean wants a cradle,   5
            An' the cradle wants a cod,
            An' I'll no gang to my bed
            Until I get a nod.

Father, quo' she, Mither, quo' she,
    Do what ye can,   10
I'll no gang to my bed
    Till I get a man.
            The wean &c.

l hae as gude a craft rig
    As made o' yird and stane;
And waly fa' the ley-crap   15
    For I maun till't again.
            The wean &c.

There's news lasses news. *Text from SMM, 1803 (589; unsigned;* Written for this
Work by Robert Burns)
    16 till't] till'd *SMM*

604. O that I had ne'er been Married

O THAT I had ne'er been married,
     I wad never had nae care,
Now I've gotten wife and bairns
An' they cry crowdie ever mair.
          Ance crowdie, twice crowdie,   5
          Three times crowdie in a day;
          Gin ye crowdie ony mair,
          Ye'll crowdie a' my meal away.

Waefu' Want and Hunger fley me,
     Glowrin' by the hallan en';   10
Sair I fecht them at the door,
     But ay I'm eerie they come ben.
          Ance crowdie &c.

O that I had ne'er been Married. *Text from SMM, 1803 (593; unsigned;* Corrected
by R. Burns; *ll. 9–12* Added by BURNS). *The* old Scots ballad (*ll. 1–8) is quoted by
Burns in the Lochryan MSS (letter to Mrs. Dunlop, 15 December 1793)*
     4 An'] *not in Loch*   5 Ance . . . crowdie,] Crowdie! ance; Crowdie! twice;
Loch   6 Three times crowdie] Crowdie! three times *Loch*   7 Gin] An
Loch

605. The German lairdie

W<small>HAT</small> merriment has taen the whigs,
　I think they be gaen mad, Sir,
Wi' playing up their whiggish jigs,
　Their dancin may be sad, Sir.—

Chorus

Sing heedle liltie, teedle liltie,　　　　5
　Andum tandum tandie;
Sing fal de dal, de dal lal lal,
　Sing howdle liltie dandie.—

The Revolution principles
　Has put their heads in bees, Sir;　　　10
They're a' fa'n out amang themsels,
　Deil tak the first that grees, Sir.—
　　Sing heedle, &c.

The German lairdie. *Text from the Hastie MS, f. 144*ᵛ

XIV

UNDATED POEMS AND *DUBIA*

606. Epitaph for H—— L——, Esq., of L——

HERE lyes Squire Hugh——ye harlot crew,
  Come mak' your water on him,
I'm sure that he weel pleas'd would be
  To think ye pish'd upon him.

607. A Ballad—

WHILE Prose-work and rhymes
  Are hunted for crimes,
And things are — the devil knows how;
  Aware o' my rhymes,
  In these kittle times,   5
The subject I chuse is a ——.

Some cry, Constitution!
  Some cry, Revolution!
And Politicks kick up a rowe;
  But Prince and Republic,   10
  Agree on the Subject,
No treason is in a good ——.

Th' Episcopal lawn,
  And Presbyter band,
Hae lang been to ither a cowe;   15
  But still the proud Prelate,
  And Presbyter zealot
Agree in an orthodox ——.

Poor Justice, 'tis hinted—
  Ill natur'dly squinted,   20
The Process—but mum—we'll allow—
  Poor Justice has ever
  For C—t had a favor,
While Justice could tak a gude ——.

Epitaph for H—— L——. *Text from* The Court of Equity, *1910*
A Ballad. *Text from the Young MS* (*Dewar; Berg collection, New York*)

Now fill to the brim—   25
To her, and to him,
Wha willingly do what they dow;
And ne'er a poor wench
Want a friend at a pinch,
Whase failing is only a ——.   30

608. Muirland Meg

Tune—Saw ye my Eppie M'Nab

AMANG our young lassies there's Muirland Meg,
She'll beg or she work, and she'll play or she beg,
At thretteen her maidenhead flew to the gate,
And the door o' her cage stands open yet.—

Her kittle black een they wad thirl you thro',   5
Her rose-bud lips cry, kiss me now;
The curls and links o' her bonie black hair,
Wad put you in mind that the lassie has mair.—

An armfu' o' love is her bosom sae plump,
A span o' delight is her middle sae jimp;   10
A taper, white leg, and a thumpin thie,
And a fiddle near by, an ye play a wee!

Love's her delight, and kissin's her treasure;
She'll stick at nae price, an ye gie her gude measure.
As lang's a sheep-fit, and as girt's a goose-egg,   15
And that's the measure o' Muirland Meg.

Muirland Meg. *Text from the Rosenbach MS, collated with MMC (pp. 16–1 8).
MMC has a chorus:*
        And for a sheep-cloot she'll do 't, she'll do 't,
        And for a sheep-cloot, &c.
        And for a toop-horn, she'll do 't to the morn,
        And merrily turn and do 't and do 't.
  5 you] ye *MMC*   6 me now] me just now *MMC*   11 taper,] taper
MMC   12 an] can *MMC*   16 And] O *MMC*

609. The Patriarch

Tune—The auld cripple Dow

As honest Jacob on a night,
 Wi' his beloved beauty,
Was duly laid on wedlock's bed,
 And noddin' at his duty:
  Tal de dal, &c.

'How lang, she says, ye fumblin' wretch,   5
 'Will ye be f——g at it?
'My eldest wean might die of age,
 'Before that ye could get it.

'Ye pegh, and grane, and groazle there,
 'And mak an unco splutter,   10
'And I maun ly and thole you here,
 'And fient a hair the better.'

Then he, in wrath, put up his graith,
 'The deevil's in the hizzie!
'I m—w you as I m—w the lave,   15
 'And night and day I'm bisy.

'I've bairn'd the servant gypsies baith,
 'Forbye your titty Leah;
'Ye barren jad, ye put me mad,
 'What mair can I do wi' you.   20

'There's ne'er a m—w I've gi'en the lave,
 'But ye ha'e got a dizzen;
'And d——n'd a ane ye 'se get again,
 'Altho' your c——t should gizzen.'

Then Rachel calm, as ony lamb,   25
 She claps him on the waulies,
Quo' she, 'ne'er fash a woman's clash,
 'In trowth, ye m—w me braulies.

The Patriarch. *Text from MMC (pp. 19–21), endorsed* Burns *by Scott Douglas in his copy*

'My dear 'tis true, for mony a m–w,
    'I'm your ungratefu' debtor;   30
'But ance again, I dinna ken,
    'We'll aiblens happen better.'

Then honest man! wi' little wark,
    He soon forgat his ire;
The patriarch, he coost the sark,   35
    And up and till 't like fire!!!

610. The Trogger

Tune—Gillicrankie

As I cam down by Annan side,
    Intending for the border,
Amang the Scroggie banks and braes,
    Wha met I but a trogger.
He laid me down upon my back,   5
    I thought he was but jokin,
Till he was in me to the hilts,
    O the deevil tak sic troggin!

What could I say, what could I do,
    I bann'd and sair misca'd him,   10
But whiltie-whaltie gae'd his a—e
    The mair that I forbade him:
He stell'd his foot against a stane,
    And doubl'd ilka stroke in,
Till I gaed daft amang his hands,   15
    O the deevil tak sic troggin!

Then up we raise, and took the road,
    And in by Ecclefechan,
Where the brandy-stoup we gart it clink,
    And the strang-beer ream the quech in.   20

The Trogger. *Text from MMC (pp. 25–26). Marked* Burns *by Scott Douglas in his copy of MMC, with a note* This is certainly by Burns

Bedown the bents o' Bonshaw braes,
    We took the partin' yokin';
But I've claw'd a sairy c—t synsine,
    O the deevil tak sic troggin!

611. Godly Girzie

Tune—Wat ye wha I met yestreen

THE night it was a haly night,
    The day had been a haly day;
Kilmarnock gleam'd wi' candle light,
    As Girzie hameward took her way.
A man o' sin, ill may he thrive!   5
And never haly-meeting see!
Wi' godly Girzie met belyve,
    Amang the Cragie hills sae hie.

The chiel' was wight, the chiel' was stark,
    He wad na wait to chap nor ca',   10
And she was faint wi' haly wark,
    She had na pith to say him na.
But ay she glowr'd up to the moon,
    And ay she sigh'd most piouslie;
'I trust my heart's in heaven aboon,   15
'Whare'er your sinfu' p——e be.'

Godly Girzie. *Text from MMC (pp. 27–28), collated with a transcript of Burns's
holograph* (Burns Chronicle, *1894, p. 142; ll. 1–8 only; BC*). *Title in BC* A new Song
—From an old Story
    3 Kilmarnock] *alternative to* The winnocks *in BC*   4 As] When *BC*
5 man o' sin] ploughman lad *BC*

612. The Jolly Gauger

Tune—We'll gang nae mair a rovin'

And we'll gang nae mair a   ro - vin'.

T HERE was a jolly gauger, a gauging he did ride,
And he has met a beggar down by yon river side.
An' we'll gang nae mair a rovin' wi' ladies to the wine,
When a beggar wi' her meal-pocks can fidge her tail sae
fine.

Amang the broom he laid her; amang the broom sae green,
And he's fa'n to the beggar, as she had been a queen.
An' we'll gang, &c.

My blessings on thee, laddie, thou's done my turn sae weel,
Wilt thou accept, dear laddie, my pock and pickle meal?
An' we'll, &c.

Sae blyth the beggar took the bent, like ony bird in spring,
Sae blyth the beggar took the bent, and merrily did sing. 10
An' we'll, &c.

The Jolly Gauger. *Text from MMC (pp. 31–32). Marked* Burns *by Scott Douglas in his copy of MMC*
2 beggar] *Scott Douglas adds* lass   3 *et passim* An' we'll] And weel *MMC*

My blessings on the gauger, o' gaugers he's the chief.
Sic kail ne'er crost my kettle, nor sic a joint o' beef.
An' we'll, &c.

613. Wha'll m—w me now

Tune—Comin' thro' the rye

O WHA'LL m—w me now, my jo,
    An' wha'll m—w me now:
A sodger wi' his bandileers
    Has bang'd my belly fu'.

O, I hae tint my rosy cheek,   5
    Likewise my waste sae sma';
O wae gae by the sodger lown,
    The sodger did it a'.
      An' wha'll, &c.

Now I maun thole the scornfu' sneer
    O' mony a saucy quine;   10
When, curse upon her godly face!
    Her c—t's as merry's mine.
      An' wha'll, &c.

Our dame hauds up her wanton tail,
    As due as she gaes lie;
An' yet misca's [a] young thing,   15
    The trade if she but try.
      An' wha'll, &c.

Our dame can lae her ain gudeman,
    An' m—w for glutton greed;
An' yet misca's a poor thing
    That's m——n' for its bread.   20
      An' wha'll, &c.

Wha'll m—w me now. *Text from MMC (pp. 51–52)*
  14 due . . . lie] *Scott Douglas emends to* oft as down she lies *in his copy of MMC*
16 try] tries *MMC*

Alake! sae sweet a tree as love,
Sic bitter fruit should bear!
Alake, that e'er a merry a—e,
Should draw a sa'tty tear.
An' wha'll, &c.

But deevil damn the lousy loun,   25
Denies the bairn he got!
Or lea's the merry a—e he lo'ed
To wear a ragged coat!
An' wha'll, &c.

614. O saw ye my Maggie—

I

Saw ye my Maggie?
Saw ye my Maggie?
Saw ye my Maggie?
    Comin oer the lea?

2

What mark has your Maggie,   5
What mark has your Maggie,
What mark has your Maggie,
    That ane may ken her be?

O saw ye my Maggie. *Text from the Abbotsford MS, collated with MMC (pp. 60–62).
Lines 21–28 added in margin in the MS. Tune in MMC* Saw ye na my Peggy.
*Sequence in MMC ll. 1–20, 29–32, 25–28, 21–24, 33–36, with an additional stanza
after l. 8:*

Wry-c——d is she,
Wry-c——d is she,
Wry-c——d is she,
    And pishes gain' her thie.

See Commentary

3

My Maggie has a mark,
Ye'll find it in the dark,　　　10
It's in below her sark,
　A little aboon her knee.

4

What wealth has your Maggie,
What wealth has your Maggie,
What wealth has your Maggie,　　　15
　In tocher, gear, or fee?

5

My Maggie has a treasure,
A hidden mine o' pleasure,
I'll howk it at my leisure,
　It's alane for me.　　　20

6

How loe ye your Maggy,
How loe ye your Maggy,
How loe ye your Maggy,
　An loe nane but she?

7

Ein that tell our wishes,　　　25
Eager glowing kisses,
Then diviner blisses,
　In holy ecstacy!—

8

How meet you your Maggie,
How meet you your Maggie,　　　30
How meet you your Maggie,
　When nane's to hear or see?

9

Heavenly joys before me,
Rapture trembling o'er me,
Maggie I adore thee,　　　35
　On my bended knee!!!

615. Gie the lass her Fairin'

Tune—Cauld kail in Aberdeen

O GIE the lass her fairin', lad,
  O gie the lass her fairin',
An' something else she'll gie to you,
  That's waly worth the wearin';
Syne coup her o'er amang the creels,   5
  When ye hae taen your brandy,
The mair she bangs the less she squeels,
  An' hey for houghmagandie.

Then gie the lass a fairin', lad,
  O gie the lass her fairin',   10
An' she'll gie you a hairy thing,
  An' of it be na sparin';
But coup her o'er amang the creels,
  An' bar the door wi' baith your heels,
The mair she gets the less she squeels;   15
  An' hey for houghmagandie.

616. The Book-Worms

THROUGH and through the inspired leaves,
  Ye maggots, make your windings;
But, oh! respect his lordship's taste,
  And spare his golden bindings.

Gie the lass her Fairin'. *Text from MMC (pp. 79–80). Marked* Burns *in Scott
Douglas's copy of MMC*

The Book-Worms. *Text from Cunningham, 1834 (iii. 293). There is a transcript of
another version in Syme's MSS* (Burns Chronicle, *1932, p. 15):*

> Free thro' the leaves ye maggots make
>   your windings,
> But for the Owner's sake oh spare the
>   Bindings!

617. On Marriage

THAT hackney'd judge of human life,
　The Preacher and the King,
Observes: 'The man that gets a wife
He gets a noble thing.'

But how capricious are mankind,　　　　　　　5
　Now loathing, now desirous!
We married men, how oft we find
The best of things will tire us!

618. [Here's, a bottle and an honest friend]

HERE'S, a bottle and an honest friend!
　What wad ye wish for mair, man?
Wha kens, before his life may end,
　What his share may be of care, man.

Then catch the moments as they fly,　　　　　5
　And use them as ye ought, man:—
Believe me, happiness is shy,
　And comes not ay when sought, man.

619. Fragment

HER flowing locks, the raven's wing,
　Adown her neck and bosom hing;
How sweet unto that breast to cling,
　And round that neck entwine her!

On Marriage. *Text from H–H.* (*ii. 261; MS not traced*). *In l.* 7 We *corrects* Ye
(*H–H.*)

Here's a bottle. *Text from Cromek,* Reliques, *1808 (p. 440), collated with the Aldine
edition, 1839 (from a MS, with the epigraph:*

　　　　There's nane that's blest of human
　　　　　kind,
　　　　But the cheerful and the gay, man.
　　　　　　　　Fal lal, &c.)

Fragment. *Text from Cromek,* Reliques, *1808 (p. 445)*

Her lips are roses wat wi' dew,   5
O, what a feast, her bonie mou'!
Her cheeks a mair celestial hue,
A crimson still diviner.

620. A Tale—

'Twas where the birch and sounding thong are plyed,
     The noisy domicile of Pedant-pride;
Where Ignorance her darkening vapour throws,
And Cruelty directs the thickening blows;
Upon a time, Sir Abece the great,   5
In all his pedagogic powers elate,
His awful Chair of state resolves to mount,
And call the trembling Vowels to account.—

First enter'd A; a grave, broad, solemn Wight,
But ah! deform'd, dishonest to the sight!   10
His twisted head look'd backward on his way,
And flagrant from the scourge he grunted, AI!

Reluctant, E stalk'd in; with piteous race
The jostling tears ran down his honest face!
That name, that well-worn name, and all his own,   15
Pale he surrenders at the tyrant's throne!
The Pedant stifles keen the Roman sound
Not all his mongrel diphthongs can compound;
And next the title following close behind,
He to the nameless, ghastly wretch assign'd.   20

The cob-webb'd, Gothic dome resounded, Y!
In sullen vengeance, I, disdain'd reply:
The Pedant swung his felon cudgel round,
And knock'd the groaning Vowel to the ground!

A Tale. *Text from the Huntington Library MS, collated with Cromek,* Reliques,
1808 (p. 406). Title in Cromek The Vowels. A Tale
  19 And . . . close] *correcting* Then siez'd the name that follow'd next *in MS*
23 Pedant] *correcting* tyrant *in MS*

In rueful apprehension enter'd O,   25
The wailing minstrel of despairing woe;
Th' Inquisitor of Spain the most expert
Might there have learnt new mysteries of his art:
So grim, deform'd, with horrors, entering U,
His dearest friend and brother scarcely knew!   30

As trembling U stood staring all aghast,
The Pedant in his left hand clutch'd him fast;
In helpless infant's tears he dipp'd his right,
Baptiz'd him EU, and kick'd him from his sight.

621. The Henpeck'd Husband

CURS'D be the man, the poorest wretch in life,
The crouching vassal to the tyrant wife,
Who has no will but by her high permission;
Who has not sixpence but in her possession;
Who must to her his dear friend's secret tell;   5
Who dreads a curtain-lecture worse than hell.
Were such the wife had fallen to my part,
I'd break her spirit, or I'd break her heart;
I'd charm her with the magic of a switch,
I'd kiss her maids, and kick the perverse b—h.   10

622. On a dog of Lord Eglintons

I NEVER barked when out of season,
    I never bit without a reason;
I ne'er insulted weaker brother,
    Nor wronged by force or fraud another.
We brutes are placed a rank below;   5
    Happy for man could he say so.

26 wailing] *correcting* rueful *in MS*   33 In] *correcting* And *in MS*
infant's] infants' *Cromek*

The Henpeck'd Husband. *Text from Stewart, 1801 (p. 50)*

On a dog of Lord Eglintons. *Text from the Grierson Papers (see* Robert Burns: His
Associates and Contemporaries, *ed. R. T. Fitzhugh, 1943, p. 27). Editor's punctuation*

623. [Epitaph]

L o worms enjoy the seat of bliss
  Where Lords and Lairds afore did kiss.

624. Delia

F AI R the face of orient day,
  Fair the tints of op'ning rose;
But fairer still my Delia dawns,
More lovely far her beauty blows.

Sweet the Lark's wild-warbled lay,   5
Sweet the tinkling rill to hear;
But, Delia, more delightful still,
Steal thine accents on mine ear.

The flower-enamour'd busy Bee
The rosy banquet loves to sip;   10
Sweet the streamlet's limpid lapse
To the sun-brown'd Arab's lip;

But, Delia, on thy balmy lips
Let me, no vagrant insect, rove!
O let me steal one liquid kiss!   15
For Oh! my soul is parch'd with love!

625. The Tree of Liberty

H EAR D ye o' the tree o' France,
  I watna what's the name o't;
Around it a' the patriots dance,
  Weel Europe kens the fame o't.

Epitaph. *Text from the Grierson Papers (see* Robert Burns: His Associates and Contemporaries, *ed. R. T. Fitzhugh, 1943, p. 28*)

Delia. *Text from Stewart, 1802 (p. 223). Published in the* Belfast News Letter, *2–5 June 1789, and Magee's Belfast edition, 1793 (ii. 89)*

The Tree of Liberty. *Text from Chambers, 1838 (pp. 86–87*), here printed for the first time, from a MS in the possession of Mr James Duncan, Mosesfield, near Glasgow. *See Commentary*

It stands where ance the Bastile stood,   5
  A prison built by kings, man,
When Superstition's hellish brood
  Kept France in leading strings, man.

Upo' this tree there grows sic fruit,
  Its virtues a' can tell, man;   10
It raises man aboon the brute,
  It maks him ken himsel, man.
Gif ance the peasant taste a bit,
  He's greater than a lord, man,
An' wi' the beggar shares a mite   15
  O' a' he can afford, man.

This fruit is worth a' Afric's wealth,
  To comfort us 'twas sent, man:
To gie the sweetest blush o' health,
  An' mak us a' content, man.   20
It clears the een, it cheers the heart,
  Maks high and low gude friends, man;
And he wha acts the traitor's part
  It to perdition sends, man.

My blessings aye attend the chiel   25
  Wha pitied Gallia's slaves, man,
And staw a branch, spite o' the deil,
  Frae yont the western waves, man.
Fair Virtue water'd it wi' care,
  And now she sees wi' pride, man,   30
How weel it buds and blossoms there,
  Its branches spreading wide, man.

But vicious folks aye hate to see
  The works o' Virtue thrive, man;
The courtly vermin's banned the tree,   35
  And grat to see it thrive, man;
King Loui' thought to cut it down,
  When it was unco sma', man;
For this the watchman cracked his crown,
  Cut aff his head and a', man.   40

27 staw] staw'd *Chambers*

A wicked crew syne, on a time,
   Did tak a solemn aith, man,
It ne'er should flourish to its prime,
   I wat they pledged their faith, man.
Awa' they gaed wi' mock parade,   45
   Like beagles hunting game, man,
But soon grew weary o' the trade
   And wished they'd been at hame, man.

For Freedom, standing by the tree,
   Her sons did loudly ca', man;   50
She sang a sang o' liberty,
   Which pleased them ane and a', man.
By her inspired, the new-born race
   Soon drew the avenging steel, man;
The hirelings ran—her foes gied chase,   55
   And banged the despot weel, man.

Let Britain boast her hardy oak,
   Her poplar and her pine, man,
Auld Britain ance could crack her joke,
   And o'er her neighbours shine, man.   60
But seek the forest round and round,
   And soon 'twill be agreed, man,
That sic a tree can not be found,
   'Twixt London and the Tweed, man.

Without this tree, alake this life   65
   Is but a vale o' woe, man;
A scene o' sorrow mixed wi' strife,
   Nae real joys we know, man.
We labour soon, we labour late,
   To feed the titled knave, man;   70
And a' the comfort we're to get
   Is that ayont the grave, man.

Wi' plenty o' sic trees, I trow,
   The warld would live in peace, man;
The sword would help to mak a plough,   75
   The din o' war wad cease, man.

Like brethren in a common cause,
   We'd on each other smile, man;
And equal rights and equal laws
   Wad gladden every isle, man.   80

Wae worth the loon wha wadna eat
   Sic halesome dainty cheer, man;
I'd gie my shoon frae aff my feet,
   To taste sic fruit, I swear, man.
Syne let us pray, auld England may   85
   Sure plant this far-famed tree, man;
And blythe we'll sing, and hail the day
   That gave us liberty, man.

626. Broom Besoms (A)

I MAUN hae a wife, whatsoe'er she be;
An she be a woman, that's eneugh for me.

Chorus

   Buy broom besoms! wha will buy them now;
   Fine heather ringers, better never grew.

If that she be bony, I shall think her right: 5
If that she be ugly, where's the odds at night?
   Buy broom &c.

O, an she be young, how happy shall I be!
If that she be auld, the sooner she will die.
   Buy broom &c.

If that she be fruitfu', O! what joy is there!
If she should be barren, less will be my care.   10
   Buy broom &c.

If she like a drappie, she and I'll agree;
If she dinna like it, there's the mair for me.
   Buy broom &c.

Broom Besoms. *Texts from Davidson Cook's transcripts from the Law MSS* (Burns Chronicle, *1926, pp. 60–61*)

Be she green or gray; be she black or fair;
Let her be a woman, I shall seek nae mair.
    Buy broom &c.

627. Broom Besoms (B)

YOUNG and souple was I, when I lap the dyke;
    Now I'm auld and frail, I douna step a syke.
    Buy broom &c.

Young and souple was I, when at Lautherslack,
Now I'm auld and frail, and lie at Nansie's back.
    Buy broom &c.

Had she gien me butter, when she gae me bread,   5
I wad looked baulder, wi' my beld head.
    Buy broom &c.

628. [Fragment]

Now health forsakes that angel face,
    Nae mair my Dearie smiles;
Pale sickness withers ilka grace,
    And a' my hopes beguiles:
The cruel Powers reject the prayer   5
    I hourly mak for thee;
Ye Heavens how great is my despair,
    How can I see him die!

629. Epigram on Rough Roads

I'M now arrived—thanks to the gods!—
    Thro' pathways rough and muddy,
A certain sign that makin roads
    Is no this people's study:
Altho' I'm not wi' Scripture cram'd,   5
    I'm sure the Bible says
That heedless sinners shall be damn'd,
    Unless they mend their *ways*.

Fragment. *Text from the Alloway MS*
Epigram on Rough Roads. *Text from Scott Douglas (ii. 15)*

630. On the Duchess of Gordon's Reel Dancing

SHE kiltit up her kirtle weel
     To show her bonie cutes sae sma',
And walloped about the reel,
     The lightest louper o' them a'!

While some, like slav'ring, doited stots   5
     Stoit'ring out thro' the midden dub,
Fankit their heels amang their coats
     And gart the floor their backsides rub;

Gordon, the great, the gay, the gallant,
     Skip't like a maukin owre a dyke: 10
Deil tak me, since I was a callant,
     Gif e'er my een beheld the like!

631. To the Memory of the Unfortunate Miss Burns 1791

LIKE to a fading flower in May,
     Which Gardner cannot save,
So Beauty must, sometime, decay
     And drop into the grave.

Fair Burns, for long the talk and toast   5
     Of many a gaudy Beau,
That Beauty has forever lost
     That made each bosom glow.

Think, fellow sisters, on her fate!
     Think, think how short her days!   10
Oh! think, and, e'er it be too late,
     Turn from your evil ways.

On the Duchess of Gordon's Reel Dancing. *Text from the* Star, *31 March 1789. See Commentary*

To the Memory of . . . Miss Burns. *Text from the Grierson Papers (see* Robert Burns: His Associates and Contemporaries, *ed. R. T. Fitzhugh, 1943, p. 27). Editor's punctuation*
    8 That] What *Fitzhugh*

Beneath this cold, green sod lies dead
That once bewitching dame
That fired Edina's lustful sons,   15
And quench'd their glowing flame.

632. [Bonnie Peg]

As I cam in by our gate-end,
    As day was waxen weary,
O wha cam tripping down the street
But bonnie Peg, my dearie!

Her air sae sweet, and shape complete,   5
    Wi' nae proportion wanting,
The queen of love did never move
    Wi' motion mair enchanting.

Wi' linked hands we took the sands
    Adown yon winding river;   10
And, oh! that hour, and broomy bower,
    Can I forget it ever!—

                        Cætera desunt.

Bonnie Peg. *Text from the* Edinburgh Magazine, *January 1818, collated with the longer version in the same periodical, January 1808 (o8). See Commentary*
  1 cam in] gaed up *o8*   our] yon *o8*   2 As] The *o8*   3 O . . . street] Wha did I meet, upon the way, *o8*   4 bonnie] pretty *o8*   4 *Additional stanza in o8:*

> The music of her pretty foot,
>   On my heart it did play so,
> For ay she tipp'd the sidelin's wink,
>   Come kiss me at your leisure.

5 sae . . . and] so . . . her *o8*   7 did] could *o8*   8 *Additional stanza in o8:*

> Her nut-brown hair, beyond compare,
>   Was on her bosom straw'd so,
> And love said, laughing in her looks,
>   Come kiss me at your leisure.

10 Adown] Down by *o8*   11 And, oh! that] Oh that happy *o8*   broomy] shady *o8*   12 it ever!] it ?—Never *o8*   12 *Additional stanza in o8:*

> The conscious sun, out o'er yon hill,
>   Rejoicin' clos'd the day so,
> Clos'd in my arms, she murmur'd still,
>   Come kiss me at your leisure.

XV

APPENDIX

THE following poems have been admitted at various times to the canon of Burns's work, either wrongly or on inadequate evidence. They are arranged in order of publication. Titles and opening lines are given for identification.

633. The Captive Ribband

DEAR Myra, the captive ribband's mine,
'Twas all my faithfull love could gain. . . .

SMM, 1790, no. 257; 4 stanzas, unsigned. 'Another unclaimed production of Burns' (Stenhouse, *Illustrations*, p. 241). But 'Dr B[lacklock] gave the words' (Burns, Law MS—list of titles for *SMM*, iii—no. 27).

634. Fine Flowers in the Valley

SHE sat down below a thorn,
Fine flowers in the valley. . . .

SMM, 1792, no. 320; 7 stanzas, unsigned. Stenhouse says that the words and air were communicated by Burns (*Illustrations*, p. 308), but there is no manuscript evidence. A related fragment, in four stanzas with a different refrain, is in Herd's *Ancient and Modern Scottish Songs*, 1776 (1869 rpt., ii. 237–8). For later versions, see Child, no. 20.

635. O'er the Moor amang the Heather

COMIN' thro' the craigs o' Kyle,
Amang the bony blooming heather. . . .

SMM, 1792, no. 328; 5 stanzas and chorus, unsigned. Collected by Burns from the author, Jean Glover, an itinerant whore and thief (*Notes*, p. 57).

636. Donald Couper

O DONALD Couper and his man,
Held to a Highland fair, man. . . .

SMM, 1792, no. 334; 2 stanzas and chorus, unsigned. Taken by Stenhouse
(*Illustrations*, p. 316) to be Burns's revision of a fragment in Herd's *Ancient
and Modern Scottish Songs*, 1776 (1869 rpt., ii. 229); but there is no manuscript evidence.

637. The Tears I shed

THE tears I shed must ever fall,
I mourn not for an absent swain. . . .

SMM, 1792, no. 340; 5 stanzas, unsigned. Burns says that the song was
written by a Miss Cranston, and that he added four lines to accommodate the
music (*Notes*, p. 59):

No cold approach, no alter'd mien,
Just what would make suspicion start;
No pause the dire extremes between,
He made me blest—and broke my heart!

638. The tither Morn

THE tither morn,
When I forlorn
Aneath an aik sat moaning. . . .

SMM, 1792, no. 345; 3 stanzas, unsigned. 'This tune', says Burns, 'is originally
from the Highlands. I have heard a Gaelic song to it, which I was told was
very clever, but not by any means a lady's song' (*Notes*, p. 59). Attributed to
Burns by Stenhouse (*Illustrations*, p. 322) and H–H. (iii. 379), apparently
on stylistic grounds. But in the Law MS (titles for *SMM*, iii), no. 32, Burns
marks the song 'Printed'.

639. O Fare ye weel my auld Wife

O FARE ye weel, my auld wife!
Sing bum bi bery bum. . . .

SMM, 1792, no. 354; 2 stanzas, unsigned. Attributed to Burns by Barke
(Burns's *Poems and Songs*, 1955, p. 452), apparently on Stenhouse's assertion
that he 'slightly retouched' the song for *SMM*; but Stenhouse says also that
it was communicated, with the air, by Herd (*Illustrations*, p. 327).

640. Hey, how Johnie Lad

HEY, how, my Johnie lad, ye're no sae kind's ye sud hae been;
Gin your voice I had na kent, I cou'd na eithly trow my een. . . .

SMM, 1792, no. 357; 4 stanzas, unsigned. Attributed to Burns by Barke (see **639**, note), p. 451. But ll. 1–8 and 13–16 are in Herd (ii. 215–16), and there are no grounds for ascribing the third stanza in *SMM* to Burns.

641. Deluded Swain

DELUDED Swain, the pleasure
The fickle Fair can give thee. . . .

SC, 1798, no. 33; 4 stanzas, alternative words to **339**. Scott Douglas, iii. 157–8, 'merely an improvement on an old English song'; Chambers–Wallace, iv. 53; H–H., iii. 217. But this is an early eighteenth-century song, quoted by Burns as an 'old Bacchanal' (Letter 588 and Ferguson's note).

642. Song—The carlin of the glen—

YOUNG Jamie pride of a' the plain,
Sae gallant and sae gay a swain. . . .

SMM, 1796, no. 420; 2 stanzas, unsigned; Hastie MS, f. 122. Described by Stenhouse as 'another unclaimed production of Burns' (*Illustrations*, p. 378), apparently on the evidence of the Hastie MS. But Johnson was anxious to mark as many as possible of the songs in this volume of *SMM*, 'Written for this Work by Robert Burns', unless they were recognizably revisions of 'old words'; and no 'original' for **642** has been recovered.

643. Wantonness for ever mair

WANTONNESS for ever mair,
Wantonness has been my ruin. . . .

SMM, 1796, no. 422; a 2-stanza fragment, unsigned. Attributed to Burns by Stenhouse (*Illustrations*, p. 379), without evidence. The air, with the *Museum* title, had appeared earlier in Aird, 1788, iii. no. 443; the stanza is not characteristic of Burns, and looks like a muddled version of a late medieval form; and the sentiment in ll. 5–8, 'I hae lo'ed the Black, the Brown . . . the Fair, the Gowden', is a classical commonplace (cf. Ovid, *Amores*, II. iv. 39–40, 'Candida me capiet . . .'; Donne, *Songs and Sonets*, 'The Indifferent', 'I can love both faire and browne . . .'). The piece is apparently a traditional fragment.

644. Wherefore sighing art thou

WHEREFORE sighing art thou, Phillis?
Has thy prime unheeded past. . . .

SMM, 1796, no. 460; 2 stanzas, unsigned; followed by an alternative, 'Powers celestial, whose protection'. Both songs are attributed to Burns by Stenhouse (*Illustrations*, p. 404). No holograph of **644** is known; but the second song, which has been traced to the *Edinburgh Magazine*, 1774 (*H–H*. iii. 426), is in the Hastie MSS (f. 139) with Burns's instruction that it is to follow 'Wherefore sighing &c.'.

645. The broom blooms bonie

IT's whisper'd in parlour, it's whisper'd in ha',
The broom blooms bonie, the broom blooms fair. . . .

SMM, 1796, no. 461; 3 stanzas, the second and third followed by asterisks; unsigned. A ballad fragment said by Stenhouse to have been recovered, with its air, by Burns; but there is no manuscript evidence.

646. Could aught of song

COULD aught of song declare my pains,
Could artful numbers move thee. . . .

SMM, 1796, no. 493; 2 stanzas, signed 'B'. 'Written for this Work by Robert Burns'. Cf. Stenhouse, *Illustrations*, pp. 432–3. The song is in the Hastie MSS (f. 159), but it was copied from the *Edinburgh Magazine*, 1774 (H–H., iv. 75), and is attributed by Thomson to Dr. Beattie in *SC*, 1798, no. 32 (alternative words to **483**).

647. Evan Banks

SLOW spreads the gloom my soul desires,
The sun from India's shore retires. . . .

SMM, 1796, no. 500; 4 stanzas, signed 'B'. 'Written for this Work by Robert Burns'. Cf. Stenhouse, *Illustrations*, p. 438. The song is in the Hastie

MSS (f. 163), but was copied by Burns for the author, Helen Maria Williams (H–H., iv. 75). On Miss Williams, see *Letters*, ed. J. De L. Ferguson, 1931, ii. 375–6.

648. Scenes of woe

SCENES of woe and scenes of pleasure,
Scenes that former thoughts renew. . . .

SMM, 1803, no. 517; 3 stanzas, 'Written by R. Burns'. Stenhouse, however, had a manuscript of the song in the handwriting of the Edinburgh poet Richard Gall (1776–1801) and says, on the authority of one of Gall's friends, that it was sent anonymously to Johnson as Burns's work (*Illustrations*, pp. 457–8).

649. The Queen of the Lothians

See **503**, introductory note.

650. The Lochmaben Harper

O HEARD ye of a silly Harper,
Liv'd long in Lochmaben town. . . .

SMM, 1803, no. 579; 21 stanzas, unsigned. Said by Stenhouse to have been recovered, with its air, by Burns (*Illustrations*, p. 497); but there is no manuscript evidence for this, although Burns and Johnson had some correspondence in 1795 about the loss of the air for this 'famous old song' (Letter 667). **650** corresponds closely to the longer of the two versions gathered from oral tradition by Robert Riddell (see Child, no. 192), and there is nothing to indicate that Burns even communicated it to Johnson directly. Cf. **558**, introductory note.

651. As I lay on my bed

As I lay on my bed on a night,
I thought upon her beauty bright. . . .

SMM, 1803, no. 581; a fragment in 3 stanzas, unsigned. Said by Stenhouse to have been recovered by Burns (*Illustrations*, p. 498); but there is no manuscript evidence.

652. I rede you beware o' the Ripples

I REDE you beware o' the ripples, young man [*bis*];
Tho the saddle be saft, ye needna ride aft,
For fear that the girdin' beguile ye, young man. . . .

MMC, pp. 5–6; 4 stanzas, marked 'Burns' in Scott Douglas's copy. But the
air prescribed, *The Taylor's faun thro the bed*, &c., dates from the late seven-
teenth century with the title of **652** (see **286**, note); and it is likely that this
is a traditional song, which Burns parodied in a suggestive one of his own (see
190).

653. The lass o' Liviston

THE bonny lass o' Liviston,
    Her name ye ken, her name ye ken;
And ay the welcomer ye'll be,
    The farther ben, the farther ben. . . .

MMC, pp. 6–7; 3 eight-line stanzas, marked 'Old song revised by Burns'
in Scott Douglas's copy. But in his notes on Scots songs (Edinburgh University MSS, Laing III. 586) Burns quotes ll. 1–2 and 5–6 as 'the old song, in
three eight-line stanzas', 'well known, and has merit as to wit and humour;
but is rather unfit for insertion' (*Burns Chronicle*, 1922, p. 10). The quotation
is probably an abbreviation, not indicating any reshaping by Burns. There
are two stanzas in autograph, opening with ll. 1–2, in the Watson MSS (1144);
Burns notes, 'The rest is lost I suppose'.

654. She's hoy'd me out o' Lauderdale

THERE liv'd a lady in Lauderdale,
    She lo'ed a fiddler fine. . . .

MMC, pp. 7–8; 3 stanzas, marked 'Old song revised by Burns' in Scott
Douglas's copy. But there is no evidence of this. For the theme, see **280**,
introductory note.

655. Errock Brae

O ERROCK stane, may never maid,
    A maiden by thee gae;
Nor e'er a stane o' stanin' graith,
    Gae stanin' o'er the brae. . . .

MMC, pp. 11–12; 6 stanzas and chorus; marked 'Old song revised by Burns'
in Scott Douglas's copy; but without evidence. Cf. **611**, introductory note.

656. For a' that and a' that

PUT butter in my Donald's brose,
For weel does Donald fa' that. . . .

MMC, pp. 15–16; 4 stanzas and chorus; marked 'Old with revision' in Scott Douglas's copy, possibly because of a reference in Letter 676. But see **84.** 208 *n*. There is no evidence to support this. The imagery of the song has a 'Burnsian' power; but so has that of the best traditional bawdry.

657. Green grow the Rashes

O WAT ye ought o' fisher Meg,
And how she trow'd the webster, O. . . .

MMC, pp. 28–29; 4 stanzas and chorus; marked 'Burns' in Scott Douglas's copy. But see **124**, introductory note.

658. Comin' thro' the Rye

O GIN a body meet a body,
Comin thro the rye. . . . .

MMC, pp. 39–41; 5 stanzas and chorus, marked 'old with Burns' revisions' in Scott Douglas's copy. See **560**, note.

659. Dainty Davy

BEING pursu'd by the dragoons,
Within my bed he was laid down. . . .

MMC, pp. 67–68; 4 stanzas and chorus ('O leeze me on his curly pow'); marked 'old' in Scott Douglas's copy and related to a song in Herd's MSS (ed. H. Hecht, 1904, p. 140) with the same chorus, 'made upon Mass David Williamson on his getting with child the Lady Cherrytree's daughter, while the soldiers were searching the house to apprehend him for a rebel' (Herd). Cunningham took **659** for Burns's work in his transcript of the Gracie MS (see G. Legman, *The Horn Book*, 1964, pp. 131 ff.); for Hecht's argument that it is Burns's revision of Herd's text, see the *Merry Muses*, 1959 edn., p. 74. But in his manuscript notes on Scots songs, Burns relates the story of Williamson (see **84.** 197–8 *n*.) and adds: 'A mutilated stanza or two are to be found in Herd's Collection, but the song consists of five or six stanzas, and has merit in its way. The first stanza is—'Being pursued by the dragoons . . . [**659.** 1–4]' (*Burns Chronicle*, 1922, p. 12).

660. Our John's brak Yestreen

TWA neebor wives sat i' the sun,
A twynin' at their rocks. . . .

MMC, pp. 76–77; 4 stanzas; marked 'Burns' in Scott Douglas's copy, but
without evidence. The song is a traditional 'wives' brag', a medieval kind still
current in folk poetry.

661. Tail Todle

OUR gudewife held o'er to Fife,
For to buy a coal-riddle;
Lang or she came back again,
Tammie gart my tail todle. . . .

MMC, pp. 111–12; 3 stanzas and chorus; marked 'Burns' in Scott Douglas's
copy. Douglas also inserted the name of the air *Chevalier's Muster-Roll*, and
amended a line of the chorus; and he may have seen a holograph. But there
is nothing to suggest Burns's hand in the style of the song. There is, moreover,
a disjunction in the sequence which is typical enough of folk-song but which
Burns usually tried to amend.

662. To the Owl—By John M'Creddie

SAD bird of night, what sorrow calls thee forth,
To vent thy plaints thus in the midnight hour. . . .

Cromek, *Reliques*, 1808, pp. 412–14; 9 stanzas. Found among Burns's MSS
'in his own handwriting, with occasional interlineations, such as occur in
all his primitive effusions', and attributed to him 'notwithstanding the evidence'
of the heading. 'Those who give the verses to Burns would give him anything'
(H–H., iv. 108).

663. Young Hynhorn

NEAR Edinburgh was a young son born,
Hey lilelu an' a how low lan. . . .

Cromek, *Select Scotish Songs*, 1810, ii. 204; 16-stanza fragment. Holograph
in the Watson MSS (1143). Reprinted by Dick, no. 348; and by Barke
(1955), pp. 484–6. But sent with **664** and **665** to Tytler of Woodhouselee
in August 1787, as 'a sample of the old pieces that are still to be found among

our Peasantry in the West. I once had a great many of such fragments; and some of these here entire; but as I had no idea then that any body cared for them, I have forgotten them.—I invariably hold it sacriledge to add anything of my own to help out with the shatter'd wrecks of these venerable old compositions; but they have many various readings' (Letter 126). Cunningham points out that at this time Burns was restoring a good many 'shatter'd wrecks' for Johnson (1834; viii. 154). But his letter to Tytler, as from one antiquary to another, is in terms which prohibit the attribution of these three pieces. For other versions of **663**, see Child, no. 17.

664. Nae birdies sang the mirky hour

NAE birdies sang the mirky hour
Amang the braes o' Yarrow. . . .

Cromek, *Select Scotish Songs*, 1810, ii. 196; 10 stanzas, fragments. Holograph in the Watson MSS (1144). Reprinted by Dick, no. 352; and by Barke (1955), pp. 455–6. But see **663**, note. This is a defective version of *The Duke of Athole's Nourice* (Child, no. 212), with two stanzas of *Rare Willie* (Child, no. 215).

665. Rob Roy

ROB Roy from the Highlands cam
Unto the Lawlan border. . . .

Cromek, *Select Scotish Songs*, 1810, ii. 199; 9 stanzas; reprinted by Dick, nos. 353 and 354. Holograph in the Watson MSS (1144). But see **663**, note. For other versions of this ballad, see Child, no. 225.

666. Thanksgiving for a National Victory

YE hypocrites! are these your pranks?
To murder men, and give God thanks. . . .

Works, ed. Hogg and Motherwell, 1834–6, ii. 71, and later collected editions; 1 stanza. But published as 'Vile wicked Whigs, are these your pranks . . .' in the *Belfast News Letter*, 11 September 1746, entitled *Lines nailed on the New Church at Manchester on the day before Thanksgiving Day for Culloden Moor* (see *Burns Chronicle*, 1955, pp. 17–18).

667. On Grizel Grim

HERE lies with death auld Grizel Grim. . . .

Works, ed. Hogg and Motherwell, 1834–6, ii. 86. But see **530**, note.

668. On seeing his Favourite Walks despoiled

As on the banks of winding Nith
Ae smiling simmer morn I stray'd. . . .

Works, ed. Hogg and Motherwell, 1834–6, v. 406 (probably from the *Scots Magazine*, July 1803; H–H., iv. 106); Scott Douglas, iii. 10–12; H–H., iv. 53–55; 6 stanzas. 'My first acquaintance with Dr. Currie, the biographer of Burns,' says Henry Mackenzie, 'was on occasion of a *jeu d'esprit* of mine, some stanzas which I passed as written by Burns in a fit of indignation at the wood on the river Nith being cut down by the Duke of Queensberry, which I read at the Royal Society. On being told that the Doctor proposed inserting those verses in a new edition of Burns, I thought it right to undeceive him as to their author' (*Anecdotes and Egotisms*, ed. H. W. Thompson, 1927, p. 173).

669. The Kiss

HUMID seat of soft affection,
Magic ointment, virgin kiss. . . .

[*Variant*: Humid seal of soft affections,
Tend'rest pledge of future bliss. . . .]

Chambers, 1838, and other collected editions; 4 stanzas (variant, 3 stanzas). Published as 'anonymous' in the *Belfast News Letter*, 25 November 1791 (Egerer, pp. 343–4), the Della Cruscan *Oracle*, 29 January 1796—'and it has the right Anna Matilda smack throughout' (H–H., iv. 107); the Liverpool *Kaleidoscope*, attributed to Burns (ibid.); and Maria Riddell's *Metrical Miscellany*, 1802, p. 102, attributed to Sheridan.

670. Elegy

STRAIT is the spot, and green the sod,
From whence my sorrows flow. . . .

Works, ed. Alexander Smith, 1865, ii. 343; Scott Douglas, ii. 77–79; H–H., iv. 46–50 (an 'improbable'); 10 stanzas. An abridgement of a 20-stanza poem by the Revd. John Mackenzie of Portpatrick, published in the *Scots*

Magazine, March 1769; transcribed in *2CPB*, pp. 8–11, as 'the work of some hapless, unknown Son of the Muses, who deserved a better fate'; and sent to Mrs. Dunlop on 8 July 1789 (Letter 351).

671. The other night

T H E other night, with all her charms,
My ardent passion crowning. . . .

Scott Douglas, vi. 288; 6 stanzas, sent to Thomson in September 1793 as 'pickt up in an old Collection' while Burns was 'turning over some volumes of English songs' (Letter 588). Thomson notes on this letter that none of the songs in it are 'Mr. Burns's own, except [671], which is too warmly coloured' (Dalhousie MS); but the song is Tom Brown's *Cælia's Rundlet of Brandy* (*Pills*, iv. 185–6) with a variant opening stanza and an additional one which Burns probably had in a miscellany reprint.

672. Elibanks and Elibraes

O, E L I B A N K S and Elibraes
It was but aince I saw ye. . . .

J. D. Law, *Here and There in Two Hemispheres*, 1903, pp. 463–4; reprinted by R. D. Thornton in the *Burns Chronicle*, 1950, pp. 30–38; 3 stanzas, from a manuscript. Law suggests that these are 'decent' verses written by Burns as alternative to the traditional bawdy song *Elibanks and Elibraes* (*MMC*, pp. 35–37); and Thornton asks, further, whether they are the song Burns took up and could not finish in (?) November 1791. But it is almost certain that what he took up on that occasion was the traditional song: 'When I tell you even [Bawdry] has lost its power to please, you will guess something of my hell within, and all around me.—I began "Elibanks and Elibraes", but the stanza fell unenjoyed, and unfinished from my listless tongue . . .' (Letter 482). Thornton offers two subsidiary arguments: Law's text is signed 'Johnnie Faa', a signature Burns used in writing to Sharpe in April 1791 (Letter 446); and the first lines of **672** may refer to 'sweet Isabella Lindsay', 'with whom Burns enjoyed the country near Elibanks'. But (i) the gipsy signature is part of the role of wandering minstrel which Burns assumes, jocularly, in his letter to Sharpe; (ii) Burns met Isabella Lindsay at Jedburgh, during his Border tour, on 9 May 1787, left her there 'with some melancholy, disagreable sensations' on 11 May, and saw 'Elibanks and Elibraes so famous in baudy song' from the road between Selkirk and Innerleithen on 14 May (*Journal*, ed. J. De L. Ferguson, in Fitzhugh, pp. 111–14). Law's song, moreover, looks like a piece of bad conventional verse in the Scottish nineteenth-century style; and I should be reluctant, even if confronted with Burns's holograph, to ascribe it to him.

(Scott Douglas, in his copy of *MMC*, has marked the first two stanzas of the bawdy song as published in Dublin in 1769. But at the end of the book (ff. 76ᵛ–77ʳ), after a note on Burns's sight of Elibanks and a transcript from Letter 482, he gives a heavily corrected version of the same song. It is possible that this is a copy of Burns's autograph revision of the old bawdy song; but it may equally well be Scott Douglas's own draft.)

673. To Mr. Gow visiting in Dumfries

THRICE welcome, King o' Rant and Reel!
Whaur is the bard to Scotia leal
Wha wadna sing o' sic a chiel. . . .

J. D. Law, op. cit., pp. 464–6, rptd. Thornton (see **672**, note); J. Barke's edition, 1955, pp. 495–7; 5 12-line stanzas on the pattern $a_4a_4a_4b_3$ twice repeated, said to be signed 'R.B.' and docketed 'From the Poet'. Gow was in Dumfries in (?) October 1793 and Burns, who thought him 'a man of great genius in his way', 'spent many happy hours with him' (Letter 591). But (i) the stanza, which is not Burns's usual one for epistles, has none of the metrical variety he delighted in when trying out longer verse-forms; (ii) the poem contains a suspiciously large number of rhymes and phrases used elsewhere by Burns; and (iii) it is flat, loose, and conventional in both content and diction, and suggests a nineteenth-century forgery (cf. **672**, note). In the weakest of Burns's epistles there is nothing like this:

> It's but a weary warl' at best,
> Wauf an' weary—aften dreary—   [worthless
> It's but a weary warl' at best,
>   A wauf and weary widdle!
> It's but a weary warl' at best,
> Gang north or sooth or east or west. . . .

674. Look up and see!

Noo, Davie Sillar, that's the plan,
Quo' I, last night, when in my han
I gaed your latest screed a scan. . . .

Poems and Songs, ed. J. Barke, 1955, pp. 255–8; 21 stanzas. No authority given for this text, which I believe to be based on a forgery. (i) It contains a number of uncharacteristic forms and spellings: e.g., 'her man or lang *begood* to ail' (l. 44), 'Aloo'd' (l. 46), 'deeins' (doings, l. 65), 'pree' ('pry',

investigate, l. 82), 'gat stown Bath-Sheba twice wi' bairn' (l. 86); (ii) there
are several unlikely words and phrases—e.g., 'A cruel curse at her he shot'
(l. 41), 'parsons' (l. 79; not otherwise used by Burns); (iii) the tag, 'Look
up and see', is used forcedly as a refrain to every stanza; and (iv) much of the
writing, when compared with that of the Ayrshire epistles, is clumsy and flat.
This is not the kind of burlesque versifying Burns did in his lighter moments
(ll. 97–102):

> Foul-mouth'd auld Davie also was
> And mony proofs your Bible has
> O' his inspired profaneness as
> Ye maun agree
> If 'tis as in my copy 'twas—
> Look up and see!

675. Epistle to Dr. John Mackenzie

DEAR Thinker John,
Your creed I like it past expression,
I'm sure, o' truth, it's nae transgression. . . .

Poems and Songs, ed. J. Barke, 1955, pp. 263–5; 13 stanzas. This epistle,
on the familiar themes of religion and hypocrisy, may be Burns's work; but
Barke gives no authority for his text. A transcript is in the Watson MSS
(1086).

676. To Robert Aiken

ASSIST me, Coila, while I sing
The virtues o' a crony. . . .

Poems and Songs, ed. J. Barke, 1955, pp. 271–3; 6 eight-line stanzas. Reprinted in the *Scots Chronicle*, 1951, pp. 95–96, from the 'Mavisgrove
MSS' (not traced). Cf. **679**. I believe this to be a forgery. The stanza form is
untypical, and the style—loose and conventional—is well below the level
of Burns's vernacular epistles of his Ayrshire period. The final stanza is
utterly out of character:

> The time will come when I'll be deemed
> A poet grander, greater,
> Than ever prophesied or dreamed
> The loodest, proodest prater. . . .

Cf. the Prefaces to *86* and *87*; **57**. 49 ff.; **62**. 247–58 *n*.

677. On Wedding Rings

SHE asked why wedding rings are made of gold;
I ventured this to instruct her. . . .

Poems and Songs, ed. J. Barke, 1955, p. 357; 6 lines. This is unlikely to be
Burns's work: it does not take the almost invariable form of his acknowledged
epigrams, and the conceit of gold as the 'conductor' of love, the soul's 'electric
flame', suggests a later date. 'Conductor' in this sense was still a new technical
term in the 1780's.

678. To —— of C—der, on some Gentlemen being refused Permission to take a View of the Architecture, &c., of C—der-House

WHY shut your doors and windows thus,
    With such a jealous dread?
We are no children come to eat
    Your works of gingerbread.

Poems and Songs, ed. J. Barke, 1955, p. 357. No authority is given for this
epigram, but it is not improbably Burns's work.

679. Ever to be near ye

EVER to be near ye!
Whaur ye bide or whaur ye stray,
To comfort and to cheer ye. . . .

Poems and Songs, ed. J. Barke, 1955, pp. 494–5; 3 stanzas. From the 'Mavisgrove MSS' (untraced); see **676**, note. It is made up of weakly vernacular
commonplaces, and is apparently a nineteenth-century vamp of **444**.

680. Wanton Willie

O WANTON Willie yir wame rins out,
O wanton Willie &c. . . .

G. Legman, *The Horn Book*, 1964, p. 136; Cunningham's transcript of the
Gracie MS, bound in a copy of the *Merry Muses* (?1827), pp. 135–6; 3
stanzas of bawdry. Possibly collected by Burns, but there is nothing in the
poem to suggest his hand.

681. Wat ye what my Minnie did

O WAT ye what my minnie did

*   *   *   *   *

My minnie did to me jo. . . .

G. Legman, *The Horn Book*, 1964, p. 137; Cunningham's transcript, pp. 136–8 (see **680**, note); 8 stanzas. Legman attributes this to Burns on grounds of style, and because 'it is written *from the woman's point of view*, a frequent device of Burns's'. But the style, and the central sexual image of the girl's 'needle e'e', are quite traditional; and I hesitate to use Legman's second argument as a criterion. The song was, however, collected by Burns in his manuscript notes on Scots song (Edinburgh University MSS, Laing III. 586; *Burns Chronicle*, 1922, p. 7).

682. Whirlie-Wha

THE last braw wedding that I was at
Was on a Hallow day. . . .

G. Legman, *The Horn Book*, 1964, p. 138; Cunningham's transcript, pp. 139–40 (see **680**, note); 3 eight-line stanzas. The song is metrically clumsy, and dully obvious in content; there are no grounds for ascribing it to Burns, though he may have collected it.

683. A Masonic Song

IT happened on a winter night
And early in the season
Some body said my bonny lad
Was gone to be a Mason. . . .

Communicated to Kinloch (see G. Legman, *The Horn Book*, 1964, pp. 139 ff.) by Robert Pitcairn, W.S., 'who received [it] from the friend of Burns to whom [it was] sent'; Harvard MS 25242.12, dated 1829; 11 stanzas. The song shows some ingenuity in using the terms of masonry as sexual metaphors —'jewels', the badge of the order; 'siege', the stone-cutter's 'block-bench' for hewing; 'gage'; 'plummets', leaden balls used on a line for determining a vertical; and 'broacher', a pointed stone-chisel. But it is metrically and verbally clumsy, closer to the style of the street ballads built on 'trade' metaphors (see **84**. 165 *n*.) than to Burns's bawdry. The MS has the familiar (and improbable) story that Burns composed the song extempore at a masonic meeting; but I cannot regard it even as a memorial version of his work.

684. On Findlater

T H E Exciseman and the Gentleman in One:
I point thee, O Findlater, for thou 'rt the Man.

Transcript in the Cowie MSS; attributed to Burns, but metrically too clumsy for him.

685. On Tom Pain's death

A L L Pale and Ghastly Tammy Pain
    Gaed down ae night to Hell,—
The Devil shook him by the Hand
    Saying, 'Tammy—I hope ye're well'—
He shut him up in Dungeon Hot
    And [on] him [clapp'd] the Door,—
Lord! How the Devil Lap and Leuch
    To hear the B——t Roar!

Transcript in the Cowie MSS; attributed to Burns. It may be his work; but he usually managed to be wittier on this theme.

686. As I walk'd by mysel

As I walk'd by mysel, I said to mysel,
    And mysel said again to me;
Look weel to thysel, or not to thysel,
    There's nobody cares for thee.

Then I answer'd mysel and I said to mysel;
    Whatever be my degree,
I'll look to mysel, and I'll think o' mysel,
    And I care for nobodie.

Holograph owned by G. Ross Roy; probably traditional.

INDEX OF AIRS

[References are to the numbers of the songs for which the airs are transcribed, and to the accompanying Commentary. The commoner alternative titles are included.]

INDEX OF SHORT TITLES

[Poems attributed to Burns erroneously or on inadequate evidence are indexed in square brackets. Poems entitled 'Ballad', 'Song', or with first-line titles only, are omitted. References are to numbers, not pages.]

INDEX OF FIRST LINES

[Poems attributed to Burns erroneously or on inadequate evidence are indexed in square brackets.]

*Indicates fragments, &c., in textual notes.

No.   *Page*

PRINTED IN GREAT BRITAIN
AT THE UNIVERSITY PRESS, OXFORD
BY VIVIAN RIDLER
PRINTER TO THE UNIVERSITY